The
LAST WINTER
of the
WEIMAR REPUBLIC

The
LAST WINTER
of the
WEIMAR REPUBLIC

The Rise of the Third Reich

Rüdiger Barth and
Hauke Friederichs

Translated by Caroline Waight

PEGASUS BOOKS
NEW YORK LONDON

THE LAST WINTER OF THE WEIMAR REPUBLIC

Pegasus Books, Ltd.
148 West 37th Street, 13th Floor
New York, NY 10018

ISBN: 978-1-64313-849-7

10 9 8 7 6 5 4 3 2 1

Printed in the United States of America
Distributed by Simon & Schuster
www.pegasusbooks.com

CONTENTS

THE GRAVEDIGGERS

Paul von Hindenburg (*1847)
A legend of the First World War and President of the Reich, Hindenburg despised democracy.
'Hindenburg is a granite-faced, bass-voiced Field Marshal with a commanding manner that makes little corporals tremble.'
— Hubert Renfro Knickerbocker, correspondent for the *New York Evening Post*

Kurt von Schleicher (*1882)
A power-broking general who suddenly found himself becoming chancellor.
'It won't be easy to strike a deal with Schleicher. He has a clever but sly gaze. I don't believe he is honest.'
— Adolf Hitler

Franz von Papen (*1879)
A risk-taker bent on revenge
'[Papen looks] like an ill-tempered billy-goat trying to stand to attention. A character out of *Alice in Wonderland*.'
— Harry Graf Kessler, journalist and bon vivant

Adolf Hitler (*1889)
As Führer of the NSDAP, Hitler wanted to create a dictatorship.
'When finally I walked into Adolf Hitler's salon in the Kaiserhof Hotel, I was convinced that I was meeting the future dictator of Germany. In something less than fifty seconds I was quite sure I was not.'
— Dorothy Thompson, American reporter

Joseph Goebbels (*1897)
Head of Propaganda for the NSDAP
'The Führer is playing […] chess for power. It is an exciting and nerve-racking struggle, yet it also conveys the thrilling sense of being a game in which everything is at stake.'

– Joseph Goebbels

THE LIE OF THE LAND

In November 1932, fourteen years after it was put in place, Germany's first parliamentary democracy found itself mired in its deepest crisis. The election on 6 November – the second that year – proved disastrous for the moderate parties that constituted the Weimar Republic. A full third of the workforce was unemployed, more than five million people in all, and many of those still in work had been hit with punishing wage cuts. The economy was at rock bottom, and political culture had taken a cutthroat turn. On the streets of Germany's cities, the situation frequently erupted into violent conflicts that left hundreds dead. Senior politicians, businessmen and journalists spoke in hushed tones of civil war.

It was only by virtue of President Hindenburg's emergency decrees that Chancellor Franz von Papen was able to govern at all. Emergency decrees had legal authority, but were not passed by elected representatives. Article 48 of the Weimar Constitution granted that power to the head of state, and since 1930 Hindenburg had been making generous use of the privilege.

Parliament could annul the emergency decrees or force the government to step down with a motion of no confidence – the checks and balances of a constitution designed to maintain an even keel. To avert this, the president had already dissolved Parliament twice and called fresh elections. What resulted was the unprecedented paralysis of German politics.

The German electorate had just voted once again. In Parliament, Chancellor Franz von Papen – a committed monarchist – found himself facing a hostile majority; like Papen, they were only too willing to dispense with democracy entirely, but on *their* terms. This majority consisted mainly of Communists and National Socialists, extremists on the left and right who were united only in their hatred of the system.

The president wanted clarity once and for all, while the chancellor needed allies – but only the German National People's Party, the DNVP, stayed loyal. They had fifty-one out of 584 representatives, laughably few. Now Papen was counting on the NSDAP to support his policies. Since July of that year, the Nazis had been by far the strongest faction in Parliament. If the worst came to the worst, Papen was even prepared to make their leader, Adolf Hitler, Vice-Chancellor: he hoped that would bring the German Fascists to heel. He had just made another attempt to woo the NSDAP, calling their proposed collaboration the 'aggregation of all national forces'. Hitler, however, flatly rebuffed him.

The German Reich in November 1932 was in an alarming state. In his book *The German Crisis*, which had been published a few months earlier and had already been reprinted several times, the American reporter Hubert Renfro Knickerbocker wrote that 'Fifty thousand Bolsheviks made the Russian revolution. Germany has an estimated six million voters for its Communist Party. Five hundred thousand Fascists put Mussolini in power in Italy. Adolf Hitler has a possible twelve million voters behind the National Socialist Party in Germany. How long can the life of the German republic last?'

That was the question. The coming winter would settle the fate of the Weimar Republic.

THE BRINK

17 NOVEMBER TO 1 DECEMBER 1932

THURSDAY 17 NOVEMBER

Chancellor on the Brink!
Decision Today
– Der Angriff

Papen Offers Resignation
Entire Cabinet to Step Down? – Hindenburg Speech Today
– Vossische Zeitung

The German Reich was ruled from the Prussian capital of Berlin. More specifically, power resided in a handful of adjacent buildings in an area referred to by the name of the nearest street: Wilhelmstrasse.

If you walked out of the Reichstag, strolled through the Brandenburg Gate and took a right behind the Hotel Adlon on Pariser Platz, you were already as good as there. Head past the British embassy and the Ministry for Agriculture, and you'd soon catch sight of the palace buildings on your right, with the Chancellery extension, built a year earlier and clad in travertine, sticking out like a sore thumb.

From the street the facades looked forbidding, but behind them stretched old, expansive gardens. Subterranean corridors led from building to building on the western side of Wilhelmstrasse, and a secret passageway was rumoured to weave among the attics. Even the gardens were connected via gates through which a person might slip unseen.

The cabinet meeting that derailed Franz von Papen's career and brought General Kurt von Schleicher out of the shadows took place, as far as we know, in the garden room of the Chancellery. In the brighter months it was flooded with light through west-facing, floor-to-ceiling windows; even on that November morning the room was lit with a mild radiance. It was a fresh and sunny autumn day. Leaves glowed on oaks, elms and lindens, trees that had been ancient in the days when Frederick the Great walked among them on his morning stroll.

The terracotta eagles of Imperial Prussia still kept watch on the rear wall bordering Friedrich Ebert Strasse, their heads adorned with gilded bronze crowns. Otto von Bismarck, first Chancellor of the German Empire, had lived in this set of buildings for twenty-eight years. According to the children of the staff, who played there often, his faithful mastiff was buried somewhere in the garden, as was the Trakehner stallion that had carried him across the fields of Königgrätz in 1866. An eighteen-year-old Paul von Hindenburg had taken part in the same battle – on foot – as a lieutenant in the Third Prussian Regiment of Guards.

On 17 November Hindenburg was eighty-five years old and the most important man in Germany. During the First World War he had commanded his troops to victory at the Battle of Tannenberg, and was later made head of the Supreme Army Command. He was still living off the reputation he had earned in his glory days. With his impressive moustache, steel-wool hair and the deep grooves around his mouth, in peaceful moments he resembled his own memorial. President of the Reich since 1925, Hindenburg was an elderly man now, but he still had all and sundry vying for his favour – including the ministers and undersecretaries gathered in the garden room that morning.

Abraham Plotkin, an American trade-union functionary, had been meandering through Paris since the day before. He had arrived at Le Havre on a cargo boat from New York, one of five passengers. The frugal crossing, devoid of creature comforts, was his preferred mode of travel – and all his budget allowed. Plotkin, forty years old, had lost his job with the textile union back home, the victim of a financial crisis that left no industry unscathed.

When he was a boy, his family had emigrated to America from Tsarist Russia. Now Plotkin had returned to Europe, bringing little more than the clothes on his back, his walking stick and his typewriter.

Shortly after his arrival he started a diary. Plotkin was inquisitive and eloquent, with an eye for the circumstances of ordinary folk. But he hadn't come to Europe to stay in France, and within four days he was travelling onwards.

His goal was Germany, where he hoped to witness the struggle of average citizens for their rights. He'd heard that political radicals on the left and right were clashing on the streets of Berlin, that there had been deaths. The capital exerted a magical force: Plotkin had devoured Alfred Döblin's *Berlin Alexanderplatz*. Now he wanted to immerse himself in the environment Döblin had so vividly depicted. He wanted whores and shopkeepers, beggars and hoodlums. He wanted to see these National Socialists, the ones everybody was talking about in voices half afraid and half fascinated. Joseph Goebbels' speech at the Berlin Sportpalast, they said, had been unparalleled in its sweeping power. For any other tourist, November – usually the month in which winter unfolds in all its majesty across the city – might not have been the best time to explore Berlin. But Plotkin didn't care. Plotkin had come to learn from the Germans.

Defence Minister Kurt von Schleicher, fifty years old and running to fat, entered the garden room. In photographs he appears ungainly, his smile rigid, although there is generally a flash in his eyes. Most people meeting him for the first time were impressed less by his looks than by his vibrant personality. Bald and short-statured, he was nonetheless a surprise hit with the ladies. Those ill-disposed towards Schleicher told tales about his shifting romantic intrigues. How he sent bouquets of flowers to married women, including the wives of influential men. How he made lifelong enemies in the process.

In Wilhelmstrasse he had acquired a reputation as a confirmed bachelor who knew how to make the most of the unencumbered life; then, in July 1931, he married Elisabeth von Hennigs, the daughter of a general of the cavalry – a woman from a military family.

Kurt von Schleicher had military origins, too. His great-grand-father had died in 1815 during an assault on Napoleon's troops at the Battle of Ligny, two days before Waterloo. Schleicher's father had also been a soldier and eventually a lieutenant-colonel.

Like President Hindenburg, Schleicher had begun his military career in the Third Regiment of Foot Guards, where he befriended Hindenburg's son and adjutant, Oskar, as well as Kurt von Hammerstein-Equord, who in 1932 was head of the German armed forces.

During the First World War, Schleicher rapidly made a name for himself. He served as part of various military staffs, organising, planning, guiding and acquainting himself with generals who appreciated him and furthered his career. Generalmajor Wilhelm Groener became his mentor, a father figure who gave Schleicher extensive latitude, even outside the chain of command. Towards the end of the First World War, Schleicher came to serve under Paul von Hindenburg, then the head of the German General Staff, and they remained close.

From then on, Schleicher worked in the dim hinterlands where politics and military business overlapped. He became head of the Ministerial Office, an important post that afforded ample opportunity for string-pulling. He met all the senior party figures and forged close personal bonds with many, including Friedrich Ebert, a Social Democrat and President of the German Reich. The 'Department of the Wehrmacht', a part of the ministry that he set up personally, was under his direct command: this was where German military politics was brokered and still is today.

Schleicher often worked long into the night, sleeping little; at daybreak he would take an hour-long ride through the Tiergarten – and yet he seemed unfazed by his exacting workload. A maestro of the small gathering, he was a forceful speaker, holding forth with charm or chutzpah as the mood took him. No German citizen had ever been given the chance to vote for Kurt von Schleicher in an election, yet it was he who had put forward Papen's name as chancellor to Hindenburg in the summer of 1932. Of that there could be no doubt.

That morning he arrived punctually in the garden room for the cabinet meeting at eleven a.m.

Chancellor Franz von Papen, the gathering's fifty-three-year-old host, entered the room a few minutes later. According to witnesses he sat at the centre of the table, opposite the high windows, treating himself to a view over the garden. To his left sat Schleicher, the friend who had brokered his remarkable promotion six months earlier. Six months had proved long enough for Papen to usurp Schleicher's place as the president's crony-in-chief – and long enough to turn a friend into an enemy.

Only a few steps away, President Paul von Hindenburg was brooding over paperwork in his office. Bismarck, the great uniter of the German Reich, surely hadn't had as tough a time as this. Germany was a crisis-ridden nation at odds with itself, the parties elected by its citizens were jockeying for power, and the inner unity of the Volk was gravely endangered. No one but Hindenburg could bring together a majority. No one but Paul von Hindenburg could save Germany.

At the beginning of June he had moved out of the presidential palace, which was sorely in need of renovation – the furniture had to be propped up on little blocks, because in many places the wooden flooring sagged alarmingly – and had been working and taking meetings at the Chancellery ever since.

The Reichstag was due to reconvene on 6 December, three weeks' time, and by then the new chancellor had to be in place. But who should Hindenburg appoint? Custom dictated that the individual tasked with forming a government ought to be whoever represented the largest faction in Parliament. That would be Adolf Hitler, Führer of the NSDAP, the National Socialist German Workers' Party (NSDAP), his erstwhile opponent from the presidential election in April. In Parliament, Hermann Göring had already been selected as President of the Reichstag, one of the most senior offices in the Reich. But NSDAP party members were forever heckling and fomenting dissent, upsetting the political process; on one occasion, they had beaten a leftist journalist in the parliamentary restaurant so badly that the man had to be hospitalised – they were an appalling bunch. It seemed scarcely conceivable that the business of state would be in good hands with those two representatives. Hindenburg would have preferred to

retain Franz von Papen as chancellor, a conservative whose perpetually cheery disposition continued to reassure him. Then there was
Kurt von Schleicher, a staunch believer in the military. Some people
said Schleicher was acid-tongued and devious, but Hindenburg had
long relied on his vigilant, resourceful brain.

Politics is tricky, especially for a career soldier like Hindenburg.
Compromises don't simply materialise to order, and democracy is the
most complicated form of politics. Whatever decision he made, Hindenburg felt compelled to safeguard the German people.

And his own reputation, of course.

Hindenburg's man in the garden room was Otto Meissner, head of the
Office of the President since 1920. The son of a postal worker from
Alsace, the fifty-two-year-old Meissner spoke fluent French and Russian. He held a doctorate in law and before the First World War had
worked for the General Directorate of the Imperial Railways. During
the war itself he was promoted to captain, and it was in 1915 that he
first met Hindenburg.

Meissner was a pragmatic man. As early as 7 May 1932 he had met
with influential National Socialists, including Adolf Hitler, accompanied by General Schleicher and by Hindenburg's son and adjutant,
Oskar. The subject of their discussion? How the cabinet, then led by
the wilful Chancellor Heinrich Brüning, could be most deftly forced
to resign, clearing the ground for a fresh start.

The plan went off without a hitch. Now, only a few months down
the line, the slippery Papen was himself under pressure.

Carl von Ossietzky, editor of the left-leaning intellectual journal *Weltbühne* (World Stage), had been sitting in prison for six months on
charges of treason and disclosing military secrets. He'd published an
article about how the army was clandestinely rearming, entitled 'Win-
diges aus der Luftfahrt' (The Winds of Aviation). Ossietzky, a pacifist,
had long been hated by the military, and now they'd hit back.

'Traitor to the Fatherland' was one accusation levelled against Ossietzky, although it was the army that had broken the law. By stealthily rearming, they were undermining the Treaty of Versailles, an issue that had already been raised in Parliament. All the documents quoted in the *Weltbühne* article – all the facts and figures – had previously been made public. Hardly secrets.

Still, a second case being brought against him was quashed. His most important writer, Kurt Tucholsky, had proclaimed in *Weltbühne* that 'soldiers are murderers'. The military took this as an offence to its honour.

Ossietzky, forty-three years old, was kept in solitary confinement, suffering dreadful rations and forbidden to smoke. Among intellectuals and leftists, he was considered a martyr. In May, when he began serving his sentence, numerous writers accompanied him to Tegel Prison in Berlin, among them Arnold Zweig, Lion Feuchtwanger, Erich Mühsam and Ernst Toller. Ossietzky gave a brief address, announcing that he was going as a deliberate demonstration on behalf of the eight thousand political prisoners 'who are languishing unknown in the darkness of the prison system'. He would demand no special privileges. He would, Ossietzky insisted, be 'unreformed' upon his release.

His release, however, wouldn't be until 10 November 1933. Nearly one whole year to go.

Nobody had reckoned with Franz von Papen. Installed as chancellor in June 1932 from the right-leaning fringes of the Centre Party, he was in no hurry to relinquish power. Papen had reputedly been chosen as chancellor primarily because Schleicher considered him tractable.

In November 1932 Papen was supposed to be in Mannheim for the official opening of a new bridge across the Rhine, and he was also expected on 'state visits' in Württemberg and Baden, as the newspapers crowed. All cancelled. On 16 November, the leader of the conservative Centre Party had informed him that although they 'fundamentally agreed with the notion of a policy of national aggregation', Papen wasn't the right chancellor for such a coalition. Chaos might loom if he stayed, they hinted, so it would be best for Papen to step down at once. The Social Democrats and National Socialists wouldn't even agree to a meeting.

Papen had taken note of everything. Of course, the Centre Party lot were sulking: he had been one of their own, after all, and now they were feeling betrayed.

During the war, he'd been a faithful officer of the Emperor – as an agent and saboteur in Washington, as a commander on the Western Front and as a major in Turkey. As a Member of Parliament he had tended to favour reactionary, nationalistic positions. And now, as chancellor of an unloved republic, he was governing without a majority. Papen had constitutional reform in mind: paralyse the Reichstag for six months, present the electorate with a new constitution then put it to the vote. In this way he hoped to sweep aside the pesky disadvantages of parliamentarianism.

Papen came from an affluent, aristocratic family. At the age of eighteen he'd been a page at the Imperial Court in Berlin. His wife was the heiress to the ceramics manufacturing company Villeroy & Bosch. Money had never been a concern. Those inclined towards mockery called Papen a 'gentleman jockey', although Berlin was hardly short of equestrians. When Papen went horse riding through the Tiergarten, clad in his rakish cap and bow tie, his skill was evident.

The constitutional reforms he hoped to push through would represent a first step back towards the monarchy – or at least towards an authoritarian government. Papen's dream – if, admittedly, a kind of coup.

Meanwhile, Frederic M. Sackett, the American ambassador in Berlin, was facing a problem. His office was appallingly badly staffed, and there was constant chivvying from the gentlemen in Washington: they weren't receiving enough situation reports, analyses and assessments from Berlin.

Only a few weeks earlier he'd written to the State Department that Hitler was 'one of the biggest show-men since P. T. Barnum', referring to Joseph Goebbels in the same communication as Hitler's 'silver-tongued lieutenant'. Sackett had arrived in Berlin in 1930, making him an embassy veteran. Hardly any of the diplomats there had lived in Germany long, and fewer still were competent German-speakers. Budgetary cuts had been felt at all levels. Many of his staff were young and inexperienced. Intelligence operations were non-existent. In a word, the US embassy, recently relocated to Bendlerstrasse, was a shambles.

The sixty-three-year-old Sackett felt personally aggrieved. He'd been on excellent terms with Chancellor Brüning, and his whole strategy was based on their close relationship: assisting Brüning's government, stabilising the German economy, supporting the sensible course Brüning was charting against the extremist parties – that had been his credo.

Since June 1932, however, the situation had been turned on its head. Brüning was out. His successor, Franz von Papen, was *persona non grata* to the Americans. During the First World War Papen had been a military attaché in Washington, secretly building up a spy ring for the Germans, although his conduct was so brazen that he was eventually caught and booted out of the country. How, then, could Sackett deal with Papen? Ignoring him was the only option.

In recent weeks Sackett had been in America, wearing himself thin campaigning for his friend, President Herbert C. Hoover – in vain, as it turned out. Now he was back in Berlin, trying to get to grips with the turbulent times. The notion that the Nazis might come to power didn't bear thinking about.

Papen needed support more than ever if he didn't want to be coerced into stepping down. In the garden room, he began to speak.

The President of the Reich, he argued, must turn once again to the party leaders and advocate for a government of 'national aggregation' with himself as chancellor; at the same time, however, the cabinet must avoid giving the impression that they were clinging to power. Surprisingly, Defence Minister Kurt von Schleicher concurred.

Only the resignation of the entire cabinet, he said, could forestall political 'mudslinging' in nationalist circles. By mudslinging he meant the
rumours that the government was the reason why there was still no
consolidated national front.

There were murmurs of agreement from around the table. Theirs
was the 'cabinet of the barons', as they were popularly known. Most
of their surnames were prefaced with 'von', indicating that they came
from aristocratic families. Yet Papen had selected them for more than
their lineage: many were respected experts in their fields.

Fine, said Chancellor Papen.

Evidently he was giving up.

He would inform the president, he said, that his entire cabinet
was ready to step down.

There was silence in the room. Outside, in the garden, slanting
rays of sunlight caught the foliage. None of his ministers were prepared to argue. Schleicher hid his satisfaction. Papen had long ago
revealed himself a dilettante when it came to political manoeuvring, a
man incapable of forging broad alliances.

Papen nodded. Was it over? Had the highest office in the land
already slipped through his fingers?

Professor Carl Schmitt, a political theorist and expert in constitutional
law, was currently advising the government in an immensely complex
case known nationwide as the Preussenschlag, or Prussian Coup. In
July, President Hindenburg had issued an emergency decree to relieve
the Prussian government of their duties and install his confidant, Chancellor Papen, as Commissioner, thereby destroying a bulwark of the
Social Democratic Party and the Weimar Republic. His justification?
The Social Democrats had failed to prevent Communist violence, and
the domestic situation within Prussia was spiralling out of their control. Eighteen people had been killed a few days earlier during a Nazi
demonstration in a predominantly Communist area, a clash that came
to be known as 'Altona Bloody Sunday'. Nearly all the dead had been
shot by police officers firing indiscriminately during the riots.

The Social Democrats had not responded to Papen's assault with violence: they had not mobilised their paramilitary wing, the Reichsbanner Schwarz-Rot-Gold, nor had they called for a general strike, as with the Kapp Putsch of 1920. They continued to support the state – even though that state had turned on them. Instead, they resorted to legal action. As faithful republicans, they believed in the independence of the justice system, and Otto Braun's deposed Prussian government went to the Constitutional Court in Leipzig: Bavaria and Württemberg, too, appealed to the most senior judges in the Republic, fearing they might be next in line.

Had Adolf Hitler's hour arrived?

The Nazi Führer wanted power at last. His most recent communication with Papen had been blunt: 'The only thing that fills me with bitterness is having to stand and watch as, day after day, your cack-handed governance, Herr Chancellor, squanders a national asset that I played a genuine part in creating, as German history will testify.'

Hitler was severing a working relationship that had scarcely begun. They were strong words, one forceful response of many during those weeks. Yet while his determination may not have been faked, his confidence almost certainly was.

In fact, the Nazi party was getting jumpy. For the first time since 1930, they had lost massive numbers of votes – two million! – at the elections on 6 November, and the peak of their public support seemed to be behind them. The party was also dogged by serious financial concerns. The election campaigns had been horrendously expensive, and Hitler had spent weeks on aeroplanes, day after day, darting from one appearance to the next in an attempt to seem omnipresent. Tens of thousands of Sturmabteilung (SA) troops weren't about to march for free: room and board for the SA had cost the party vast sums. The banks weren't giving any more credit, and their industrialist donors were withholding additional funds. Within the organisation itself, Hitler's adversary Gregor Strasser was causing trouble, arguing the case for pragmatism. He'd already got several members of Parliament and a number of Gauleiter – heads of the regional NSDAP branches – behind him.

The cash-flow situation at the most important regional branch of the NSDAP in Berlin was equally wretched – Joseph Goebbels, its leader, obtained a report on the subject from his staff. 'Nothing but debts, dues and obligations,' he subsequently complained in his diary. 'And the total impossibility of raising any serious amount of money anywhere after this defeat.'

So Goebbels sent the SA back out into the streets with their begging bowls – better visible as beggars than not visible at all. If their bid for power didn't work this time, the National Socialist movement could easily lose its momentum, its appeal and its credibility over the coming winter. It might, eventually, collapse.

FRIDAY 18 NOVEMBER

No Public Support: Chancellor Throws in the Towel
Papen Government to Step Down?
– *Völkischer Beobachter*

Proletarian Offensive Blows Papen Cabinet Apart
Papen Government Resigns – Schleicher Press Demands Hitler
for Chancellor – Working People in Extreme Danger
– *Die Rote Fahne*

Negotiations to form a new government started late that morning, as Hindenburg started casting about for a solution. He was hoping to forge what he termed 'a national aggregation of forces spanning the Centre to the Nazis'. The first person he met, around half past eleven, was Alfred Hugenberg, leader of the conservative DNVP, the German National People's Party. Hugenberg, well known for being particularly blinkered when it came to defending his interests, functioned largely as a mouthpiece for Germany's landowners and captains of industry. He expressed serious reservations about Hitler.

Although frequently mocked – he was a perennial favourite of caricaturists – Hugenberg was a powerful man. One of Europe's biggest media tycoons, with an empire of newspapers, magazines and film production companies, Hugenberg was well aware of his ability to wield print media and film to influence public opinion and, thus, politics. At this juncture, a right-wing government without the DNVP seemed impossible to countenance.

At six o'clock, Ludwig Kaas, head of the Centre Party, arrived for his presidential visit. He suggested a 'loyalty pact' between three or four 'brave party leaders'. Hitler did not seem to faze him. Eduard Dingeldey of the German People's Party was next up; as far as he was concerned, appointing the next chancellor was a matter for the president. His party, he announced, would support Hindenburg's candidate. Moreover, he added: 'Personally I would have not the least objection to entrusting the role to Papen once more.'

For Hindenburg, the process of democratic wrangling had always been a tortuous affair. Prior to his first presidential elections in 1925, he had sought the blessing of the former Kaiser, Wilhelm II, who was at that point exiled in the Netherlands. Politics had not made a republican out of Hindenburg, but he did possess a sense of duty and a deep affection for the Fatherland – he knew his responsibilities as president. And his rights, of course. He was under no obligation to hold talks with just anyone.

He did not, for instance, invite the Social Democratic Party to the table. The SPD, nearly seventy years old, had given birth to the Weimar Republic, but the party was now at daggers drawn with virtually everyone, and especially with the Communists. They had supported Hindenburg during his re-election campaign in April 1932 as part of a calculated ploy to stymie his rival, Hitler, but the old man had never shown them any gratitude. On the contrary. 'Who elected me? The Socialists elected me, the Catholics elected me,' Hindenburg once complained to his press secretary. 'My people didn't elect me.' His people – monarchists, conservatives, opponents of the Republic – had largely transferred their backing to Hitler. For the president, votes from supporters of the Social Democrats were an embarrassment.

He may, too, have still been in a huff because the SPD had flatly rejected an invitation from the chancellor to enter into talks on the fate of the government only a few days earlier. 'We're not going to Papen,' Kurt Schumacher had declared at a meeting of the SPD's executive committee.

Bella Fromm, a woman with a coquettish mouth and dark eyebrows, was the forty-one-year-old society reporter for the *Vossische Zeitung*. The newspaper was required reading for anyone in Berlin involved in politics, as well as anyone who played or hoped to play a prominent role on the social scene, including ministers, members of Parliament and their assistants, civil servants, military men, lobbyists, diplomats and their respective spouses.

Fromm had become a journalist more out of necessity than passion. Born into the Jewish upper classes, her parents ran a successful international business trading wines from Main and the Moselle. They sent their daughter to study at a conservatory in Berlin. Shortly before the outbreak of the First World War, Bella married and gave birth to a daughter, Gonny, but the relationship quickly soured. Getting a divorce required her to prove her husband's infidelity – which she succeeded in doing. Subsequently married and divorced a second time, she enjoyed only a brief glimpse of freedom before inflation spiralled out of control and she lost the majority of her inherited wealth (although the money still stretched to a villa in Berlin, a sports car and two horses). Fromm needed a source of income, and as she moved in the capital's more elevated circles she began to write about their lives. From 1928 onwards she was a columnist for the *Vossische Zeitung*, while also writing for the *Berliner Zeitung* and several other papers owned by the Ullstein publishing company.

Bella Fromm's column 'Berlin Diplomats' in the *Vossische Zeitung* proved popular with readers. Most of what she reported was friendly gossip about foreign emissaries, staff at the Foreign Ministry and politicians in Berlin; she let slip none of her poison-tongued political analysis in the papers. That was reserved for her diary.

Fromm considered the idea that the Nazis could be neutered by integrating them into government extremely dangerous. Four days earlier, at the Kaiserhof Hotel, she had bumped into the former President of the National Bank, Hjalmar Schacht, who was on his way to see Hitler. 'I'd like to know what he wants there,' she noted. 'Surely nothing that bodes well for decent people.' Her readers in the *Vossische Zeitung*, however, were not privy to musings such as these.

Fromm was never one to shy away from undercover work if it helped her get a scoop. One year earlier, at a reception given by the president for the diplomatic corps (to which the press were not invited), she had slipped into men's clothing and mingled with the curious onlookers outside the presidential palace to see who arrived when and with whom – and, above all, who left when and with whom. For the most part, however, she had no need to resort to stratagems. The gentlemen at the Foreign Office and the Chancellery were particularly susceptible to her charm.

She also kept herself well informed about frequent visitors to the Kaiserhof, including Hitler. Among her close circle of friends, Fromm referred to the Führer as 'Kaiser Adolf', and, whenever Kaiser Adolf held court at the luxury hotel, she could often be found in the lobby, observing the spectacle.

On one occasion, she bided her time there for several hours. At first nothing happened. Hitler was fond of making people wait. Amped-up Nazis, expecting an audience, settled at the bar and tried to drown their impatience in beer. Correspondents from foreign newspapers poked their heads through the door, loitered for an hour or so, then gave up.

Finally, at seven o'clock, the doors opened and senior party leaders in brown shirts poured into the lobby. The whole rigmarole reminded Fromm of a country fair, the men wearing badges and insignia in sky blue, garish red, golden yellow and a rainbow of other colours.

As the Brownshirts 'strutted around like peacocks', Fromm thought it was lucky they didn't realise how absurd they appeared. 'Their large brown trousers,' she scoffed, 'were of such widely exaggerated cut that they seemed to bear wings on either side.'

Their feet clattering, the party members shuffled into rows. A murmur filled the room, and then the man himself made his appearance. She noted the grave, belligerent expression on his face, watched arms shoot aloft, heard the men roaring 'Heil'. A single word crossed Bella Fromm's mind: 'Manitu'.

Hitler strode across the room without bothering to glance left or right – then vanished through a side door.

Once the apparition had passed, a few observers began to laugh. All of them foreigners. They could afford to, thought Fromm.

That day, Friday 18 November, Hitler was expected back in Berlin. The Kaiserhof was already trembling with anticipation.

Whenever Hitler – only a German citizen since February 1932 – was in Berlin, he stayed at the Kaiserhof as a matter of principle. In recent months he had visited the city often, entering into secret negotiations with representatives of the government, holding audiences with Hindenburg, and conferring with his entourage. High-ranking guests, journalists and political opponents were received in his suite. The hotel, with its heavy chandeliers and stuccoed walls, had become the Nazis' de facto campaign headquarters. A highly symbolic site, it was an ideal base for them. The main attraction of the building was its dining room, an airy, vaulted space where sumptuous meals were served. Even when it opened fifty years earlier, the hotel had offered an array of modern conveniences, including pneumatic lifts and private radiators in each of the 230 rooms. And the location was unbeatable. You could see straight across onto Wilhelmstrasse 77.

Hitler had only to step out of the Kaiserhof and stand beneath its porticoed entrance, and there it was, almost within his grasp: the Chancellery of the Reich.

The fifth division of the High Court at Leipzig sentenced three Communists to lengthy spells in prison, accusing them of 'high treason in coincidence with crimes against the Explosives Act and offences against the Firearms and Military Equipment Act'. A thirty-one-year-old carpenter was handed six years in prison and ten years deprived of his civil rights, including the right to vote; two construction workers, twenty-five and twenty-eight, were jailed for three years each. The police had found the men in possession of sixty-five kilograms of explosives, as well as rifles, pistols and ammunition, and the judges assumed the convicted men were planning to launch an attack.

In Hofgeismar, not far from the city of Kassel, four National Socialists were standing trial. They had built an armoured vehicle, complete with bullet-proof cladding and shooting slits, which the police seized in the early hours of 1 August. The accused claimed in court that the vehicle was intended to protect the NSDAP from Communist violence. The public prosecutor proposed fines of between 50 and 200 marks for the men, who were members of the SA.

For Harry Graf Kessler, once a diplomat and now an art collector and intellectual, this was a red-letter day. Papen had *finally* resigned. That reckless, perpetually grinning dilettante had wreaked more havoc in six months than any chancellor before him. Worst of all, perhaps, he'd made Hindenburg – that hero of the First World War – look like a fool. A few months earlier Kessler had written that Papen looked 'like an ill-tempered billy-goat in a silk-lined black Sunday suit trying to stand to attention. A character out of *Alice in Wonderland*.'

Kessler, a member of the Reichsbanner – the paramilitary wing of the Social Democrats – had voted for the SPD in the November elections, as had 20 per cent of the German electorate. After all, the SPD was one of the only parties still trying to defend the Republic.

Fromm wasn't mourning the departed chancellor either. Papen had mainly represented the interests of the major landowners in eastern Germany, who, in November 1932, were eagerly scrabbling for power. She believed 'they underestimated the radical movement', meaning the Nazis.

Two months earlier she'd spent a Sunday with Schleicher and Papen at the racetrack. The chancellor had approached her as she stood with Schleicher and a female friend. Papen kissed her hand – he could be gallant, on occasion. 'Frau Bella, would it not be a marvellous idea to take a group photograph for your newspaper?' he asked. His object, of course, was to make people believe he was still on the best of terms with the Defence Minister, thought Fromm. It was all for show. She knew the two men had fallen out long before.

At Karstadt's Lebensmittel, the comestibles department at the vast department store near Hermannplatz Station, a pound of top-quality butter cost 1.44 marks, a pound of pork belly 64 pfennigs and a litre of wine from Edenkoben 60 pfennigs, assuming you could buy ten.

The average worker earned 164 marks per month.

'This is how they live every day,' announced a leaflet Communists were handing out on the streets of Berlin. 'Hitler's bill at the Kaiser-hof: 1 breakfast, 23 marks – times twelve, 276 marks! And 28,890 marks for the room! All while you're going hungry!'

Propaganda or truth? At the end of 1931, we know the Nazis paid a sum total of 650.86 marks for three nights and seven rooms, including food and service. Although it's also true that the Kaiserhof was among the most expensive hotels in the city.

That said, Hitler frequently abstained from the chef's famous dishes at the Kaiserhof: after all, you never knew what kind of mischief people might be planning. He also had a better alternative. Magda Goebbels' cooking was exquisite, and she prepared vegetarian meals just the way the Führer liked them. The Goebbels lived only a few minutes' drive away, in Charlottenburg, not far from Berlin's largest sports stadium. Their spacious, high-ceilinged apartment was originally Magda's, paid for by her ex-husband, the millionaire Günther Quandt. A grand piano stood in the salon.

The address had a nice ring to it: Reichskanzlerplatz 2.

Joseph Goebbels was thirty-five years old, a small, slight man with a weedy torso, a large head, brown eyes and black hair. Club-footed, he walked with a limp, courtesy of a childhood attack of bone-marrow inflammation. His adversaries referred to him mockingly as a 'shrunken Teuton', a term that became increasingly common in Nazi Germany for men of short stature. At the podium, however, he radiated power; he was a demagogue whose oratorical skill had won over thousands of new supporters for the Nazis in Berlin. When he took over the Berlin branch of the NSDAP in November 1926 it was a bickering mess; by 1932 he was the undisputed master of its well-organised ranks.

More than a few Berliners were afraid of him, of his radicalism, his unscrupulousness, his cunning. Goebbels was pathologically ambitious, a megalomaniac and workaholic desperate for recognition. And he sought the favour of one man above all others: Adolf Hitler. He was willing to use any means to aid Hitler's rise to power, convinced that one day, when his Führer became Führer to all Germans, his own brilliance would truly come to shine. Hitler? 'A wonderful man!' noted Goebbels in November 1932. 'For him I would willingly be quartered.' He hoped that when Hitler and Hindenburg stood face to face once more, shook hands and looked each other in the eye, they would trust each other. Although Hindenburg, it was rumoured, referred derisively to Hitler as the 'Bohemian lance corporal'.

At one o'clock an aeroplane coming from Munich landed at Tempelhof Airfield. On board were Adolf Hitler, Wilhelm Frick, head of the NSDAP parliamentary group in the Reichstag, Gregor Strasser, organisational director, and Ernst 'Putzi' Hanfstaengl, senior foreign press secretary. They had come to arrange their rise to power. Hitler was driven from the airport to Goebbels' house, where Goebbels updated his guest on the events of the past few days.

The question was, what was Kurt von Schleicher thinking? Always whispering in Hindenburg's ear. In conversation with English-speaking informants, Hanfstaengl only ever referred to the Defence Minister as 'Mr Creeper', a literal translation of his surname that made him sound like some whimsical creation out of a Dickens novel. Hanfstaengl was a cultured man, the son of a prominent art dealer and a keen if unsubtle pianist. His renditions of Wagner's magnificent arias, hammered out on the keyboard, moved Hitler profoundly.

How did Hitler, Austrian by birth, acquire German citizenship so quickly? Without it, he would have been ineligible to stand for president. More than a few people in Germany were wondering the same thing, including Oskar Thielemann, an SPD politician.

The official explanation? That the Free State of Brunswick had given Hitler an advisory role in local government and granted him

German citizenship for his 'valuable services'. Valuable services? What kind? Thielemann put the question to the Nazi-led Interior Ministry of the Free State: 'What contracts has Councillor Hitler secured for the economy of Brunswick, and what work, if any, has he carried out for the State of Brunswick thus far?'

The answer arrived on 17 November: 'The Interior Minister of Brunswick has communicated that Councillor Hitler provided valuable services to him in his role as special adviser on economic issues, in particular regarding the preservation of the mining industry in Unterharz.'

Hitler, an expert on mining? The news must have come as a surprise to more people than just Thielemann.

Abraham Plotkin was a riddle unto himself. In his writing he tried to explore what was driving him, tried to probe what he was seeking in Europe. His family had fled from the 'dark shadows of terror' in Tsarist Russia for America when he was a child. 'Now I am going back. What for? I hardly know. Perhaps I am going so as to escape the humdrum of everyday city life in my own country. [...] Perhaps later when and if I become aware of it I'll feel as silly as I look. One never can really tell how foolish one is.'

Around midnight Hitler returned to Reichskanzlerplatz, where the Goebbels were expecting him. First their guest told them a little of what had happened that day. He seemed entirely at ease. The government would declare another 'truce' the next morning: there were to be no demonstrations and no open-air rallies until 2 January. Gregor Strasser, meanwhile, was getting on the Führers' nerves. Recently Hitler had sounded contemptuous whenever his name was mentioned. But enough of all that – it was time for music. Why else was there a grand piano in the salon?

Goebbels himself was a keen accordion-player. Music, he observed, was the only indulgence Hitler permitted himself after a dogfight.

SATURDAY 19 NOVEMBER

Hitler Visits Hindenburg Today
— *Vossische Zeitung*

After Papen Resigns: No Half Measures!
History Demands Action
— *Völkischer Beobachter*

Central Committee Calls for United Front:
Join Forces to Battle Fascist Dictatorship!
— *Die Rote Fahne*

The negotiations to form a government continued at a frenetic pace, despite Hindenburg's advanced age. Visiting the president on 19 November was a guest he only reluctantly received: Adolf Hitler had asked Otto Meissner, head of the office of the President and Hindenburg's most senior member of staff, for an interview with Hindenburg alone. They agreed on strict confidentiality.

At half past eleven, the leader of the Nazi party arrived as agreed. The president made it clear to Hitler that he wanted to adhere to the principle of a non-partisan government. A government led by Herr Hitler, however, would be a single-party administration. Still, he added, Hitler could achieve his goals another way, by agreeing to a government led by a non-partisan. In return, Hindenburg would allocate Hitler's party some ministerial posts.

Hitler, having arrived with sky-high expectations, struggled to conceal his indignation. He would only join a cabinet, he insisted, if he was given the reins of power. Moreover, he followed this up with a threat: 'A non-partisan cabinet may be able to govern for a while by authoritarian means, supported by the instruments of state power, but it wouldn't last long-term. By February there would be a new revolution, and Germany would cease to be a significant force in world politics.'

The president demurred.

Yet he continued to observe the proprieties. The man sitting before him was a candidate for chancellor, after all – at least in theory.

The conversation lasted not fifteen minutes, as agreed, but sixty-five. It was only their fourth private meeting. Meissner noted that sort of thing. Meissner noted everything. Afterwards Hindenburg recounted to him every twist and turn of the discussion.

Hitler had suggested that Hindenburg sign an 'enabling act', a legal step – taken years earlier, for example, under the liberal Chancellor Gustav Stresemann – that would give a chancellor governing without a majority sweeping plenary powers and allow the president to withdraw from the day-to-day minutiae of politics. It would also require the dissolution of Parliament. True, Stresemann's situation in 1923 had been somewhat different, what with hyperinflation and the Occupation of the Ruhr by the French, but, in both cases, there was serious internal unrest caused by both the left and the right.

An enabling act. Yes, perhaps that might work.

Around half past twelve Hitler left the Chancellery and climbed into his car. Outside the entrance on Wilhelmstrasse, a crowd had gathered. They had broken through the chain of police officers and surged towards the gate, but gradually they cleared a path, and the car edged its way through. Outside the Hotel Kaiserhof, the mob was in a festive mood. 'Heil Hitler!' they bellowed, most of them men in brown shirts.

Hitler didn't address them; he had nothing to report. Instead, he was whisked into the hotel, leaving murmurs of hope and impatience in his wake. Only briefly did the Führer make an appearance at his window.

At five o'clock that afternoon, Fritz Schäffer of the Bavarian People's

Party arrived at Wilhelmstrasse 77 for a meeting with the president. Hitler, Schäffer felt, gave less cause for alarm than those around him. The man only needed a strong counterweight.

Thank you, said Hindenburg, and continued to brood.

Each party was concerned solely with furthering its own advantage, and there were also the personal grudges or compacts among the relevant actors to be considered, which were difficult to judge. How could Hindenburg make a decision that would bring Germany together instead of splitting it further apart? Uniting the people – that was the most important thing of all.

At two o'clock, in the Kammersäle in Teltower Strasse the nineteenth district conference for the Berlin-Brandenburg–Lausitz–Grenzmark branch of the German Communist Party, the KPD began. More than a million KPD voters lived in this area, which was the most important party district in Germany. Roughly eight hundred delegates were in attendance, and they were confident. The chaos at Wilhelmstrasse could only drive more voters into their arms.

At the top of the agenda was 'the political situation and our next task'. Comrade Walter Ulbricht, a member of the Central Committee of the KPD, addressed the assembly. During the transport workers' strike in early November he had joined forces with Joseph Goebbels in leading the charge; now Ulbricht warned against sharing power with the NSDAP.

Of primary concern to the Communists, however, was an altogether different enemy: the Social Democrats. The comrades who had erred from the righteous socialist path – in the eyes of the KPD, at least, and in their propaganda. Yet not all of those sympathetic to the party understood why their leaders were campaigning more resolutely against the Social Democrats than against the Nazis. In reality, the senior figures in the KPD were not free to decide how they should treat the Social Democrats. Strategic decisions were made by Moscow, and Moscow's strategy required that the Nazis assume control of the German government. At first, anyway. Hadn't Marx and Engels predicted that the counterreaction would smooth the Communists' way into power? As soon as the NSDAP ruled Germany, thousands of workers would transfer their allegiance to the KPD.

That was the plan.

A letter arrived at Hindenburg's office in Wilhelmstrasse. By no means all of Germany's most prominent industrialists had signed it, but a considerable number had. 'Your Excellency, most honoured President of the Reich! Like Your Excellency, we are imbued with a passionate love of the German people and the Fatherland, and we the undersigned are hopeful regarding the fundamental transformation in the leadership of state business that Your Excellency has initiated.' One of the signatories was Kurt Freiherr von Schröder, a Cologne-based banker who was influential in the Rheinland. He had big plans for Hitler.

Similar letters arrived from leading businessmen such as Fritz Thyssen, Erwin Merck and the former banker Hjalmar Schacht. They, too, wrote that 'the National Socialist German Workers' Party fundamentally' approved of Hindenburg's policies. 'Entrusting the leadership and responsibilities of a presidential cabinet endowed with the best practical and personal talents to the leader of the largest nationalist group will eliminate the detritus and drawbacks that inevitably cling to every mass movement, and will sweep along with it millions of people who are currently standing back, making them a positive force.'

Hindenburg was very impressed, as he confessed to his inner circle, particularly because one of the signatories was Eberhard Graf von Kalckreuth, president of the National Rural League and one of the most influential landowners in Prussia.

Details remained sketchy regarding the 'detritus and drawbacks'.

Reinhold Georg Quaatz, a nationalist, conservative-leaning Member of Parliament, was nervous. If Hitler and Schleicher reached a deal, they could conceivably marshal a majority in the Reichstag. If so, they would be in the president's good books. Quaatz, a member of the DNVP, observed: 'If that happens, we'll end up squashed against the wall.'

Everybody was talking about Schleicher, Schleicher, Schleicher. He didn't think much of the former military man. Did he have the toughness required to see through a grand plan? Moreover, Quaatz had heard that Schleicher was ill.

'What do you reckon?' he'd asked Otto Meissner. 'Does Schleicher want to be chancellor?' Meissner and Quaatz knew each other well, and spoke candidly.

'Schleicher's intentions are always obscure,' replied Meissner. Personally, he added, he objected 'sharply' to the idea of the man becoming chancellor. But it wouldn't come to that – Hindenburg wanted to save the General for a military government.

Hitler's visit to the president was already common knowledge. Harry Graf Kessler – who enjoyed a fierce exchange of opinions – had invited Georg Bernhard to dinner. Bernhard was senior publisher at Ullstein, a defender of free speech and opponent of the National Socialists. A man after Harry Graf Kessler's own heart. Bernhard invited several other guests: the author Heinrich Mann, whose novel *Untertan* (The Subject) had delivered a devastating critique of Prussian militarism; Wolfgang Huck, newspaper magnate and one of Berlin's biggest taxpayers; Hans Schäffer, who had been responsible for the national budget at the Finance Ministry until the spring of that year and was currently head of the Ullstein publishing house; and Bernhard Weiss, erstwhile Deputy Chief of Police in Berlin, whom Papen had hounded out of office. Also present was Rudolf Hilferding, a Marxist theorist who had twice served as Finance Minister for the SPD, as well as various other politicians, journalists and diplomatic staff. It was an illustrious gathering, one generally abreast of the latest news – and usually with an accurate sense of everything else.

Even here, however, Kessler didn't really find out what Hindenburg was thinking. Nothing but rumours. Huck said the meeting between Hindenburg and Hitler had been quite civilised – very different from their previous encounters. Bernhard announced that Papen's resignation was merely a ruse! He'd be back. Several other gentlemen believed a general strike was unavoidable if the National Socialists took power.

But who was going to be chancellor?

'Nobody knew anything,' wrote Kessler in his diary at the evening's end. 'Everything is more or less down to chance and the whims, good or bad, of four or five people.'

Hindenburg, Meissner, Schleicher, Hitler – and Papen? Or was Kessler thinking of someone else? Either way, it had nothing to do with transparent democratic decision-making.

At midnight Joseph Goebbels appeared before the leaders of the SA in Berlin. The Sturmabteilung had invited him to a cordial social gathering, although it turned out to be anything but. After months of waiting, the party soldiers were itching to finally get their hands on power. Goebbels knew many of them hoped for senior posts to reward their loyalty. They were the ones who'd risked their necks, who'd taken brutal, hospitalising beatings for their Führer and the party or served their adversaries the same treatment. The events of August, when Hitler had seemed on the verge of becoming chancellor, had been a bitter disappointment for them, too.

It was now or never: Hitler must finally become chancellor. And it wasn't just the SA finding the tension unbearable. 'The whole city was in a state of tremulous agitation,' as Goebbels wrote.

SUNDAY 20 NOVEMBER

Papen's Legacy:
SPD Threatens Political Mass Strike – Communists
Step Up Civil War Agitation
– *Völkischer Beobachter*

You Can't Deny That Every Day
The Red Wall's Taller and Wider.
The First's Already Smacked His Head
Now Bring on the Next Rider!
– *Die Rote Fahne*

Totensonntag – Sunday of the Dead. The day when Germany commemorates its departed. Families make pilgrimages to graveyards. The journalist Alfred Kerr once described the atmosphere in the capital as follows:

Cemeteries in Berlin are less cemeteries … than convenient places for the accommodation of lifeless bodies.

They sprawl (in the city) flat and indifferent. Trains on metal girders thunder past; opposite are distilleries.

On the Sunday of the Dead all are drawn to these railway tombs: widows, sons, fiancées, daughters, mothers; with flowers.

Berlin's instinct towards orderliness: the graves are tidied. Almost soaped down … only then does grief make its presence truly felt.

Cleaning, here, is a profession of the heart.

Sunday of the Dead. Some think of those they have lost – those who have died, though they still live and walk among us.

Sunday, a day suspended, a day of quiet, private conversation. But, in November 1932, there was no peace in Berlin.

At noon Meissner arrived at the Kaiserhof. He had come to meet Hitler and arrange another interview with the president for the following day.

Many National Socialists sensed their moment approaching. Goebbels, however, took a cooler-headed view of what was happening at the Chancellery. Did the president really intend to hand Hitler the reins of power? Or was he simply trying to assimilate the party into his government in order to curb its momentum? 'Everybody mistrustful of Schleicher', he noted in his diary. He counselled against optimism and overconfidence.

Hindenburg might have been hoping Hitler would fall in line, but Goebbels knew his Führer's stubbornness.

He suspected, moreover, that General Schleicher was secretly in talks with other senior politicians in the NSDAP. Schleicher's goal was obvious: to sow discord and division among the Nazis. Left-leaning Gregor Strasser, the second strongest man in the party, was currently enjoying his 'obligatory fling', as Goebbels called it. Roughly half the branch leaders of the NSDAP seemed to be on Strasser's side. Opposed to Hitler's all-or-nothing strategy, they wanted compromise, and the instant gratification that a scrap of power would bring. How would they respond if Strasser brought the conflict into the open? The air was thick with gossip.

All the parties in the Reichstag were dodging and feinting, wheeling and dealing. The Centre Party signalled its willingness to tolerate Hitler as chancellor. The DNVP wouldn't even accept the Nazis' invitation to talk. While Hermann Göring was negotiating with other party leaders, Goebbels went to the Kaiserhof to consult with Hitler and his most faithful followers. 'From now on the Führer is playing chess for power,' he later wrote. 'It is an exciting and nerve-racking struggle, yet it also conveys the thrilling sense of being a game in which everything is at stake.'

What was the right move? A few months earlier Goebbels had written in his diary: 'Legal? With the Centre Party? It's enough to make you vomit!'

In any case, Hitler would carry out all future negotiations in writing. Goebbels was sure of that. No unnecessary emotion, no ill-considered turns of phrase. Every nuance mattered.

Being the French ambassador in Berlin had been a challenge even before the economic crisis, but the political situation was now utterly confused. The peace agreed at Versailles more than thirteen years earlier was still as much of a bone of contention as ever, resentment centring on the loss of territories like Alsace and all of Germany's colonies, the issue of war guilt and the high reparations paid to France. André François-Poncet had known Germany since his youth, having attended school in Offenburg before becoming a student of German Studies, and had been injured in battle during the First World War. He was motivated by one primary goal: to improve Franco-German relations and prevent yet another war. He hoped to achieve a modus vivendi in which both countries could coexist peacefully side by side.

François-Poncet had been ambassador for just over a year. He threw countless receptions and parties, while his sweet-natured wife gained a reputation as 'the most marvellous hostess in Berlin', as Bella Fromm put it. François-Poncet was greying at the temples and his hair was thinning at the back – but, then, he was nearing his mid-forties. He set great store by an elegant appearance, and the tips of his moustache were always delicately twirled.

News of Papen's resignation had reached him that same evening. The ambassador had never thought especially highly of Papen, once remarking that the man was 'superficial, quarrelsome, false, ambitious, conceited, devious and scheming'. Papen pretended to be a friend to France, but François-Poncet was sure he was longing for the moment when the German army could exact its revenge and surge triumphantly into Paris.

Then there was Kurt von Schleicher. As François-Poncet well knew, there were many who considered him a realist and above all a cynic, a past master of intrigue. The military had no affection for him because his career had been made in the back office rather than at the front or the barracks. So what kind of impression did the Defence Minister make? The ambassador described him as follows: 'Bald, with a shaved head, of striking pallor, wan, his expression like a mask with two gleaming, piercing eyes; his features are ill-defined in his bloated face, and his narrow lips are barely visible. None of this speaks in his favour. In one aspect, however, he is distinctive: his beautiful hands.' Schleicher, observed the ambassador, spoke brusquely and without mincing words, but in conversation he often revealed a sharp wit. Oh, and one more thing about the General: 'He likes to laugh. Loudly.'

MONDAY 21 NOVEMBER

Hindenburg Offers Hitler Mandate:
Is Stable, Working Majority Feasible for Hitler Cabinet?
– Hitler to Give Written Reply This Afternoon
– Vossische Zeitung

Hitler Visits Hindenburg Again
– Der Angriff

Police were deployed outside the Kaiserhof that morning. SA men in brown shirts had gathered, shifting from one foot to the other. Hitler, they believed, was nearly at the finish line, and they were eager to cheer him on.

His limousine was already waiting outside. The Chancellery was only a hundred paces away, but Hitler preferred to be driven; he climbed out of the car on the other side of the street like the statesman he wanted to be.

The spoken word counted for little when it came to power. Instead, writing was read out and notes exchanged – the consequence of 13 August 1932, when Hitler had considered himself as good as chancellor, only to find that Hindenburg had changed his mind at the last minute, despite all assurances to the contrary from the president's camp. It had been a plot, he was sure of it. Who was behind it? Papen? Schleicher? Hitler didn't trust either of them an inch. Carefully considered letters were now his instruments of choice.

At their meeting, which began at half past ten, Hindenburg informed Hitler that he had until Thursday evening to establish 'whether and under what conditions' he could obtain 'a stable, working majority in the Reichstag with a clear, consolidated agenda' under a Hitler-led cabinet. As it happened, Hitler had already handed him his response in a letter at the beginning of their conversation.

'I have only one request for Your Excellency,' wrote Hitler.

> At least give me the authority and status given to the men before me, who could not contribute as much to the great value of the authority and significance of Your Excellency's name as I can. … My own name and the existence of this greatest of German movements are themselves security, but they would necessarily be destroyed if our efforts led to an unfavourable outcome. In that case, Herr President, I see not a military dictatorship following after us but Bolshevist chaos.

Did that cut any ice? Many German citizens were, in fact, afraid of the Communists. The clock was ticking. Hitler had been given Hindenburg's mandate in writing – and he now had eighty hours to think it over.

In Tegel Prison, Carl von Ossietzky signed a statement drafted for him by his lawyer. The editor-in-chief of the *Weltbühne* was facing another accusation, this time for having published a series of critical articles about Reemtsma, a tobacco company, which uncovered corruption and sleaze within the industry and the Finance Ministry. The libel suit was currently being heard, and Ossietzky was being held responsible for the journalistic content of his magazine. For the third time in a few months, he was having to defend himself. It was the second time he was doing so from prison.

It was unnerving. What should he do? Ossietzky distanced himself from the two articles on Reemtsma that he himself had put into the magazine. Was he getting tired of fighting? 'The thick wall never fails to make its presence felt,' he had just written to his friend Kurt Tucholsky in exile.

Defence Minister Schleicher still hadn't come to terms with the fact that his predecessor and long-time boss and mentor Wilhelm Groener no longer wanted to speak to him. True, one of Schleicher's intrigues had played a role in Groener's resignation, and Groener had been unable to quell the scurrilous rumours that he was going senile – perhaps somebody close to him had even spread them – but that was how politics worked. Did he have to be so bitter?

On 21 November Schleicher tried again to save their old friendship, and congratulated Groener on his upcoming sixty-fifth birthday, both personally and in the name of the Wehrmacht.

'Most honoured Excellency!' wrote Schleicher. 'I hope that this new year of Your Excellency's life will lead to the discussion I have long awaited, as I believe I have a right at least to learn the reasons for our estrangement, which are unknown to me.'

Did Schleicher's letter change anything? Groener knew him better than most. At the end of May 1932 – almost three weeks after he stepped down as Defence Minister and Minister of the Interior – he had explained Schleicher's motives in a letter to one of his allies: 'It's not that he's trying to get the Nazis into power; he wants it for himself, and he wants to do so through Hindenburg. With the aid of Hindenburg's son, a close friend, he wields great influence over the president. Meissner, who cares for nothing but his little job, is only too willing to assist.'

Moreover, Groener added, 'Schleicher has long dreamed of governing via the military, without the Reichstag. But his plans, which obviously he no longer shares with me, are deeply obscure, and perhaps the Nazis will prove more cunning even than he.'

Some time later, on 18 June 1932, more than two weeks after the downfall of Chancellor Brüning, Groener wrote to the same friend:

> When I think back on recent developments, Schleicher seems to me more and more of a puzzle. When we dined at the Russian embassy about ten weeks ago, he told several German guests (you can ask Schäffer) that the military would never tolerate the Nazis coming to power, and that over there (Hammerstein)

was the man whose ruthless energy would prevent it. Perhaps it was all a sham.

'Hammerstein'. Groener meant Kurt von Hammerstein-Equord, Commander-in-Chief of the German armed forces. Elsewhere, Groener had commented that 'Hammerstein follows his friend Schleicher like a well-behaved hunting dog.'

Four Nazis attacked a newspaper seller on Friedrichstrasse who was distributing Social Democratic papers on behalf of the Reichsbanner. The twenty-nine-year-old was left with serious head injuries. The attackers fled when the police arrived.

It was a test of the party's nerve. By all appearances, Hindenburg still wanted nothing to do with a presidential dictatorship. The leaders of the NSDAP withdrew once again to the fourth floor of the Kaiserhof to confer. Gregor Strasser stuck his neck above the parapet: they had to negotiate with the DNVP. The time had come for a coalition!

Hitler rebuffed the idea. He would make no compromises.

From outside they could still hear their supporters baying as they gazed up at the top floor of the hotel where the National Socialists were gathered.

'Heil Hitler,' they roared.

The mood in the street was one of feverish anticipation, as though their moment was finally near at hand. More than a few members of the party itself were also convinced that Hitler was already chancellor.

'Poor deluded lot!' thought Goebbels. 'He was never further from it.'

Yet, in theory, their calculation was paying off. The pressure on the street was growing, the SA was ever-present, the Communists were making a racket, as they'd hoped. It all helped. Surely there had to be some way to break the old man's resolve?

TUESDAY 22 NOVEMBER

Highest Alert!
Hindenburg's Task for Hitler – Hitler Orders SA Terror
Workers of Germany, Unite in the Struggle!
– Die Rote Fahne

Hitler Hesitates
– Berliner Tageblatt

The state crisis won't end until a new system has stabilised,
be it through a right-wing or left-wing victory. Until
then every government will feel like a stopgap.
– Die Weltbühne

Abraham Plotkin was taking the night train from Paris to Berlin. The wooden benches in third class made it impossible to rest – he'd barely managed a wink of sleep. Travel in France was an altogether different affair. The seats there were upholstered, even in the cheapest classes, while the wood on German trains was so hard that his buttocks hurt and so smooth it was impossible to find a comfortable position. Disembarking at Potsdamer Bahnhof at 7 a.m. the next morning, Plotkin rubbed the drowsiness from his eyes. The city was cast in a leaden light. Here and there, men were cycling to work. Policemen surveyed him warily. A few beggars lay on the pavement. Plotkin was astonished that there weren't more – nothing like back home in New York or San Francisco, although Germany, too, had been hit hard by the economic crisis. Plotkin had come to meet trade-union allies and because he wanted to see how a welfare state could function despite empty government coffers. Functioning it apparently was.

The city was still asleep, the shops shut. He dropped off his bags and went for a walk, eventually reaching the Brandenburg Gate then

Unter den Linden. It was raining, but that didn't bother him. The sky was beginning to brighten, although the streetlamps were lit and mist drifted through the wide streets. The light struck him as unreal, bathing the trees and buildings in a strange gloaming.

Plotkin decided to find the Hotel Adlon. He must have realised he was in the centre of political Berlin's beating heart, yet he couldn't have heard about the poker game going on just a few hundred yards away down Wilhelmstrasse.

Fatigue overwhelmed him. Plotkin dragged himself into the hotel café and took out his travel typewriter, which lent him the aura of a busy writer, but before he could order a coffee or write a line his eyelids dropped shut. One could sleep well in an Adlon armchair, and no one there was going to wake him.

Many Berliners were marvelling at the National Socialists' latest act of heroism. To make sure he was on time for the most recent discussions about forming a new government, Hermann Göring had cut short his visit to Benito Mussolini in Italy and made a special trip on the Italian dictator's plane from Rome to Venice, where a Ju 52 was waiting for him – the same aircraft Hitler had used to wage his legendary electoral campaign that summer. Göring, a former fighter pilot, had flown the plane himself; or that was how he told the story later, anyway.

Rome to Berlin in under six hours! A record, naturally. Göring had been awarded the *Pour le Mérite*, the Reich's highest honour for bravery, for his actions on the Western Front during the First World War. A flying ace.

The headline splashed across the *12-Uhr-Blatt* in Berlin:

If Hitler Fails …
Meissner for Chancellor?

Not, the newspaper added, that Meissner needed it: 'his role as head of the office of the President affords him virtually as much influence over political affairs'. Meissner was a member of the 'camarilla', as the Berlin journalists liked to call it, the small circle of intimates who advised Paul von Hindenburg. Or manipulated him, if you believed the more critical voices.

To observers of the political scene, Meissner was as sinister as he was indispensable – devoted to his master, fanatically dutiful, terrifyingly well informed and well connected, with no apparent interests of his own. The factotum of power, and an expert in constitutional law, to boot.

Meissner was a man who hedged his bets. His eyes were vigilant, protected behind their spectacles. His thin, pursed upper lip was covered with a grey moustache, the corners of his mouth drawn down. His head appeared retracted into his neck, like a boxer readied for the next punch. His suits, which he liked to wear with a pocket handkerchief, always seemed to be a size too small, and the knot of his tie nestled tightly against his throat. Those who saw how much lobster he could put away at a buffet were astonished to witness such an eruption of greed in a man who otherwise kept his own interests firmly under wraps.

Otto Meissner, they said, had advised the president to make Hitler chancellor. Or perhaps that was just another rumour.

Schleicher had helped him draft the most recent letter to Hitler, lending a hand with the wording.

That was a fact.

The *12-Uhr-Blatt* lay on a table chez Meissner. A servant had bought the newspaper near the Adlon because of the headline. The lady of the house, Hildegard Meissner, blanched as she read. Her voice was barely audible. 'Anything but that,' whispered Frau Meissner. 'Dear God, please spare us!'

At the Kaiserhof, another note arrived from Meissner. It instructed

Hitler to find coalition partners – or keep his mitts off power. Rather more politely phrased, of course.

Hitler felt attacked, and Goebbels, too, was incensed. To unwind, the two of them attended the opera at Unter den Linden. Staged that night was Wagner's *Die Meistersinger von Nürnberg*, a piece calculated to raise even the most dejected spirits. Later, well after the final curtain, Goebbels noted: 'The orchestra played more beautifully and impressively than ever before. Wagner's eternal music gives all of us renewed strength and endurance. At the great "Awake" chorus we all felt our hearts swell.'

Abraham Plotkin found a place to stay on the corner of Friedrichstrasse and Dorotheenstrasse, a room that cost him 2.50 marks per night. He then called the editorial department at *Vorwärts* (Onwards), the daily newspaper of the SPD, to ask for the telephone number of Raphael Abramovitch, whom he'd met in the USA. Abramovitch, a Russian living in exile in Berlin, was one of the Mensheviks who had lost the tussle for power with the Bolsheviks in the revolution of 1917. Since then, men like him had been threatened, persecuted, locked up and even murdered in Russia.

His voice sounded friendly down the telephone line. Did Plotkin have any news from America?

Of course, said Plotkin. For his part, he was eager to learn what was going on in Germany. They arranged to meet the next day.

Afterwards Plotkin took a stroll down Friedrichstrasse. It was unbelievable how well dressed most people were. At the same time, he'd heard that roughly a third of Germany's more than sixty million inhabitants were currently reliant on state support. How could the government be pulling it off? Plotkin was deeply impressed. Wherever he looked that night, he could find no signs of poverty. Not in that part of town.

WEDNESDAY 23 NOVEMBER

Hitler to Answer Today
Expected to Reject Government Mandate
– Vossische Zeitung

Presidential Principle or Parliamentary Majority?
President's Mandate Unclear
Führer Expecting Clarification
– Völkischer Beobachter

In the town of Gladbach-Rheydt, a special court sentenced a member of the SPD's Reichsbanner to ten years in prison. Along with some fellow members of the paramilitary organisation, the man had been caught fighting Nazis on the street. He'd beaten one opponent with a stick and thrown stones at him. The new emergency decree against political terror was used to convict him, although it had not yet been in force at the time of the offence.

Hitler met with Schleicher. The president had asked his devoted general to sound out Hitler on the possibility of working together for the good of the Fatherland. Without putting anything in writing.

Schleicher was only too happy to seize the opportunity. If he couldn't undermine the Nazis, then perhaps he could at least exploit them for his own gain. 'If they weren't there one would practically have to invent them,' he had written in a letter that March. It was their existence that prevented the Communists from attracting even more angry, jobless young men.

The Sturmabteilung, the military arm of the Nazi party, had about 445,000 men in its ranks. To the General, the idea of integrating them into the military was compelling: the Treaty of Versailles had left the military so depleted that if war broke out Germany would be unable to defend itself, let alone go on the attack. A hundred thousand men on land and fifteen thousand on water was all the country had been allotted. They'd been secretly rearming for years, of course, but the military was still anything but fighting fit.

'Herr Hitler,' asked Schleicher, 'would you join a cabinet under myself as chancellor?'

The two had first met a little over a year earlier. Schleicher's assessment? 'An interesting man and an outstandingly gifted speaker. Tends to get carried away with his own plans. Needs to be yanked back down by the coat-tails to solid, factual ground.'

Hitler, for his part, had told party members: 'It won't be easy to strike a deal with Schleicher. He has a clever but sly gaze. I don't believe he is honest.'

'No,' replied Hitler.

Their conversation lasted three hours.

The discussion earned Schleicher a presidential rebuke. He was supposed to sound him out, yes, but not to suddenly put himself forward as chancellor and certainly not to make any offers!

Hindenburg never showed that side of himself in public. The blustering, authoritarian bruiser was known only to his inner circle.

Ever since the NSDAP's electoral success, there had been a stream of people keen to meet with the Führer, including industrialists, diplomats and politicians from other parties. Most of these guests would be ushered in through the back doors or meet Hitler at some remote location. Many of them found him interesting. But being seen with him? Well, there was no need for that.

Such was the American ambassador Frederic M. Sackett's way of thinking, at any rate. Not originally trained as a diplomat, Sackett's methods were unorthodox. He was the son of a prosperous wool manufacturer from Kentucky and had been a businessman before he was elected to the Senate as a Republican. For the past few months he'd got into the habit of finding out where the Nazi leaders were going to be dining and then turning up as though by sheer coincidence. He particularly liked to keep an eye on Hermann Göring that way – a dazzling fellow.

Sackett's British colleague, Sir Horace Rumbold, refused to meet with Hitler or any other Nazi. Sackett, on the other hand, had already gone to meet him one year earlier, on 5 December 1931, at the house of Emil Georg von Stauss. Stauss, a friend of the Nazis, was on the board of various major German companies. Sackett had brought someone from the embassy to translate, and both men had their wives with them as cover – as though this were a social occasion, not a political one.

The door was flung open. Rudolf Hess, Hermann Göring and Ernst Hanfstaengl appeared. At their side was a man introduced as 'Herr Wolff'. Adolf Hitler. It was a major political event, this encounter between the US ambassador and the leading member of the German opposition, and one kept strictly confidential. It had been arranged by bankers close to the Nazis, who were concerned about the vast amounts of American credit held in German companies.

It was a trying afternoon, which had the effect of convincing Sackett that there was little to fear from Hitler. Although the Führer did speak – and he spoke a lot, in declamatory style, as though before a vast public – he wouldn't look the ambassador in the eye. A fanatical crusader, thought Sackett. Certainly not the type from which statesmen evolved.

The Nazis he considered ruffians, symptoms of a radical change, not an independent political force. He was far more afraid of the Communists – and he knew the White House shared those fears.

Raphael Abramovitch was looking tired. He was a small man in his fifties, and Plotkin saw trepidation in his eyes. In Russia his host had founded an underground movement that aided political prisoners, helping many of them to escape. When he gave lectures in America, Communists rioted.

Next to Abramovitch sat a young refugee from Russia. Tea was served. They talked about America, the economic crisis, the trade unions. Why had Plotkin come to Berlin? And why now? 'The possibility', replied the American, 'of real developments in Germany this winter. If anything happens, I want to be on the ground.' He was tired, he added, 'of reading about things that happened elsewhere'.

'Make no mistake,' cautioned Abramovitch, 'Hitler is dangerous. He is the most dangerous enemy of trade unionism, social democracy and the Republic that there is in Germany today.'

In Germany, 156,000 more people were unemployed than in the previous month, bringing the total to 5,265,000. Many of those were breadwinners. Still, the rate of increase had slowed.

Newspapers in Berlin had reported that morning that lower-level NSDAP party leaders had got into a scuffle outside the Kaiserhof the night before. Hitler, they wrote, had gone to the theatre out of sheer resentment and bitterness, escaping the wretched state of his party. For Goebbels, these were lies spread by 'Berlin's Jewish press'.

When he arrived at the hotel, Hitler dictated another missive to Hindenburg. The Führer sounded truculent, despite his 'expression of deepest devotion', and he argued his case once again. Shortly after four in the afternoon, Hitler had finished the letter. A masterpiece of political strategy, thought Goebbels.

Göring, President of the Reichstag, handed over Hitler's letter in person late that afternoon, long before the period he'd been given to think had come to an end. In it, Hitler rejected the offer to form part of a government – 'owing to its inherent unfeasibility'. Instead, the head of the NSDAP suggested he submit a policy programme within forty-eight hours and a list of ministers within twenty-four. He renewed his demands for plenary powers, which 'have never previously been denied even to parliamentary chancellors in such critical and difficult times'.

Was this desperate determination a calculated political decision – or merely a farce? Did the Nazis really believe that the legendarily obstinate Hindenburg could be defeated by still-greater obstinacy?

Meissner's response was swift, and none too diplomatic:

> The president has dismissed this suggestion, as he does not believe he would be able to defend before the German people granting presidential powers to the leader of a party that has repeatedly emphasised its exclusivity ... he fears that a presidential cabinet led by Herr Hitler would inevitably develop into a party dictatorship with all that would entail in terms of badly exacerbating the rifts within the German people. The president can take responsibility neither before his oath nor before his own conscience for bringing about such a situation.

Shortly after Göring's departure, several hundred Communists suddenly materialised on Wilhelmsplatz outside the Kaiserhof. 'Down with Hitler!' they screamed. National Socialists surged onto the square, and the two groups rapidly came to blows outside the luxury hotel. After a while the police intervened, driving the men apart and breaking the deadlock.

The pressure on the streets – how long could a teetering society withstand it?

There was an equally heated duel at the Sportpalast. The BSC, the Berlin Ice-Hockey Club, beat Pötzleinsdorf from Vienna 3–1. A test of German against Austrian mastery. Only in the last fifteen minutes did the Berliners turn up the heat.

The tickets were relatively cheap, but many seats in the stadium remained empty all the same.

Despite the flurry of activity, Goebbels decided, the situation that evening was unchanged. The waiting was almost unbearable. Would Hindenburg capitulate, ground down by the urgent need to present the German people with a government? Goebbels studied the evening papers in his apartment and was amused. 'The press is in a state of feverish tension. The most wonderful canards are being spread by means of their printing ink,' he observed.

Then the man he referred to even in his personal diaries as 'the Führer' appeared. They chatted, listened to music and, for the time being, avoided discussing their plans to conquer Wilhelmstrasse.

Schleicher's network of informants was more vigilant than ever. Rumour had it his eyes and ears were everywhere. His confidants had even been in talks with supporters of Gregor Strasser, Hitler's great adversary in the NSDAP, and the signals were highly encouraging. A brief drawn up by the Ministerial Office for General Schleicher announced that 'They expressed themselves very explicitly, indicating that they were authorised to say that Strasser's support for Hitler is due solely to party solidarity. Strasser was not involved in the various letters and memoranda of the past few days. He is ready to step in personally should Hitler's efforts come to nothing.'

At Vossstrasse 3, just around the corner from the Chancellery, the Bavarian envoy, Konrad von Preger, was taking his leave of Berlin. Two hundred and fifty guests were celebrating his retirement. Almost the whole cabinet was present, including Chancellor Papen.

Around the same time, *Die glückliche Reise* (The Happy Journey) was being premiered at the Theater am Kurfürstendamm. It was an operetta by Eduard Künneke, and its subject – how could it be otherwise? – was love. The audience was enchanted by its lively, swinging rhythms, which even incorporated a touch of the blues. At the end of the piece the heroes left Germany for Buenos Aires, still searching for happiness.

That night, the windows of the synagogue on Prinzregenten-strasse in Wilmersdorf were smashed by person or persons unknown – for the third time within a few days. The police suspected young National Socialists. They announced they would be boosting patrols.

THURSDAY 24 NOVEMBER

Hitler Rejects Mandate
Wants to Lead a Presidential Cabinet
– *Vossische Zeitung*

Former Reichsbank President Dr Schacht on Berlin Negotiations:
'Only One Man Can Be Chancellor: Adolf Hitler'
– *Völkischer Beobachter*

The 'Kaiserhof' in Berlin, the NSDAP's headquarters, looks
like a fortress besieged on all sides. There are currently two
things this country would be unable to withstand: a presidential
crisis and the disintegration of the NSDAP, which would
give tremendous impetus to the Communist movement.
– *Tägliche Rundschau*

Hitler sat upstairs at the Kaiserhof. The decision-makers sat across
the street. Another day's waiting, another day's brooding. Was Hindenburg on the verge of cracking? Surely he *had* to be. Was he still
not under enough pressure? By now the NSDAP even had influential
industrialists on its side.

At three o'clock, Meissner's next message arrived. The president
had given it to be known that his door was always open to Hitler and
that he would always be ready to hear his views on the outstanding
issues. Hindenburg, he continued, did not want to give up hope 'that
in this way it will, in time, be possible to prevail upon you and your
movement to cooperate with all the other forces in the nation willing
to work constructively together'.

Hitler's answer, a long-winded, self-justifying screed, declared the
discussion closed. 'As ever, I also ask you to convey my deepest devotion to His Excellency, Herr President.'

What now? What should be done? How many more weeks would the National Socialist movement be able to persevere in the teeth of such opposition? How long would Joseph Goebbels continue to fight for power, especially when power might never come? 'Schleicher,' he noted grimly, 'that eternal schemer, has emerged victorious once more. Until he, too, is devoured by the revolution.'

And Hitler himself? Was his enthusiasm dwindling, as so many journalists had been predicting for months?

Who was this Adolf Hitler? For more than nine years, ever since his failed power grab in Munich, the Beer Hall Putsch, he had been a controversial figure on the political scene. Numerous foreign correspondents in Berlin had long believed his time was coming, and doggedly tried to arrange interviews. Ernst Hanfstaengl, meanwhile, was convinced that the Nazis ought to be winning over the American public.

Dr Ernst F. Sedgwick 'Putzi' Hanfstaengl was married to an American woman, Helene. On his father's side, his family had been advisers to the aristocratic House of Wittelsbach – Bavarian royalty – while one of his great-uncles on his mother's side was General John Sedgwick, who had been killed by Confederate sharpshooters during the American Civil War. Hanfstaengl had studied at Harvard, where one of his fellow students was the recently inaugurated President Franklin D. Roosevelt. He made cautious attempts to explain to Adolf Hitler what kind of country they were dealing with – this was a nation that, during the First World War, had mustered millions of soldiers nearinstantly and dispatched them across the Atlantic. The United States was a new kind of world power.

Hitler, for his part, was excited about the Klu Klux Klan, the skyscrapers and the anti-Semitic Henry Ford. That was more or less all he knew of America – although, of course, he also realised that the German economy was heavily dependent on American credit and that America's interest in the National Socialist movement was accordingly significant.

On 24 November 1931, therefore, he had agreed to an interview with Dorothy Thompson for *Cosmopolitan*. One year later he was still seething.

Thompson, a New Yorker then thirty-seven years old, and the daughter of a Methodist preacher, was a frequent contributor to the *Philadelphia Public Ledger* and the *New York Evening Post*. She spoke fluent German and was adept at mimicking both the Berlin and the Viennese dialects. Wilhelmstrasse held a special place in Thompson's heart. It was there, at a reception given by Gustav Stresemann in 1927, that she had met her future husband, the Nobel Prize-winning author Sinclair Lewis.

Hanfstaengl was known to enjoy keeping journalists on tenterhooks. He made them wait and hope and pray, and only those who passed this test were granted access to the Führer. Thompson was among them.

Her book *I Saw Hitler*, published in late 1932, was less an interview than the chronicle of a failed interview – and an unconventional portrait of the man.

She had spent years fighting for a meeting, but even the groundwork proved irritating. 'I had rather expected a clipped "Appear!"' wrote Thompson. 'Instead, I must present questions. Written out, and twenty-four hours beforehand. No trickery allowed. ... Then, later, I was informed that the questions must be reduced to three.' Being treated like children tended to put experienced journalists on the defensive, rather than making them more respectful, but Thompson arrived at the hotel as agreed.

She was kept waiting in the upstairs lobby. Suddenly, Hitler bustled past, accompanied by a bodyguard. She continued to wait. An Italian journalist was shown in before her. At last, however, her turn came. And what did Thompson make of Hitler? Mostly, she was disappointed. 'When finally I walked into Adolf Hitler's salon in the Kaiserhof Hotel, I was convinced that I was meeting the future dictator of Germany. In something less than fifty seconds I was quite sure I was not. It took just about that time to measure the startling insignificance of this man who has set the world agog.'

Thompson described Hitler as 'almost faceless, a man whose

countenance is a caricature, a man whose framework seems cartilaginous, without bones'. Harsher still: 'He is inconsequent and voluble, ill poised and insecure. He is the very prototype of the little man.'

He did possess a certain charm, she admitted, but 'it is the soft almost feminine charm of the Austrian!' Only his eyes were notable. 'Dark grey and hyperthyroidic, they have the peculiar shine which often distinguishes geniuses, alcoholics, and hysterics.'

For Thompson, Hitler gave 'the impression of a man in a trance'.

The DNVP, as rapt as they were jittery, observed these proceedings. Their party was too elitist for the masses, and Hindenburg detested their leader, the enterprising media tycoon Alfred Hugenberg.

In the battle for power, that was not an advantage.

Quaatz, a fellow party member, noted in his diary: 'The crisis continues. Hitler declines again, as on 13.8, after protracted toing and fro-ing. Goebbels (said to be an agent of Moscow) and Strasser fighting over the poor soul. Goebbels won, as Hitler himself is probably afraid of the responsibility. He's the archetypal "rascal".'

Goebbels, an agent of Moscow? Who was spreading those rumours? Did the German conservatives really have such fertile imaginations? Surely Goebbels and his Communist counterpart Walter Ulbricht were at each other's throats? Goebbels was always railing against the Communists in his speeches, whether of the Russian or the German variety, and he made it painfully clear what he'd do with them if he had his way.

And yet.

Soviet intelligence was surreptitiously abetting the German Communists – that was an open secret. The problem was, nobody knew precisely which social circles their agents had managed to infiltrate. Only that they'd succeeded.

The painter Gert Caden (codename 'Cello'), for example, was assigned responsibility for 'special connections' and given lodgings with the family of an army officer by the name of Rinck von Baldenstein. The latter's acquaintances included General Friedrich von

Cochenhausen, President of the German Society for Military Policy and Military Science, as well as other senior officers. The Soviets also sought contacts in the networks around Franz von Papen and Kurt von Hammerstein-Equord.

Caden was soon deftly navigating this social world, becoming a member of the Stahlhelm (Steel Helmet), a right-leaning group of soldiers that worked hand-in-glove with the DVNP, and cultivating a relationship with the Wallenbergs, a family of bankers linked to Kurt von Schleicher. He was given the opportunity to observe military training exercises and was a welcome guest at all sorts of receptions.

Such was the calibre of the Communist Party's informants. But Goebbels?

The party had three hundred thousand members in Germany, but nothing was as shrouded in secrecy as its Geheimapparat, its 'secret apparatus'. That much is clear even from the names they used, which were constantly shifting. Military Apparatus. M-Apparatus. Department of Military Policy. Kippenberger Apparatus. Alex Apparatus. Adam Apparatus.

'Alex' and 'Adam' were codenames for Hans Kippenberger, the man in charge of the department. Having distinguished himself during the Hamburg Uprising of 1923, Kippenberger underwent some ideological fine-tuning in Moscow before returning to Germany.

Inside the Communists' headquarters at Karl Liebknecht House was an attic room accessible only via a concealed staircase. This was the central nervous system of the military-political apparatus of the KPD. It was from this room that the agents were managed, 112 of them since 1930, all trained in Moscow. Training focused on insurgency tactics, explosives, weaponry and telecommunications, as well as driving cars, trains and tanks. Also on the schedule were studies in dialectics, historical materialism, political economics, the history of the workers' movement, party-political techniques ... Thrilling stuff.

Several of the agents were interesting characters. Hans Hubert von Ranke – codename 'Moritz' – was the son of an imperial officer and a senior employee at Tempelhof Airport. Helga von

Hammerstein-Equord ('Grete'), daughter of the Commander-in-Chief of the German military, was a KPD informant. 'Erika' was the daughter of one of the biggest landowners in Mecklenburg, 'Liselotte' of a prominent industrialist, 'Gisela' of a German-Baltic aristocrat and 'Bover' of a major Swiss industrialist. 'Rita' worked at an embassy.

Other agents were so secret that in sources they are mentioned only by their codenames, including 'Be', 'Oskar', 'Ru 1' and 'Ru 27'. 'Be' had a good relationship with General von Stülpnagel, government press officer Erich Marcks – one of Schleicher's allies – and an adviser at the Ministry of Economics by the name of Waldeck.

'Ru 27', meanwhile, was someone in President Hindenburg's immediate circle. His reports demonstrate remarkable political insight. Or should that be her reports? Just who were 'Be' and 'Ru 27'? German counter-intelligence would certainly have loved to know.

The Prussian Judges' Association rebuked Goebbels' newspaper, *Der Angriff* (The Attack), for its abuse of various judges. Their statement deplored the 'coarse insults and malicious disparagement levelled at the court and the judiciary in general' and rejected all the accusations made by the National Socialist press. 'The Prussian judiciary serves the law and does its duty, without looking either right or left. It cannot be swayed by threats.'

Göring, President of the Reichstag, as well as MPs Frick, Goebbels and Strasser, and SA Chief-of-Staff Ernst Röhm, published a response in the *Völkischer Beobachter* and *Der Angriff*. 'The opposition press – as it has tended to do ever since the NSDAP was founded, particularly at times of political unrest – has once again published politically motivated reports in various guises on apparent differences within the National Socialist leadership.' The undersigned declared that they were 'united in their unshakeable allegiance to the Führer of the movement, and they consider it beneath their dignity to engage with such lies any further, in whatsoever form'.

Evidently Gregor Strasser was still avowing his unshakeable allegiance.

Fritz Kammler was advertising his 'balloon bicycles' in the newspaper. They were of 'excellent quality, with freewheel coaster brakes, a 3-year guarantee, part-payment permitted. 48 marks'. His shop was located at Oranienstrasse 70 in Berlin.

At five o'clock that afternoon, Göring summoned the press to the Kaiserhof. On the wall was a depiction of Frederick the Great in blue tiles. The past few days had taken their toll; that much was clear from Göring's demeanour. He was looking sluggish – flying across the lofty Alps, he must have pictured things very differently. The room was too small for the crush of people.

But Göring did what he could do better than anyone else: he introduced the Führer.

They hadn't given Hitler a chance, he shouted at the journalists. They'd thrown a spanner in the works right from the start! Hitler hadn't demanded the chancellorship at the head of a presidential cabinet, absolutely not. No, the Führer had simply made known his desire to be made chancellor. Forces that he, Göring, did not need to specify had systematically prevented Hitler from building a cabinet. Well. The National Socialists, he warned, would bring down any cabinet, just as they had done with Papen's.

'Only Hitler', concluded Göring, 'can rescue the German people.'

That evening Hans Albers was treading the boards at the Theater im Admiralspalast on Friedrichstrasse. The play, cryptically titled *Liliom*, told the story of a poor carousel barker who dies in a robbery trying to provide for his pregnant lover. It began at a quarter past eight. Originally by the Hungarian playwright Ferenc Molnár, it had been prepared for the German stage by Alfred Polgar.

Alfred Döblin, poet, psychiatrist and doctor from the east of Berlin, had written vividly about the area around Alexanderplatz, and it was because of Döblin that Abraham Plotkin now found himself in a tangle of narrow alleyways crammed with Jewish second-hand shops, brothels and pawnbrokers. Prostitutes loitered outside front doors. It reminded him of the old Hell's Kitchen in New York.

He came across a young woman selling sweets. Blonde and scrawny, she appeared no older than twenty-five. Her face was pinched, her clothes much too thin for the climate. Plotkin walked on, but he couldn't forget her face, in which he'd glimpsed 'that pallor that speaks of hunger'. Turning on his heel, he went back and bought ten pfennigs' worth of sweets.

'Have you eaten anything today?' he asked. They were standing outside Aschinger's restaurant, a chain that advertised the 'best quality at the cheapest price'.

Instead of replying the woman fainted, but Plotkin caught her before she hit the paving stones. He was astonished at how little she weighed.

He carried her into Aschinger's, followed by a policeman who asked what all the commotion was about. The woman came around, and Plotkin explained the situation. She wouldn't speak, but accepted some hot soup, spooning it down in silence. She seemed too afraid to say a word. Her sweets, which she'd dropped outside, had vanished, so Plotkin pressed money into her palm. A whole mark, he thought, 'a whole mark between herself and the possibilities of starvation!' But when he offered to walk her home she declined.

On Alexanderplatz, Plotkin realised, one did not accept help from strangers.

Entering a saloon, he fell into conversation with a prostitute. 'Have you read Döblin's *Alexanderplatz*?' she asked at some point. Startled, Plotkin looked up. 'That is why I came down here,' he replied.

'Do you remember', she went on, 'that Döblin said that time is a butcher and that all of us are running away from the butcher's knife? Well that's me, and that's all of us. You, too. I'll run until I fall. But until I fall I want to live. Will you buy me another schnapps?'

Twice he turned down her offer to spend the night. The price?

Five marks. 'The women in Wedding', she told him, 'will sell themselves for a piece of bread!'

Plotkin moved on. He wasn't there for pleasure.

The Political Police – the branch assigned to protect the interests of the state and its institutions rather than the individual – had the Communists in its sights. That year in Berlin, two-and-a-half units' worth of office staff, as well as a senior detective, six junior detectives and seventy-three ordinary officers, were deployed against the machinations of the KPD. The NSDAP, on the other hand, were allocated only one unit, a senior detective, three junior detectives and forty-nine officers. Such were their priorities.

The KPD were doing their best to combat the infiltration of their party. Only two years ago they had uncovered almost seventy informants and provocateurs – thirty-nine of whom were working for the police, three for both the police and the Nazis, two for the SPD, eleven for foreign intelligence agencies and five for various companies.

Things were getting lively in Berlin.

FRIDAY 25 NOVEMBER

Adolf Hitler Only Solution to Government Crisis!
Führer Ready to Deploy Full Weight of Himself
and Movement if His Suggestions Are Taken
– *Völkischer Beobachter*

Hindenburg's Decision: No Hitler Dictatorship
Hitler Cabinet Fails – Presidential Powers Denied
– *Vossische Zeitung*

They'd begun the preparations one week earlier. The Ministry of Defence invited experts from the police, the post office, the railways and Technische Nothilfe – an organisation set up after the First World War to provide technical support to the nation's infrastructure – to participate in a thought experiment, a simulation to run all possible configurations of the ways in which conflict might break out. It was a game of what-ifs. What threats might confront the German military, and how might it respond? What dangers might develop in the aftermath?

The simulation assumed that 'the KPD and the Free Trade Unions will push strongly for a general strike and that elements in the SA and the Nazi-orientated workforce will join them'. Their blueprint was the Berlin transport workers' strike earlier that month. The Communists and National Socialists had banded together and fought against the police. The final count? Four people dead, forty-seven injured and 583 arrested. What if they formed a similar alliance nationwide? Who would be able to hold back the extremists, left and right? And what if every worker in Germany went on strike at the same time?

The experts had played through the scenarios, weighed up the risks, calculated how badly a workers' uprising would affect the state – and debated whether the army would be able to put it down.

Now Lieutenant-Colonel Eugen Ott began to run the simulation for a civil war. Tomorrow promised more of the same – the gentlemen in uniform were scrupulously detailed.

Addressing the ministers of the current cabinet, Kurt von Schleicher declared that he would rather not be chancellor after all: the chancellor, he explained, could not also serve as Minister of Defence. The notion that he would cede his influence over the military with a civil war in the offing was unthinkable.

Then Schleicher gave them the gist of a conversation he'd had with Hitler two days earlier: the latter had declared himself categorically unwilling to join the government, even if Hindenburg picked someone besides Papen as chancellor. Nor would he permit any other National Socialist to do so.

Later that day, Colonel Ferdinand von Bredow, head of the Ministerial Office, briefed his superiors on the topic of readying the German youth for war. The army badly needed men, everybody realised that, and they had to get underway as soon as permission was granted; negotiations were currently in progress between various European foreign ministers and the USA in Geneva. A decent offer – food, a bed, proper physical training – would, moreover, get them off the streets. Less chance of them getting any funny ideas.

Above Café Kranzler, on the corner of Friedrichstrasse and Unter den Linden, Edgar Ansel Mowrer had set up an office for the *Chicago Daily News*. There, on the peaceful second floor, his compatriots could read the newspaper and swap ideas.

Events in Germany were certainly keeping the foreign correspondents on their toes. The Americans, in particular, didn't always find it easy to put the various developments in terms that made sense to their readers: in Washington there were only two major parties, the Democrats and Republicans, tussling over power, while in Germany there were many, some of which only represented the interests of a small group, yet they might still be enough to tip the scale. And the current situation was so all-or-nothing, so breathless and charged.

The Americans on the Berlin political beat were a peculiar breed. In March, after a conversation with journalists and diplomats from the USA, Goebbels had complained that he was 'squeezed dry as a lemon'. Nor were they afraid to hit below the belt. Hubert Renfro Knickerbocker, a red-haired Texan, had informed his editor at the *New York Evening Post* only that summer that 'Hitler is a homosexual, effeminate corporal with a hypersensitive political olfactory nerve. Hindenburg is a granite-faced, bass-voiced Field Marshal with a commanding manner that makes little corporals tremble.'

There was unrest fomenting in the NSDAP. Many members, both new and long-serving, were dissatisfied. After the disastrous parliamentary elections, some within the party were convinced they should at least accept power in Prussia, the most important federal state in the Republic. The party that commanded Prussia commanded its well-equipped, well-trained police force, ninety thousand strong, including twelve thousand armed officers in Berlin. Thousands of uniformed men with access to automatic weapons and tanks. That was a force to be reckoned with.

It was, indeed, tempting. Yet Goebbels thought otherwise. 'We will end up in the most embarrassing situation,' he believed. They might even have a government commissioner foisted on them. The consequences didn't bear thinking about. After all, the president had already dissolved the SPD government in Prussia that summer and installed Papen as Commissioner. Just like that – by emergency decree. All the reason they needed was that the Social Democrats had been unable to quash the Communist violence. Proof had not been required.

True, the court had partly found in the former Prussian Prime Minister's favour. But only the president could dismiss Papen as Commissioner.

Hitler's behaviour – dithering to some, deft poker-playing to others – was gleefully dissected in the liberal press. 'Now that he's miles away from the Chancellery again, even though a few days ago it was only a metre or two, he's taking revenge by lobbing a gas bomb as he scrambles to retreat,' wrote one commentator in the *Vossische Zeitung*. The writer was referring to the PR battle over how important the failed negotiations had actually been. 'Having spent years extolling his "steely energy", his "icy determination" and his daring, the moment these qualities were put to the test he started checking and comparing texts all day long, burying himself in hair-splitting examinations of the difference between presidential and parliamentary cabinets, and writing sentimental letters, when one expects action – not even heroic action, necessarily – from him.' Hitler, the writer argued, preferred the Bavarian mountains and the scrimmage of electioneering. 'He's a born drummer, and at least subconsciously he's aware of his limitations.'

Did Gregor Strasser pass the article around his group of friends? Perhaps he'd even fed information to the paper. That, at least, was Goebbels' claim.

At five o'clock in the afternoon, Hindenburg met with Ludwig Kaas, the leader of the Catholic-orientated Centre Party. They discussed the 'remaining possibilities for building a workable emergency majority in the Reichstag' in the hopes of developing 'a pragmatic emergency programme for a majority government'.

Over the course of the day, Kaas had tried to consult the heads of the National Socialists, the German National People's Party, the Bavarian People's Party and the German People's Party. The first two swiftly turned him down.

Now Kaas was politely asking the president not to make him keep trying.

This attempt, too, had foundered. The situation was a disaster. What options did Hindenburg have left?

Hindenburg! A man idolised by most Germans. Dorothy Thompson described him in terms similar to Knickerbocker: 'A face cut out of rock. No imagination in it; no light; no humor. Not exactly an appealing face. But one revealing a character so defined as to determine its owner's destiny.'

At 5.10 p.m., Scharführer Erwin Jänisch – an officer in Sturm 13 of the SA – died at Auguste Viktoria Hospital. He'd been involved in a violent clash with members of the SPD-affiliated Reichsbanner early that morning.

The NSDAP described him as the 'twenty-eighth martyr in our struggle against Marxism in Berlin'.

In Bahnhofstrasse, Abraham Plotkin had found an attic room he could rent for 48 marks a month. From his window, he felt like he could see out across half of Berlin. Humboldt University, the museums and the Imperial Palace were only a few steps away. The location was ideal and the place unexpectedly luxurious. 'Heating is 25 pfennigs extra,' he noted in astonishment. 'Good Germans are used to doing [without] it – but these foreigners are a soft lot and need more heating than a chicken's egg.'

That evening Bella Fromm attended a reception thrown by Frau Meissner, wife of Otto. The event brought various members of the diplomatic corps out of the woodwork, including the wives of the British, Turkish and French ambassadors, as well as envoys from Norway, the Netherlands, Poland, Belgium and Estonia with their wives, and the wife of State Secretary Erwin Planck.

Mrs Planck's husband, as it happened, worked hand-in-glove with the Minister of Defence. Planck had, of course, served under Kurt von Schleicher during the First World War. The son of the world-famous physicist Max Planck, he, like Ferdinand von Bredow, was a member of Schleicher's inner circle.

That evening the buildings on Alexanderplatz were bathed in the glow of floodlights. Construction had dragged on for years, but it was finally finished. Flags fluttered from the facades, and the shops extended their opening hours. Forty-one of them had hidden figures in their display windows – anybody who could work out the right number was handed a raffle ticket. The prizes? Home furnishings from R. Israel, a Singer sewing machine, a radio and 500 marks in cash.

SATURDAY 26 NOVEMBER

Kaas Fails Too
Presidential Chancellor to Be Named Today
Papen Visits Hindenburg
– *Vossische Zeitung*

National Socialists, party comrades! Our economic woes
continue, unemployment is rising, Bolshevism is spreading
in Germany and the Reich's isolation from the rest of the
world is virtually complete. Never has a German cabinet held
more power, and never has a German cabinet failed more
utterly than this government of a small, exclusive elite.
– Adolf Hitler in the *Völkischer Beobachter*

Abraham Plotkin was itching for a bath. To wash off the dust of the
streets and give himself a thorough scrubbing. He asked his new landlady to point him in the direction of the bathroom.

The woman goggled at him. Was he sure he meant 'bathroom'?

Plotkin wasn't wearing much in the way of clothes, and he held a
towel and soap in his hands.

The landlady called over her husband, while Plotkin's teeth began
to chatter. His skin was turning blue with cold.

'Don't you know?' asked the landlady's husband.

Plotkin shook his head. Know what?

They called down the lady from upstairs for reinforcements, then
conferred for several minutes.

At long last the landlady, her expression triumphant, handed Plotkin a piece of paper with the address of the nearest public swimming
baths.

The simulation was concluded, all the what-ifs mulled and discussed, the results analysed. The devastating conclusion reached by the military and their colleagues from the railways, police and postal service was that the armed forces were not currently in a position to maintain order in the country, should there be a crisis. Or they'd have to be willing to take on a majority of the population with armed force.

The Weimar Republic was only partly capable of self-defence. Not a word to anyone, of course.

It was a Saturday, but at the Ministry of Defence they weren't exactly in a weekend mood. The heads of department gathered for a meeting. Who was going to be chancellor?

Bredow, former head of military intelligence and now in charge of the Ministerial Office – making him Schleicher's Deputy Defence Minister – kept minutes. They discussed the 'three illusions' of the past few weeks: that Hitler would capitulate; that Hindenburg would appoint him anyway; that there would be a coalition after all. Only one man had not fallen prey to these illusions: Defence Minister Kurt von Schleicher. And now they were turning on him, as though he were responsible.

The group argued back and forth about parties and departmental responsibilities, about lines that had to be drawn. Yet the military was supposed to keep out of the political arena – which was why the Defence Minister couldn't also be chancellor.

Towards the end they discussed potential activity in Parliament, unrest and strikes – 'in which case, state of emergency', noted Bredow. 'Everything prepared,' he continued. 'Ott exemplary, brutal, no timidity, no worries.'

Ott was the lieutenant-colonel who had led the simulation. One of Schleicher's men.

Police officers Karl Wiehn, twenty-eight, and Erwin Kohlert, thirty, burst into 48a Kaiserallee. It was a raid. In the apartment, the officers discovered a large-scale counterfeiting operation, complete with technical machinery and chemicals. The police announced that the forgers were Communists – yet more proof of KPD treachery.

The KPD did indeed run numerous counterfeiting operations throughout the city. A special division within the office of the Central Committee was assigned to organise various illegal activities, building secret offices, procuring suitable locations and cover addresses. The division's codename was in a perpetual state of flux: I-Apparatus or Department 'Iffland', later 'Iduna'. The Communists knew what they were doing. In Berlin alone, they set up more than sixty hideouts where weapons, ammunition and explosives obtained by Department 'Wels' were stockpiled. Would it be enough to start a revolution? The KPD's official tack was scrupulously legal, of course. Just like the Nazis'.

Papen, Schleicher, Meissner and Oskar von Hindenburg convened at the office of the president. There was only one item on the agenda: the political situation. Even so, the meeting went nowhere, devolving into bickering.

Die Rote Fahne (The Red Flag), the widely read organ of the KPD, was banned from publication for three weeks on account of flagrant offences against the Law for the Protection of the Republic. The newspaper distributed almost twenty-five thousand copies in Berlin alone, and in virtually every issue the editors called for the proletariat to take up arms and revolt against the state.

SUNDAY 27 NOVEMBER

Backroom Deals as Germany's Fate Hangs in Balance
Negotiations with Hitler – 'Another Method of Sidelining Him'
— *Völkischer Beobachter*

SCHLEICHER CABINET IMMINENT?

A Schleicher cabinet does seem to be the only way
out of the current shambles. It's assumed a decision
will be made on Tuesday at the latest.
— *Tägliche Rundschau*

Hitler and Goebbels were being driven to Weimar. It was a glorious journey. The wind swept across their faces, whisking away all negativity, and Goebbels felt he could breathe freely again at last. That evening, reaching Weimar, their conversation was upbeat despite the fiasco in Berlin. Assuming the party stuck together, said Goebbels, the NSDAP's bid for power would pay off.

Later they took a stroll through the city, letting it work its magic. But there was little time to dawdle – Hitler's next stop was Munich.

Meanwhile, Abraham Plotkin was visiting the Odeon theatre, where a comedy was playing entitled *Musik von Susie* (Music by Susie). It was a modern theatre, he observed in surprise, with 'an excellent cast splendidly directed, and music that was far superior to the run of Broadway shows'.

The theatre was two blocks from Unter den Linden, yet by the time he made it back to his room he'd passed thirty prostitutes and eventually given up counting.

Germany never ceased to amaze him. As an American, so much of it was alien. 'Bread has to be ordered – and water has to be pleaded for. And so far I have not seen butter placed on the table in any of the restaurants which I have been in.'

MONDAY 28 NOVEMBER

Papen or Schleicher? – Public Interest Now
Centres on These Two Names
– Vossische Zeitung

Tremendous Speech by Adolf Hitler
'Soon They Must Call Us for the Third Time'
– Der Angriff

This was the night winter set in. It had taken its time this year, but now it had come – although not yet with the kind of continental wrath that could make the entire city grind to a frozen halt. To Plotkin it felt like an omen, although what it augured he couldn't say. He peered out of the window of his garret. 'Frost, white, almost like snow. In the distance the white-green circular roof of the Dom and the tall steeple immediately behind it pointing into a sky of pink and rose sunrise. Washed in the cold water and wondered what it would be like when real cold weather comes along.'

No, Kurt von Schleicher did *not* want to be chancellor. Definitely not. Still, it couldn't hurt to get the lie of the land. His spies were hard at work, but, meanwhile, the General decided to scout out the terrain in person.

He met with Theodor Leipart and Wilhelm Eggert, leader and deputy leader respectively of the ADGB, the Federation of German Trade Unions. At more than 3.5 million members – representing 80 per cent of organised workers – it was a group with serious clout, and the Social Democrat-affiliated ADGB was ill-disposed to Papen's government. Clear battle lines had emerged, certainly since the chancellor had overruled the collective wage agreements at the beginning of September and slashed the winter welfare budget for the unemployed.

Still, the meeting was cordial. Schleicher seemed to be a man one could talk to. A man of flexibility and good sense. One, apparently, whose beliefs were not so unshakeable that they would be obstructive. The groundwork was in place.

Also working at the ADGB was Franz Joseph Furtwängler, whose remit was statistics and public relations. A man in his late thirties, he had blue eyes and a pompadour of ginger hair. His whole body moved when he spoke. Plotkin surveyed him with a mixture of curiosity and amusement. 'A tired nervous energy, too tired to rest,' he observed. 'He had the harassed appearance of a slim, trim young American businessman who was on the verge of losing a big deal.'

Furtwängler was an expert on working conditions, a whizz with numbers and a voracious reader. They sat in a branch of Aschinger, eating sandwiches and drinking beer. After a while they continued their chat in a neighbouring café. Six hours, their conversation lasted.

There were three types of social security, explained Furtwängler. The first was provided by employers, the second by the federal states and the third by cities. The first two were limited. After twenty-six weeks state aid ceased, and the cities stepped into the breach – assuming their pockets were deep enough.

At some point Furtwängler began to work himself into a rage. 'When the city's funds are gone then we may expect desperation and rioting. It is here, at this point, that we will get much excitement this winter, excitement that in all likelihood may lead to a revolutionary movement. [...] I mean a revolutionary movement. I do not mean a revolution.'

What was the difference, Plotkin wanted to know?

'A revolution in Germany is impossible,' said Furtwängler.

'But who would lead such a revolutionary movement?'

'Anyone who promises them bread,' replied Furtwängler:

Our people are desperate now. Any addition to their misery will bring them to the breaking point. [...] Anyone who comes to them and promises them something to eat will carry them as the wind carries pollen. How else can you explain the enormous vote that the Communists and the Hitlerites have been getting? It is because the masses think that through some miracle these two groups can bring food to them. It is absurd, and the leaders of these two groups know that they are not telling the masses the truth.

Another coffee. Plotkin was a good listener. Attentive and well-informed. He got people talking. And maybe some Germans were proud that an American was showing such interest.

'Once the movement in this direction starts there is no telling how far it will go. It will inevitably mean the Polizei and the soldiery and bloodshed. Then there is the danger of contagion. These things spread from city to city, and in Germany the cities are pretty close together,' said the trade unionist. What was coming, he added, would spread 'like wildfire'.

Günther Gereke was the brains of a conservative group advocating for economic reforms to stimulate the labour market. President of the German Assembly of Rural Municipalities, he was considered a highly efficient and intelligent administrator – as well as a dyed-in-the-wool conservative who wanted to see the emergence of an authoritarian state. His suggestions, however, were objective and precise; Gereke was anything but a zealot, and he had even been mooted as a potential candidate for chancellor – although that was a long shot.

Schleicher met with the ascetic-looking Gereke that evening. 'Oskar von Hindenburg telephoned you!' he greeted him.

'Yes,' replied Gereke, 'but how did you know? Hindenburg wanted our conversation to be discreet.'

Schleicher laughed. He took out a record, placed it on the gramophone and replayed the bugged telephone conversation to an astonished Gereke. 'We in the armed forces are well-briefed on everything,' said Schleicher, not without pride.

Gereke wasn't indignant, nor did he feel it was any breach of trust. 'Then you have a first-rate intelligence service,' was his only remark. 'No doubt we'll need it.'

The election results began to roll in. At Sunday's local elections in the area around Bremen, the NSDAP had lost more than half the votes they'd achieved at the parliamentary elections on 6 November. In Geesthacht, near Hamburg, they lost a third.

Earthquakes like these were, of course, registered on the seismographs in Berlin.

At two o'clock in Berlin, a Communist pirate radio station began broadcasting. They transmitted propaganda for ten minutes before concluding the programme with a rendition of 'The Internationale'. Officials from the postal authority and the police had been trying to pinpoint the source for some time, but so far they were out of luck.

Schleicher met with an insider from the Christian Trade Unions and a gentleman from the Employers' Associations, as well as the influential Social Democrat Rudolf Breitscheid and the leader of the Centre Party, Ludwig Kaas.

He knew what he was doing.

TUESDAY 29 NOVEMBER

Whole Nation to Collapse Because of Hindenburg's Advisers?
— *Völkischer Beobachter*

General von Schleicher Negotiates Truce with
Parliament / What Will NSDAP Do?
— *Tägliche Rundschau*

Still, he reacted. Wilhelm Groener, former Defence Minister and Minister of the Interior, replied to Schleicher's congratulatory note with a letter. And what a letter it was:

Dear Schleicher!

I was genuinely pleased to receive your birthday letter, because I understand from it that you wish to renew your old relationship with me. You wish to have a discussion with me, in order to learn the reasons for our 'estrangement'. Dear Schleicher, the word 'estrangement' is altogether too mild. I'd like to be open and frank. I'm boiling with rage and fury because I was disappointed by you, my old friend, pupil, adopted son, my hope for the Volk and the Fatherland. It cannot be analysed, not with reason, and it certainly cannot be probed with exaggerated cunning. They are emotions at the very core of the soul. Perhaps I'm in the wrong, in which case I'm heartily sorry to have offended you.

If you do become chancellor, show what you can do, but be a great and whole man, one in whom utter confidence can be placed. Who has confidence in you now? Almost no one. You are considered exceptionally clever, skilful, cunning, and people expect that you will become chancellor because of your cleverness and cunning. You have my blessing. But don't work too brashly, but with softness; no more light cavalry, take one thing after another, don't try to solve everything at once from the 'authoritarian' government to the tiniest detail [...] Give the horsewhip a rest. Hitler knows how to use it, too. They don't need you for that!

There's plenty more rancour I could vent. You may have noticed that there's a volcano raging inside me. If you find my outburst unpleasant, then you can consign this letter to oblivion. Send your tasteless sycophants packing. My old Schleicher never needed such things. I'm still holding out hope for the old Schleicher, by the way.

Yours, Groener

Another conversation – one that might prove decisive – was still to come: Schleicher had agreed to meet with Gregor Strasser, eager to find out whether the NSDAP would, if the possibility arose, be willing to assume governmental responsibilities after all. Schleicher was holding out great hopes for their discussion. The messages he'd received from Hitler's adversaries had put him in an expectant mood.

Then, however, Strasser cancelled their appointment at short notice, declaring that Schleicher ought to speak with Hitler in person. What was going on?

Goebbels, who had driven back to Weimar, received a telegram from Hitler. The Führer would not, as planned, make himself available in Berlin. 'Letting Schleicher wait. Bravo!' wrote Goebbels telegrammatically in his diary. Instead, Hitler joined his head of propaganda in Weimar.

WEDNESDAY 30 NOVEMBER

Hitler Arriving This Morning for Talks with
General von Schleicher in Berlin
– Vossische Zeitung

Adolf Hitler Not in Berlin
– Der Angriff

NSDAP Will Not Tolerate Schleicher Cabinet
Transitional Schleicher Cabinet – United Reactionaries' Last Hope
– Völkischer Beobachter

Papen or Schleicher?
Negotiations Making Progress / Troublemakers at Work!
– Tägliche Rundschau

At nine o'clock Schleicher was expecting an important visitor: Adolf Hitler. But the Defence Minister waited in vain. *Der Angriff*, Goebbels' mouthpiece, wrote that the election campaign in Thuringia was more important than discussions in Berlin. Why, then, had Hitler driven from Weimar to Munich yesterday morning? And wasn't he on the night train to Berlin only hours later? The confusion in the capital was perfect.

Perhaps there was a way after all. Schleicher and Hindenburg weren't giving up – they wanted to get the National Socialists on side. Schleicher sent word to Hitler via an intermediary that he should 'present himself at the presidential office for a discussion of the political situation on Thursday 1 December at 11.30'. What did Hindenburg want now? Hitler wondered. He asked Göring to find out.

The papers in Berlin were abuzz once again with speculation about civil war: SA men had launched an attack at a KPD meeting place in Pflugstrasse. Some had opened fire, while others had beaten the Communists with their fists. Two people were badly injured, including Otto Möhle, a nineteen-year-old waiter who had been shot in the shoulder and was rushed to hospital. Meanwhile, the police investigation had come up with nothing.

In political Berlin there was only one topic of conversation: Papen or Schleicher? Who would win the race to the chancellor's office? Sources apparently on the inside told the *Vossische Zeitung* that Hindenburg no longer considered Papen an option. Schleicher, they whispered, was now the only candidate. It was a done deal.

That afternoon Hitler, Göring, Strasser and Frick convened in Weimar to discuss General Schleicher's nebulous invitation. Yet again, they found themselves at odds. Goebbels and Göring were in favour of pursuing absolute power, but Strasser urged them to abandon this all-or-nothing mentality and join a new government. Frick, likewise, thought this a sensible plan. And what did Hitler want? Both camps vied for his approval. The Führer and his subordinates conferred for four hours.

Göring's adjutant paid Meissner a visit. What would be the subject of their conversation, he wanted to know – and would Hitler be speaking with the president alone? Or could other members of the National Socialist movement attend? Meissner's answer was somewhat convoluted. Herr President wished to discuss the political situation as a whole, which would naturally entail an exchange of views regarding whether the NSDAP might be willing to tolerate a Schleicher cabinet. Herr President would prefer this conversation to be conducted alone.

The intermediary promised a swift response from Hitler. Instead, however, Göring put in a call to Wilhelmstrasse. He was phoning from Weimar, from the Thuringian regional parliament. Meissner picked up the receiver. Another visit to the president, announced Göring's voice down the telephone line, would put Hitler in an awkward position. Moreover, the president had already heard everything Hitler had to say. Another meeting would merely kindle fresh hope in the populace and, if nothing came of it, prove a fresh disappointment.

Meissner replied that the situation had changed. Hindenburg now wanted to know if and under what conditions the NSDAP would support a presidential cabinet with Schleicher at its head. Surely that was worth discussing. No subject was out of bounds, however, and Hitler could speak confidentially with the president. Göring assured him a prompt reply.

But Meissner heard nothing more from the National Socialists, until at last he left the office and went home.

Late that evening, Meissner's private telephone rang. Göring's adjutant was on the line. Herr Hitler would not be coming to Berlin. A letter turning down the invitation would be sent via courier overnight. It ought to be in Meissner's hands by 9.30 a.m. on 1 December.

What was the meaning of this performance? After all, he already knew what was in it.

Later still, Schleicher picked up the telephone and called one of his closest confidants. Eugen Ott was dispatched immediately to Weimar. His orders? To meet with Hitler and convey a message: Schleicher was offering Hitler the position of Vice-Chancellor in his cabinet. He would remain Minister of Defence, but would grant the National Socialists a number of other posts. The Minister was brief; he trusted Ott.

THURSDAY 1 DECEMBER

TWO-WEEK CRISIS — HITLER CANCELS

Despite official denials, it's clear that Hitler was supposed
to be in Berlin, that he left Munich for Berlin, and that
he changed his destination during the night.

— *Vossische Zeitung*

From one side we hear that Hitler will arrive in Berlin today, from
the other that Hitler has returned to Munich, while another version
insists that Strasser will come to Berlin instead of Hitler. All in all,
the Führer's iron reserve has left more than a few people red-faced.

— *Der Angriff*

Had Hindenburg really hoped to reel Hitler in after all? Either way,
Göring's adjutant appeared before Meissner at half past nine and
handed him Hitler's letter. 'As on top of that I am in the middle of
the Thuringian election campaign, a visit that serves merely informa-
tional purposes seems unfeasible to me, and so with great deference
I request of the honoured Herr President that he kindly refrain from
inviting me in person at the present moment.'

Meissner dismissed the adjutant and reported immediately to the
president. He outlined the situation: Hitler wasn't coming.

Two weeks ago, the government had resigned – and there was no
end in sight to the political crisis.

The NSDAP had just inducted a new member from the very highest social echelons. On 1 December, Annelies von Ribbentrop joined
the party and was assigned membership number 1411594. She followed
her husband, who had submitted his application in May. Annelies
von Ribbentrop (née Henkell) was a scion of the Henkell champagne

dynasty, and her husband Joachim ran the Berlin office. He had also set up a company that imported whisky.

The Ribbentrops were known for their lavish parties and counted several Jewish families among their old friends. It was a pity that their new acquaintances couldn't be invited to those. Instead, they arranged festivities at their villa for their like-minded pals at the NSDAP.

Ott appeared in Weimar. Schleicher's Ott, the man who had simulated civil war. The lieutenant-colonel visited Hitler in his hotel room, where their conversation lasted more than three hours. It could hardly be called a dialogue, as only one of them did most of the talking. Hitler demanded the chancellorship for himself and warned Schleicher off taking control of the government – the military would be stretched too thin, he harangued Ott, and the attempt would end in disaster. It was a threat.

All this frenzied toing and froing did not go unnoticed in Berlin. Rumours abounded. Finance Minister Schwerin von Krosigk heard an especially piquant anecdote: on Wednesday, a reception committee consisting of Gregor Strasser and Eugen Ott had turned up at Anhalter Bahnhof. They were waiting for Hitler.

But Hitler wasn't there. Göring had picked up the Führer at an earlier stop and driven him to Weimar. On the journey he reported to Hitler that Schleicher and Strasser had lied: Hindenburg was by no means immovable on the matter of Hitler's chancellorship; Papen could sort everything out. It was an amusing yarn – or was it more than that?

Journalists, too, had got wind of the story, and it was reported in all the papers. Hitler's opponents painted the scene – the Nazis arriving to pick up their Führer at the train station – in vivid technicolour: 'Not a creature was stirring in the sleeping car when suddenly footsteps came stomping down the corridor and a rasping male voice could be heard,' wrote *Vorwärts*. 'A fist thundered at the door of the compartment where the Führer was catching forty winks. Hitler appeared at the door after a few tense seconds, half dressed (Hitler as no one knows him!), and identified the rasping rabble-rouser as none other than – President of the Reichstag Hermann Göring.'

Berlin interpreted, surmised, laid bets. Who would come out on top?

> Meanwhile, the press office at the NSDAP commented: 'Regarding the accounts systematically circulated in the public sphere by politically interested sources, according to which Adolf Hitler has agreed, signalled his intention or simply purposes to come to Berlin in order to participate in negotiations with various offices to form a government, the party wishes to make clear that these accounts are pure invention, designed to confuse public opinion.'

Papen or Schleicher? Papen was in favour, ultimately, of a new constitution: a dictatorship. Schleicher wanted to prevent civil war, and he wanted a rearmed military that would subsume the various right-wing paramilitary groups; escalating matters would cause more harm than good. To Hindenburg there seemed no other alternatives. He ordered Papen and Schleicher to convene at six o'clock that evening. Meissner and Oskar von Hindenburg were also present, as they so often were. How had the French ambassador André François-Poncet described the president's son? 'Plump features, a coarse demeanour and possessing scant knowledge; as tall and as heavily built as his father, but without the latter's genteel manner [...].'

An hour and a half the meeting lasted – and neither Papen nor Schleicher were able to present a satisfactory solution. Schleicher did report that the Centre Party and the trade unions had evinced a 'pleasingly milder attitude' towards a cabinet under his leadership.

But would it convince the president?

That evening, Ott telephoned his boss, Schleicher, and related his conversations in Weimar. It was hardly a topic suitable for a telephone call, however, so Ott hopped on the train and arrived at Schleicher's office late that night.

The Defence Minister had been waiting for him. Ott gave his account: Hitler had brusquely refused to enter into a coalition; Göring had sounded less adamant; and Strasser continued to disapprove of Hitler's chosen course, doing his best to push back. They talked long into the night.

THE PLAN

2 TO 15 DECEMBER 1932

FRIDAY 2 DECEMBER

Trade Union Demands for Schleicher
Eliminate Social Hardship – Promote Public Job Creation
– Vossische Zeitung

Appointment of New Papen Cabinet Expected
– BZ am Mittag

Schleicher was on the phone to military commanders until the small hours. It was a short night. Even so, he didn't skip his morning ride through the Tiergarten: he loved those daybreak excursions.

Afterwards Schleicher was driven straight to the Chancellery. He had a tough day ahead of him. And a crucial one.

For the Americans, the spectacle of German politics was unsettling. Never before had the Weimar Republic found itself so deeply ensnared in a political quagmire, thought Ambassador Frederic Sackett.

Did it all boil down to Schleicher?

Sackett had heard Hindenburg was torn, worried about where the General's restless energy and aptitudes might lead. In power, he'd be little better than Hitler. But Sackett was convinced Schleicher was of an altogether different calibre to Papen.

At the Chancellery, the interim cabinet – still governing – reconvened. By nine o'clock that morning all the ministers were assembled. Outside, the clouds were gathered low. The glow of autumn was now no more than a faded memory.

The gentlemen chatted softly as they waited for the chancellor. They had been summoned late the night before: Foreign Minister von Neurath, Finance Minister Graf Schwerin von Krosigk and the other members of the cabinet. Meissner was there, too, and one of

Schleicher's confidants, Major Erich Marcks – a head of department at the Ministry and a former army comrade of the Defence Minister. He was also Papen's press secretary, and thus the spokesman for the current government. Minutes were taken by Erwin Planck, another of Schleicher's men. The general had taken care to seed his allies in positions of importance.

The chancellor appeared a few minutes after nine. Franz von Papen outlined the situation – it was looking grim. No majority in sight, no sign of cooperation.

Schleicher piped up. He had received no assurances from any side, he said, that the cabinet would be tolerated, far less supported. The National Socialists were dragging their feet. Strasser had not yet attended any discussions in Berlin, but he was expected on Sunday evening. They had to keep their nerve. Meanwhile, he advised the president to wait for the outcome of these negotiations before making a final decision.

Meissner countered that the president's current psychological state permitted no further delay.

Suddenly, Papen began to speak. The president, he announced, had entrusted him with the task of forming a cabinet. Yesterday evening. Moreover, he had been granted comprehensive plenary powers.

He asked the ministers for their response.

It was, he confessed, a surprising turn of events.

Nobody reacted. Silence.

Then Konstantin von Neurath, the oldest man in the room, with salt-and-pepper hair, a short grey moustache and a duelling scar on his cheek, did as he was asked. He spoke slowly, as though with conscious effort, saying that he would take a sceptical view of a second Papen cabinet; that he would, indeed, caution against re-entrusting Papen with the role of chancellor.

Silence fell once more across the room, until the Finance Minister, Schwerin von Krosigk, raised his voice. He asked Papen to inform the president that most, if not all, members of the cabinet shared Neurath's opinion. Papen was incensed. He glanced around the conference table. Did *nobody* think otherwise? he asked exasperatedly, clearly on the verge of losing his self-control. Only one minister reacted. Peter Paul Freiherr von Eltz-Rübenach, responsible for the postal service and transport, said he didn't think substituting Schleicher for Papen would accomplish anything.

Not exactly a ringing endorsement.

Schleicher took the floor. He summarised Lieutenant-Colonel Ott's conversation with Hitler in Weimar. The NSDAP had made it clear they weren't going down without a fight, and that could only mean one thing: civil war. The military didn't have the resources to cope – the simulation proved it!

At Schleicher's signal, Ott entered the room. His presentation lasted an hour. A level-headed man, he didn't rush to judgement – as he'd been taught in the General Staff. Many young soldiers and officers up to the rank of captain, he explained, were already committed to National Socialism. If they were attacked, they would go on the offensive against the left but defend the right.

Line by line, Ott soberly depicted a horrifying scenario: dockworkers striking, separatists rebelling in the Rhineland, Poland mobilising, a general strike, civil war. And in the middle of all this, the military stretched to breaking point.

Agitation swept across the room. The ministers had questions.

Ott explained that they couldn't hope to defeat their opponents by sheer force of arms, especially if the country were to be paralysed by a general strike, and that eastern Germany would be left undefended.

'After serious study of all these factors,' said Ott, 'it's clear that defending the eastern border while simultaneously maintaining order domestically against the National Socialists and the Communists would overtax the state's current capacity. The government is therefore advised against any measures that would lead to such a situation.'

Ott folded his notes and left the room. Some of the ministers may, perhaps, have suspected Schleicher of staging everything: the catastrophic outcome of the simulation, Ott's unfaltering performance, Neurath's verbal attack on Papen. Was the whole thing a ploy? Papen got to his feet. Failure was a bitter enough pill. Being shown up, made to look a fool – that was something else entirely.

He took his leave of the cabinet and went straight to the president.

Shortly before Papen's visit, Hindenburg had been informed that the military would be unable to defend the Reich if there was a general strike. He understood immediately what was happening: his ministers were refusing to obey him, their president. An extraordinary act of disloyalty. He must, too, have suspected who was at the bottom of it: Kurt von Schleicher.

The president told Papen he was too old to take responsibility for another civil war. 'Then in God's name we'll have to let Herr von Schleicher try his luck.'

Shortly afterwards, Schleicher paid his own visit to Hindenburg. How was he feeling? Like his goal was within his grasp? Perhaps it was a matter of duty. Was he triumphant? Afraid of his own courage?

Hindenburg received Schleicher. The president was still a tall, broad-shouldered man, and his physical presence never failed to make an impression.

Some of his visitors described afterwards in wonderment the way so many of his staff scurried around. Hindenburg's head secretary; servants, typists, clerks. Secretaries entered noiselessly, placed bits of paper on the desk and vanished just as noiselessly once more. Hindenburg was known for pencilling his notes on tiny scraps of paper. 'Leaflets', he called them.

Right and left, files were piled high on the desk. A helmet with a bullet hole from the Battle of Königgrätz in 1886 – Hindenburg's own, by all accounts. He must have cheated death by a whisker. He'd been a young man in those days.

At the 1871 Proclamation of the German Empire in the Hall of Mirrors at Versailles, Hindenburg had represented his regiment. Two years later he entered the Prussian Staff College, an educational facility for military officers, finishing his training in autumn 1876. His final assessment concluded that he was 'an independent, spirited character of great ability and with a solid military eye. Will do superbly everywhere and is chiefly suited for a command with the General Staff.' What followed was a career that made him one of the most senior officers in the Empire: a general of the infantry.

Hindenburg strove to emulate Helmuth von Moltke, the great strategist of the Wars of Unification. Yet developing his own strategies had never been among Hindenburg's strengths. Three years before the beginning of the First World War he retired, decorated with the Order of the Black Eagle, Prussia's highest honour. When war broke out in August 1914 his offer to come back was initially turned down, but later he was recalled and given a command in the army.

Hindenburg was legendarily unflappable. Even before the Battle of Tannenberg, he lunched punctually at one o'clock in the afternoon. Then he took a nap. 'I'm doing well; I sleep like a cannon,' he told journalists.

On his desk in Wilhelmstrasse was a framed motto: 'Ora et labora'. Pray and work. Next to it were photographs of his wife, Gertrud. Dead for more than eleven years now, in many ways she'd been his opposite, kindly and temperamental. She succumbed to cancer. Three of his grandchildren by Oskar lived nearby, and his two daughters often brought their children to visit.

A painting hung on the wall, depicting the burial of Field Marshal Kurt Christoph Graf von Schwerin. An eighteenth-century Prussian hero of the Silesian Wars, Schwerin died on the field of battle, sacrificing himself for the Fatherland.

And in the end, that's what it was all about. The nation. Only once in his life had Hindenburg travelled abroad, apart from in battle. 1911. Rome, Florence, Naples; with Gertrud.

The evening before, the president had settled on Papen. Once upon a time, his word had been law. Months earlier, when Schwerin von Krosigk had been on the fence about joining Papen's cabinet, Hindenburg merely remarked that an officer and a nobleman ought not to leave his old field marshal in the lurch. Lo and behold, the man ended up Finance Minister.

Now Hindenburg had been betrayed by his ministers and caught unawares by a general who thought and acted like a politician.

Schleicher entered the room.

Hindenburg was too disciplined to betray how he felt, and entirely too certain that emotions had no place when it came to action. 'Soppy sentimentalism', he had often said, 'achieves no positive results in practical life; world history teaches as much on all sides.' Now he addressed the next chancellor like a senior officer, his tone peremptory.

It was time for Schleicher to become Chancellor of the Reich. Yet the General hesitated.

'Herr Field Marshal, I'm the last horse in your stable,' he said, 'and I ought to be kept hidden.'

'You will not desert me now!' replied Hindenburg. Loyalty, that was the most important thing. Fealty. Doing one's duty.

Yet Schleicher still seemed unpersuaded, so the president promised to grant him the power to dissolve Parliament at any time, should that prove necessary.

Those were the magic words. They implied unconditional confidence, although Hindenburg had almost certainly already lost such confidence in Schleicher.

The question was, how quickly would he use it? How much time did Hindenburg have until he found out? Power was always a matter of timing.

The president issued the letter of appointment, but inside he was fuming. Schleicher, chancellor? It was an outrage.

Still, Hindenburg spared a thought for Franz von Papen. He sent him a photograph, a signed portrait of himself. On it he wrote: 'I had a comrade!'

It was a gesture out of character for the old man. He no longer cultivated friendships, but he was fond of Papen. Best to keep him close at hand. You never knew. These days reliable men were thin on the ground.

Oskar Loerke, an editor at S. Fischer Verlag, a publishing house, and secretary of the Poetic Arts Division of the Prussian Academy of Arts, was sauntering through Berlin. All these new buildings – Berlin was transforming into a world city. Loerke mentioned nothing besides the walk in his diary, having written not a word about politics for several weeks. He'd been more forthcoming over the summer. On 22 July he'd been listening to the radio to find out the latest developments. His summary? 'The government's out of its mind again.' Then, on 4 August: 'Can't help but think of leaving. Feeling: I will be driven out. Germany's gravediggers will bury me alive, too.' And now, in December? Nothing but strolls, the weather and everyday minutiae from the publishing house. Loerke had turned away from politics. He wanted to keep his distance from the gravediggers.

By early afternoon, word of the new appointment was spreading across the clacking network of telex machines. Kurt von Schleicher had been named twelfth chancellor by the president, charged with forming what would be the Weimar Republic's twentieth government.

He would be the second general to rule Germany. The first had been Leo von Caprivi, chancellor from 1890 to 1894, who had succeeded Bismarck in the days of empire.

Harry Graf Kessler was relieved: Schleicher was chancellor. 'After looming till the bitter end, the spectre of Papen has at last been banished,' he noted. 'It has been spat out in disgust by the German people, much as old Hindenburg may regret that.'

Nearly all the prominent National Socialists were actively involved in the Thuringian elections, including Joseph Goebbels. Still, he took the time to dictate an editorial for *Der Angriff*:

> One thing has been achieved. General von Schleicher, previously content to stand in the background and cast his shadow

over the events of the day, has now come to the fore, into the glaring spotlight of the public gaze. We do not believe this will prove to his advantage; it is well known that a man's shadow is always bigger than the man himself.

Schleicher's first meeting that afternoon was with influential trade unionists. They were debating sociopolitical questions. Schleicher – very much the military academy-trained officer – outlined his 'cross-party front' strategy. The plan relied on backing from the trade unions, the Social Democrats and the leftist fringes of the National Socialists, as well as from various business associations and the military. This relationship would, he hoped, allow parliamentary business to proceed more smoothly.

The leftist-orientated Free Trade Unions made a string of demands, which Schleicher could have read in the morning edition of the *Vossicher Zeitung* even before the meeting. Several emergency decrees were to be lifted, including one from 5 September, which permitted employers to cut wages earned between the thirty-first and the fortieth hour of the working week. Moreover, the working week should not amount to more than forty hours. And there must be better provision for the unemployed during the winter months.

Feeding information to the press, hours before a confidential meeting? Was that a way for prospective allies to behave?

For those who'd had enough of Berlin, there was always skiing. 'There's snow on the slopes!' an advertisement in the *Tägliche Rundschau* promised. 'Christmas – New Year. Sudeten Mountains/Gr. Aupa-Petzer. Excellent value trips with ski courses and guided tours for beginners, advanced and touring skiers, led by experienced, qualified instructors in association with the German Gymnastic Association, Gau Mittel-Elbe. For more information contact Gerhard Scheer, Quersprung-Scheer, Dresden, Amalienstrasse 18.'

The Sudeten Mountains. Silesia's skiing paradise. They were

roughly four hundred kilometres from Berlin – a whole day's drive. That August, between Cologne and Bonn in the west of Germany, they'd opened the first 'junction-free motor road', to use the official terminology of the day. In everyday speech, however, people usually used another word to describe these new-fangled racetracks, one that turned out to be a little catchier: 'autobahn'.

What kind of political calibre would Kurt von Schleicher reveal as chancellor? In small gatherings he was a pleasant, amusing conversationalist; he had the gift of being able to leave everyone in the room with the impression that they fundamentally saw eye to eye. Yet Schleicher, born in Brandenburg an der Havel, a small town near Berlin, also had the jaunty manner and quick, inborn wit of a Berliner. He could be as cutting as he was lively, being rarely able to resist a good line, and his brashness was legendary. Once, at a dinner party given by an industrialist rumoured to bribe all public officials who crossed his path, Schleicher raised his bowl after the soup course and asked, 'Where's the million?'

Now, as chancellor, would he be able to keep himself in check? Could the string-puller become a statesman? Perhaps his wife, Elisabeth, would be able to help him there. She was renowned in diplomatic circles for her charm, her elegance and her fashionable taste. In a photograph of them taken in 1931, Schleicher stands behind his wife with his arm around her, while she touches his left forearm. They were evidently a loving couple. That same year Schleicher wrote to a friend with a twinkle in his eye that 'I continue to be a fervent advocate of celibacy for the ranks up to that of general. For generals, a certain feminine intelligence and womanly tact is a necessary support.'

And for chancellors? In October, he had visited a health resort in Badenweiler, in the Black Forest. His constitution was weak. There's good evidence he was anaemic, an illness that saps a person of energy.

What about Paul von Hindenburg? The crisis had been resolved, but not the way he'd foreseen. Schleicher's manoeuvre – and it certainly had the stench of one of Schleicher's manoeuvres – had left him feeling humiliated. Nobody treated the Field Marshal like that.

These aftershocks did not go unnoticed in conservative circles. Gräfin Ada Westarp, whose husband Kuno had previously been party chairman of the DNVP and was a long-time presidential confidante, wrote to her daughter Gertraude that 'Hindenburg is fuming.'

SATURDAY 3 DECEMBER

It is impossible to explain how this cabinet was formed.
The story is so confused and criss-crossed with such a wide
range of influences that the knot is hard to disentangle.

– Tägliche Rundschau

SCHLEICHER'S APPROACH

What's currently happening has little to do with democracy.
Democracy in Germany has quietly withdrawn. It's sitting in the
hall, sure to return one day, but it has vacated the main room.

– Vossische Zeitung

Zero Tolerance for Schleicher!
A 'Solution' That Solves Nothing

– Der Angriff

Hermann Foertsch, a press officer at the Ministry of Defence, rubbed his eyes as he read the new cabinet restructure. Schleicher had recalled virtually all the serving ministers. Did that mean Papen's 'cabinet of barons' would simply be ploughing on under new leadership? Even close colleagues had expected a new roster. Concerned, Foertsch asked Schleicher whether he wouldn't be taking on the old cabinet's lack of popularity as well as its ministers. 'Yes, my little chap,' replied Schleicher, with the irony so feared by those who knew him. 'You're absolutely right; but I can't do without them, because I don't have anybody else.'

The first cabinet meeting began at a quarter to one. Schleicher reported that 'a large proportion of the public' considered it a 'relief' that he had taken Papen's place as chancellor. They discussed the emergency decrees, which had to be relaxed, the upcoming government statement, and the overly harsh sentences meted out to political criminals.

Schleicher was barely in office and already they'd all come running, the lobbyists and interest groups, with their demands. No warm words of welcome, scant congratulations. Maybe the occasional 'please'.

Abraham Plotkin, too, had learned that the most important German trade unions were negotiating with Schleicher. Theodor Leipart and Wilhelm Eggert from the ADGB had been to see him. Plotkin had even heard they'd reached an agreement. But was that true? He spoke to Fräulein Heinrich, secretary to Martin Plettl, the President of the German Textile Workers' Union. 'No,' replied Fräulein Heinrich. 'There is no agreement and no understanding. The unions will never come to an agreement with Schleicher.' They were only visiting him because, well, it was good manners.

Really? Was it only a matter of politeness? Plotkin managed to buttonhole Martin Plettl in person, a bald man in his early forties who was constantly twirling his thin, imposing moustache. Plettl said that Leipart and Eggert were considering questions of 'practical economics' with Schleicher; they wanted to discuss the possibility of setting up state job-creation programmes. As yet no firm conclusions had been reached, but a formal agreement was out of the question. 'We are Social Democrats, and there can be no agreement between the Social Democrats and the representatives of the military regime that Schleicher embodies.'

That afternoon, roughly two hundred Communists gathered for an illegal demonstration on Strausberger Platz in Friedrichshain. While they marched, unknown perpetrators smashed the windows of a gun shop in Frankfurter Strasse and made off with tear-gas guns and air rifles. The window of a grocer's was also broken, and ten marks' worth of sausages were stolen. The demonstration was immediately dispersed, and a KPD man was 'forcibly detained' by the police.

At a cemetery in Schöneberg in Berlin, recently murdered SA officer Erwin Jänisch was being laid to rest.

Late that night, the Reichsbanner conducted a large-scale field training exercise in Hamborn-Duisburg. After they were finished, around 350 National Socialists attacked a group of 150 Reichsbanner. The Nazis were armed with spades and belts. Nine members of the Reichsbanner were severely injured, mostly with head wounds, although one had taken a bullet to the leg.

SUNDAY 4 DECEMBER

Schleicher Cabinet Appointed
Schleicher Also Defence Minister
– Vossische Zeitung

The older generation has brought out its strongest and final
representative in the General; it now has nothing in reserve.
The last horse has been led out, and the stall is empty.
– Tägliche Rundschau

WHAT DOES SCHLEICHER'S APPOINTMENT MEAN?
Another Government Ruling Against the Will of the People!
Worst of all, the military is being dragged
into the internal struggle for power!
– Völkischer Beobachter

Reinhold Quaatz attended a church service at the Holy Trinity Church
on Wilhelmplatz, situated immediately next to the Kaiserhof.

Hindenburg, a pious, evangelical Lutheran, could often be found
in this understated church. If the president was at the service – and he
attended regularly when in Berlin – it became a kind of public spectacle. Many parents brought their children purely so they could catch
a glimpse of the living legend.

The round building, consecrated in 1739, had stood there for
nearly two centuries; Bismarck had been confirmed there. It was a
residue of old Prussia, and on Sunday it was packed. Half an hour
before the service was due to start, people were already crammed into
the galleries like sardines, clad in their Sunday best, while outside a
few hundred spectators were jostling to catch sight of the most senior
political figure in the Reich.

Police officers kept the road clear for the president, who finally drew up in his limousine. His chauffeur opened the door, and Hindenburg climbed out unassisted, tipping his hat to greet the crowd. There was a reverent silence in the church. On either side of the altar sat a number of severely disabled worshippers, most of them veterans of the First World War.

Hindenburg strode to the front, top hat in one hand and hymnal in the other, closely followed by his son and Otto Meissner. A few elderly ladies curtseyed. The priest came to meet Hindenburg, squeezing his right hand between his own – and bowed.

Space had been saved for Hindenburg and his companions in the front pew. He knew the hymns by heart, his resonant bass echoing loudly. Finally, the priest announced, 'From the depths of our hearts we ask God the Almighty to protect the grey head that bides among us.'

When the service was over, Hindenburg leant across to the veterans, who wore their medals on their chests. One or two had seen combat in the Franco-Prussian War, and they told the Field Marshal the sites where they'd been wounded, whispering the names of battlefields. Old stories, ones nobody else wanted to hear. Hindenburg wanted to hear.

He shook hands with the old men, every single one of them, and only then did he turn away.

When would it happen, the Communist uprising so many people feared? Or would the SA be first to lose their nerve? Plotkin observed uneasily that there were more police than usual out on the streets, and uniformed Nazis stood on every corner with their collection boxes. Then it dawned on him: the Reichstag was due to open in two days; no wonder they were taking so many precautions. But what were the SA up to?

Adolf Hitler was still out and about in Thuringia. Today was the election, and the Führer was touting for votes. In Eisfeld he was awarded honorary citizenship of the town by the local council. In Sonneberg he addressed more than ten thousand supporters: 'And this nation, our very lifeblood, shall I now abandon it for a mess of pottage, for titles and frivolous hopes? I cannot act otherwise today than I did four months ago. A "cabinet of social equity", they're calling the new government, and they are always finding new names to hide the inner vacuity of the whole business.'

Ernst Thälmann, Chairman of the KPD, travelled to his home town of Hamburg to attend a regional party conference in the district of Wasserkante, where he was feted as the 'Leader of the German Proletariat'. A portrait of Lenin hung in the hall. Thälmann called for a 'mass attack on the Fascist Schleicher dictatorship'.

Such was the logic of the Communists. It was the line dictated by Moscow, and the line Thälmann had drummed into his party. Everyone to the right of the Communists were Fascists.

A clandestine meeting. Schleicher and Strasser. The chancellor, a guest of the Nazi who could split the NSDAP.

Many of the district party leaders are behind me, said Strasser. They'd rather follow me than Hitler.

You could be Vice-Chancellor, said Schleicher. Maybe even Prime Minister of Prussia.

Paul von Hindenburg's farewell letter to Franz von Papen was made public, for who knows what reason. 'It is with a heavy heart, persuaded only by your personal representations and in consideration of the reasons presented to me that I allow you to be relieved of this office,' wrote the president.

> My confidence in and respect for you yourself and what you
> have accomplished remain undiminished. During your tenure
> as Chancellor of the Reich and Commissioner for Prussia,

which regrettably lasted only six months, I have come to greatly appreciate your devotion to work, your willingness to accept responsibility, your selfless love of the Fatherland and your noble character. I will never forget my time working with you. For everything you have done for our Fatherland over these difficult months, I express my deepest thanks, on behalf of the Reich as well as my own.

The German national football team played in front of fifty thousand spectators in Düsseldorf. Their opponents were the Dutch, who had brought eight thousand fans of their own. The match was a fiasco for the host team and their coach, Otto Nerz; Richard Hofmann, a German striker, had a particularly unfortunate day. They were lucky to get away 2–0.

It's hard to say how the Germans compared to other international squads. Football wasn't part of the Olympic Games that summer, and at the first World Cup in 1930 they had been put off by the three-week voyage to Uruguay.

By late evening, there was one clear loser at the Thuringian elections: the NSDAP. Goebbels had already identified the culprit: Strasser. He'd never really put his back into the campaign, Goebbels noted afterwards. Nor had he shown any enthusiasm. Was this jealousy talking? Everyone in the party knew how ambitious Goebbels was, that he coveted responsibility for the entire propaganda machine of the NSDAP. Strasser was currently entrusted with Propaganda Department II, which dealt with all the party's speakers and was in charge of their training and appearances, but Goebbels considered himself the movement's greatest agitator. After the Führer, of course.

MONDAY 5 DECEMBER

HITLER'S LOSSES IN THURINGIA

Apart from Hitler, Strasser, Frick, Göring and Goebbels also
gave numerous speeches during the campaign. The result
of these efforts has been to make the National Socialists'
defeat even more clearly and indisputably obvious.

– *Vossische Zeitung*

At approximately four o'clock in the early hours of Monday morning,
a twenty-six-year-old man by the name of Max Brien, of Feldzeug-
meisterstrasse 3 in Moabit, was found in a pool of blood. According to
the doctors at Rudolf Virchow Hospital, he'd been shot through the
lung. The man was at death's door. Was there a political motive? Brien
was apparently sympathetic to the NSDAP, but he wasn't a member.
The police's working theory was that he'd picked a quarrel with a
gang of Communist bill-posters.

Goebbels was studying the papers that morning. One topic inevita-
bly dominated: the new chancellor. All the Jewish papers, thought
Goebbels, were praising Schleicher to the skies. 'That always speaks
against a public figure,' he noted in his diary. A good word from the
Jews – there could hardly be anything worse for an anti-Semite like
Goebbels.

He promptly scribbled an aggressive article lambasting the new
chancellor. By now the distribution of roles within the party was
clear: while Goebbels went on the attack, Göring continued to negotiate with Schleicher. 'We'll soon start kicking up a fuss and squeeze
out whatever there is to be squeezed out,' Goebbels had written three
days earlier. Today he turned word into deed.

A summit of Nazi grandees was called at the Kaiserhof. There was plenty to deliberate. The new Parliament was set to convene for the first time tomorrow; just as important, meanwhile, was their lack-lustre showing at the local elections in Thuringia. How could they have they let things slide? And how should they proceed now that the General was at the helm? There was a heated discussion. The mood was jittery. They were coming to the crunch, and they all knew it. They'd waited so long for this chance.

They had met up earlier in the year, when the *Neue Illustrierte Zeitung* had dispatched a reporter to the Kaiserhof. Back then, confident of victory, the party had allowed a media presence. The article appeared shortly afterwards:

> A large round table on the right-hand side of the hall is reserved for Hitler and his staff. When political negotiations demand it, meetings are held around this table. All the well-known Führers sit down, [...] put their heads together and listen eagerly to Hitler's remarks, which are accompanied by lively gestures. Every movement sends an untameable lock of black hair falling across his brow.

The *Neue Illustrierte Zeitung*'s reporter had also been permitted into the *sanctum sanctorum*: Hitler's suite:

> Four storeys up. Telephones hum, orders are issued. People come and go. On important political days [...] there's a virtually uninterrupted telephone connection with the Brown House in Munich. The telephonist at the hotel has his hands full connecting the Führer first with a senior SA officer in the Rhineland, then with a district party leader in East Prussia. From a room somewhere there's the muffled sound of clacking typewriters. Hitler is in No. 440. A small sign hangs from the doorknob: '*Nicht stören* – don't disturb'. Important decisions are being made. Otto Meissner, emissary of the president, is paying a visit.

That was January 1932. How many conversations had there been since then? How many debates about what to do, how to achieve power? Yet there'd been nothing in comparison to the fight Gregor Strasser was about to pick.

Hitler's rivals, Strasser and Frick, urgently recommended that the NSDAP cooperate with Schleicher's government. Otherwise the chancellor would call fresh elections – and they couldn't afford to finance another campaign. That could bring the movement to its knees.

Hitler objected. Cooperating with the government – *that* would bring the movement to its knees.

During the final discussions with the members of Parliament, Strasser sat with a face of stone. It was mainly Hitler who spoke. Any compromise was an attack on the party's honour. They had to play for time.

The Christmas break would prove most convenient.

And Schleicher? He was still trying to secure backing from the party leaders, asking them to give him some initial leeway. Kaas assured him that the Centre Party would do everything in its power 'to enable a technical adjournment and thereby give the government a chance'. As long as Parliament was not in session, nobody could introduce a motion of no confidence against Schleicher's cabinet. Nobody could dislodge the chancellor. Apart from the president, of course.

In a small Jewish shop, Abraham Plotkin was being interrogated – by the owners, their son and some customers. 'Not all at once,' the son admonished the curious Germans. 'In America they don't talk at the same time.' So many questions. Is there a Fascist party in America, too? 'Do they ever throw Jews out of subway cars in New York? Do they ever come into stores belonging to Jews and tear up all the stock and break all the fixtures?' Do they boycott Jews in America?

When they heard that there was anti-Semitism in America, too, they could scarcely believe it. The son told Plotkin: 'There is hardly a Friday night that we pray without trembling.' The Jews were being driven towards something, but none of them knew what it was.

That evening, Hitler dropped in to visit the Goebbelses at Reichs-kanzlerplatz. A large circle of sympathisers was present, including artists and musicians. They were looking to unwind after the psycho-logical toll of the past few days, wrote Goebbels.

Purely to unwind? Or were a small group of them also talking about Strasser? About the spat the day before? Goebbels called Stras-ser's actions a policy of sabotage. He believed he'd finally worked out the real reason for his behaviour: Strasser had spoken to Schleicher on Sunday evening and been offered the role of Vice-Chancellor. Not only had he not turned it down, he'd even offered to run in the next parliamentary elections with a 'Strasser list'. 'That', wrote Goebbels, 'is the worst betrayal of the Führer and the party.'

TUESDAY 6 DECEMBER

ADJOURNED UNTIL JANUARY?

Schleicher's cabinet will not issue a government statement until the Reichstag reconvenes after the break, in more than five weeks' time.

– Vossische Zeitung

Out with Schleicher's Cabinet!

– Der Angriff

One hour before the opening of Parliament, a large area around the Reichstag building was cordoned off by the police.

Parliament was back in session! Abraham Plotkin saw Communists handing out *Die Rote Front* outside the university. Dozens of helmeted policemen on horseback. SA men everywhere, touting for donations, shoving their collection boxes under the noses of passersby. Plotkin's original idea had been to watch the debates, but this proved impossible – no chance of getting through the ring of police officers – so he decided to hang around near the Reichstag like the other Berliners. Roughly fifty thousand, he estimated.

Most of them were men. Young men. They were good-natured, thought Plotkin, but not loud.

What were they waiting for?

Chancellor Schleicher was nowhere to be seen in the assembly hall. He had sent a representative: Erwin Planck.

Presiding in Schleicher's absence, as the oldest Member of Parliament, was General Karl Litzmann of the NSDAP, who claimed to have made the decisive intervention at the Battle of Tannenberg in 1914. Field Marshal Hindenburg would be struck by the 'curse of world history', said his former brother-in-arms in his opening speech, if he didn't make Hitler chancellor. There was scorn from the left.

The KPD didn't hang about – they pushed immediately for a vote of no confidence. It seemed they weren't prepared to engage with the cabinet at all. The motion was voted down, however, including by the Nazis.

Hermann Göring was re-elected as President of the Reichstag, but the MPs knew that Parliament would soon be adjourned. Schleicher had already arranged it with most of the party leaders.

The Reichstag is a massive building, much bigger than the Brandenburg Gate – this comes as a surprise to most tourists arriving in Berlin for the first time. It's a short stretch from Wilhelmstrasse. Head down the road, go left at the Hotel Adlon, walk through the gate, take a right, and you're outside the mighty columns of the German Parliament building. It's maybe ten minutes from the Chancellery, if you're brisk.

Above the grand portico are the words *Dem deutschen Volke*. To the German people. Kaiser Wilhelm II had made no secret of his loathing for the place, calling it a 'talking shop'. In this building the Social Democrats had voted to approve war credits in 1914; in 1920 the Parliament of the young Weimar Republic had first set to work. It was a fateful place. A place of stone.

Indestructible, or so it seemed.

The KPD, NSDAP and SPD put forward draft amendments to a law regarding amnesty for crimes committed for political motives or for reasons of financial need. If the law passed, countless prisoners would be released. Including Carl von Ossietzky.

The police began to herd the crowd towards Tiergarten, and Abraham Plotkin was jostled helplessly along.

Slowly it grew more and more packed, and it became apparent that something was happening.

What's going on, people were asking, but nobody knew. Suddenly men began to run. Plotkin now belonged to the mob; the herd instinct was terrifying. He heard screams and shouts, and a thunderous roaring that came from the police.

Plotkin wanted to bolt – 'anything to get out of the crowd'.

Suddenly he felt a hand on the collar of his coat, a fist was jabbed into his ribs, and he found himself staring into the face of a Prussian policeman, who was shouting something at him. Plotkin yelled like he'd never yelled before, bellowing his guts out in English.

Although Schleicher was now chancellor, he remained Minister of Defence, so Bredow continued to write 'short briefings' for his boss. Today he reported that he'd heard from various visitors 'that the concerns raised in the cabinet meeting regarding the problems that would arise in a state of emergency have led to the opinion that the military would not be secure in such a situation; moreover, that it is necessary to draw on the Stahlhelm in greater numbers so that the military will have a strong reserve straight away'. There were, after all, approximately three hundred thousand battle-tested men serving in the Stahlhelm, the DNVP-affiliated paramilitary group.

In other words, these 'visitors' were recommending to Schleicher that he ally himself not with the trade unions, Social Democrats and Centre Party, but with the conservative, nationalist DNVP, the German National People's Party. The DNVP may not have been getting many votes at parliamentary elections any more – 8.7 per cent in November, to be exact – but the Stahlhelm, a closely affiliated yet independent paramilitary organisation, was a force to be reckoned with. They would be no easy adversaries in a civil war.

Whether it was hearing a person yell like that or the sound of a strange language that surprised the officer, Plotkin would never discover, but he relaxed his grip and stared with bloodshot eyes. Then he clicked his heels and explained that he couldn't possibly have known Plotkin was a foreigner. 'What difference does that make?' asked Plotkin. 'The crowd was orderly!' The officer didn't reply. Instead, he fetched a colleague and asked him to take Plotkin somewhere safe. At the Brandenburg Gate his papers were checked, and an official sent the foreigner on his way with a piece of advice: 'stay away from crowds in the future'.

The chancellor's efforts at persuasion were finally bearing fruit. Bernhard Otte, chairman of the conservative-leaning General Association of Christian Trade Unions, declared in a newspaper article:

> Nobody can deny the magnitude and difficulty of the task that lies ahead of the Schleicher government. Because of this, and because so much is at stake, it is necessary for the representatives of the people – in the interests of the economy and the Volk – to allow for a period of calm and inner composure as well as to demand of the government a less pressured and more socially responsible kind of politics.

Schleicher, it seemed, had reason to hope that his 'cross-party front' idea might be catching on.

Hitler spent another evening at the Goebbels', where they calmly mulled over the whole situation. Pondering his guest, Goebbels noted later that 'the Führer is in his whole being an artistically sensitive person. His instincts are so unerring it takes his keen mind only a moment to grasp any situation, and his conclusions are always based on absolute clarity and powerful logic. There's no getting past him with tactical dodges. And his thoroughness will be the undoing of Schleicher's cabinet.'

Goebbels worshipped Hitler.

WEDNESDAY 7 DECEMBER

BLACK–BROWN MAJORITIES

FIRST DAY OF THE NEW PARLIAMENT –

GÖRING PRESIDENT AGAIN

The inaugural session of the new Parliament was dominated
by hotly contested votes for seats on the Presidium.

– *Vossische Zeitung*

BATTLE AGAINST SCHLEICHER BEGINS

HUGENBERG THREATENS/CENTRE PARTY WAITS/SPD

REGAINS COURAGE/NSDAP WANTS OPEN WAR

These are the same parliamentary tacticians as before. If
Germany wasn't at stake, you'd let them have their open
dictatorship or their civil war – both of which have just
been avoided through Schleicher's appointment!

– *Tägliche Rundschau*

The rivals eyed each other furtively, waiting to see how Schleicher got
on. Clearly the chancellor had a plan. Moreover, he was diligent. Experienced. He seemed to be everywhere at once – negotiating, making
promises, trying to gain people's trust. He aimed to soften fronts and
rouse sympathies, but also to destabilise, to embrittle alliances, to
question certainties. Yet if his plan failed? If he couldn't win over the
moderate left as well as the centre and the valuable – from his perspective – left wing of the NSDAP, did he have an alternative? Hindenburg
had appointed him only grudgingly. How long would the president
support him?

Even if things were quiet at the Reichstag, Schleicher didn't have
much time to make his progress apparent.

It was the NSDAP again who tabled draft legislation in Parliament. Who would be in charge of state business if the president fell too ill to remain in his post? According to the current constitution, it would be the chancellor; in future, they proposed, it should be the President of the High Court.

Observers were puzzled. Was this an affront to Schleicher? Or some cunning ploy – maybe this was why Hindenburg had shrunk from making Hitler chancellor, because he would replace him as president if Hindenburg fell ill or died? The legislation was scheduled for debate during the inaugural session.

It had been suggested, in fact, two weeks earlier by Otto Meissner – Hindenburg's adviser.

While Erwin Planck was representing the government in the Reichstag, the cabinet was meeting, starting at 11.45 a.m.

Schleicher outlined to his ministers his view of the internal political situation. The Nazis had decided to tolerate his government, which meant a parliamentary majority was within their grasp. There had been a similar alliance under Brüning, who had been able to govern, more or less, using emergency decrees – although he'd had the SPD behind him, not the NSDAP.

Some in the cabinet wondered where Schleicher had got that assurance. Hadn't Hitler told him only days before that his party would recognise no government besides their own?

The Nazis would never let it come to a dissolution of Parliament, declared Schleicher, because there was currently a leadership struggle going on within the party itself.

Hitler versus Strasser.

He wasn't wrong. The infighting was getting worse.

The first debates in Parliament were relatively even-tempered, not as turbulent as expected. Outside the assembly hall, however, tensions ran high. Communist and Nazi MPs were exchanging angry words in the foyer, until finally the argument came to blows. The trigger? One of the Communists whacked a Nazi colleague over the head with a telephone. Soon spit was flying through the air, fists were swinging and MPs were arming themselves with ashtrays and desk lids. Panes of glass were shattered, and a chandelier dropped from the ceiling. Several MPs were injured.

The German Parliament was back in session.

Goebbels seemed to be enjoying the fray. In his diary, he bemoaned the tedium of parliamentary routine, of group and plenary sessions. 'In the middle, a bloody punch-up in the galleries and the foyer between the KPD and us.' One of his lot had been badly injured, noted Goebbels. Of the other side's victims he had nothing to say.

'Thunderous racket. Balkanisation continues apace,' wrote Quaatz. 'Huge punch-up between the Nazis and Sozis.'

The Nazis, he added, were nonetheless politically 'completely in servitude to the Centre Party'. Even Schleicher was 'in a bad situation, because the Centres, Nazis and Sozis aren't cheap'.

A bad situation? Schleicher had sold it very differently to his cabinet that morning.

At six o'clock that evening, the Walther Rathenau Society convened in the assembly hall of the Reich Economic Council. Harry Graf Kessler, who was being awarded the Silver Medal, gave a speech: 'Rathenau and Man in the Mechanistic Age'. Walther Rathenau had been Foreign Minister during an earlier incarnation of the Weimar Republic, before he was murdered by right-wing radicals. A widely trusted politician, he'd lent the Republic stature and a sense of sovereignty, both domestically and internationally.

The Nazis were raw-nerved. At the Kaiserhof, Hitler and Strasser had locked horns for the second time within only a few days.

Finally, Strasser picked up his belongings and left the room without a word. In his hotel suite, he sat down and penned Hitler a long letter in which he announced his resignation from all party offices.

It could have been a declaration of war, if war Strasser wanted.

What would he do now? And who in the party would follow him, if he made the break public?

THURSDAY 8 DECEMBER

Work Despite Kerfuffle
Large Majority Pro Deputisation Legislation in Reichstag
– Vossische Zeitung

Wednesday's Reichstag session got off to a flying start: Herr
Hugenberg has been elected parliamentary recording clerk, with
291 votes at that. A consolation prize, perhaps? From minister-
maker and chancellor stalwart to clerk – what a career.
– Der Angriff

Hitler received Strasser's missive that morning. In it, Strasser wrote
that he no longer wanted any part in a policy that would see Germany
descend into chaos before rebuilding it along National Socialist lines.
He was withdrawing from all party offices to become a simple soldier
in the movement.

Strasser then announced his intention to leave Berlin and travel
abroad; he assured Hitler, however, that he was still loyal to the
movement.

The letter triggered panic among the party leadership.

At midday Hitler discovered how Strasser had justified his resignation
to seven senior regional administrative officials in the party: he considered Hitler's all-or-nothing tactics – to stake everything on the role of
chancellor – a failure. The seven officials were promptly summoned
to the Kaiserhof: Hitler dismissed all criticism of his chosen course.

In those days of double-dealing, of back-room bargains and open spar-
ring, was there any common humanity?

Were there stress-induced stomach aches? Did anybody, knocking back one schnapps too many of an evening to make the mental merry-go-round stop, wonder how they could possibly stick it out? Did Hitler sleep through the night? Did he dream? Of what, and whom? And Strasser?

Strasser was a diabetic who'd walked with a cane ever since a skiing accident. Was he fretting over what to do next? Did he know what calibre of politician he'd need to be in order to defeat this particular adversary? Did he want to be a revolutionary himself? Perhaps he didn't understand that flight meant capitulation. Why did he decide to leave Berlin, to head south?

Representatives from the Christian Trade Unions of Germany were granted audience with Hindenburg. Minutes were taken by Meissner. Hindenburg was already familiar with his visitors' arguments: the people, they said, were in a state of material as well as moral abjection. He knew what they would warn him was going to happen next, and he knew what they would demand. Nevertheless, the trade unionists protested that they were keeping an open mind towards Chancellor Schleicher.

Hindenburg assured his guests that the people – and the little man – had always been near and dear to his heart. 'I have never been otherwise and will never be otherwise.'

Bella Fromm was dining with Hassan Nachat Pasha, the Egyptian ambassador. It was a pleasant group of people. Seated next to her was Karl von Wiegand, a correspondent for various newspapers published by the American media magnate William Randolph Hearst, and an old friend with an uncanny nose for the shifting balance of power. Dear Karl always popped up in Berlin, thought Fromm, 'whenever a political melodrama is about to sweep the stage'.

'When are the National Socialists going to seize the government?' Fromm asked her neighbour. 'It won't be long now,' was the reply.

Wiegand knew the NSDAP like few others. He'd interviewed Hitler for the first time back in 1921, and recognised him as a man who meant business. Bella Fromm affectionately referred to Wiegand as the 'dear old alarm signal'. Was he right? Was Hitler really so close to power? Hadn't he just failed once again?

Hitler, meanwhile, was at the Goebbels'. The atmosphere was hardly convivial; everybody was downcast, worried that the party was falling apart. That years of work would be for nothing.

The telephone rang, cutting through the gloom. An informant. The situation was coming to a head. Hitler was needed at the Kaiserhof without delay.

At two in the morning, the Goebbels' telephone rang once more. The Führer was expecting him. Immediately! Goebbels set off straight away. On reaching the hotel he bumped into Heinrich Himmler, Reichsführer of the SS, and discovered the reason for the commotion: the *Tägliche Rundschau* would be publishing an article the next morning in which Strasser announced his resignation. Consternation! Until now, the whole debacle had been kept under wraps.

They racked their brains all night long, not resting until six o'clock the next morning. This was an emergency. Wave after wave of bad news came filtering through from various regional sub-offices of the party. The NSDAP was in chaos; Strasser's gambit had shaken it to the core. Apparently he was holed up in the Hotel Excelsior, having gathered his friends and allies. What would be his next move?

The Führer was looking embittered, and, as Goebbels later remarked, 'wounded to the quick by this act of disloyalty ... We were all dumbfounded by this level of malice. Treachery! Treachery! Treachery!'

Treachery? What, exactly, had Strasser done?

Rumours spread. In the bar and corridors of the Kaiserhof, people whispered that even Wilhelm Brückner, Hitler's adjutant, was in favour of joining the government.

Hitler was seething. This was a decisive moment, that much was certain. And wasn't it moments like these that revealed a person's true colours?

'If the party falls apart, I'll end it all in three minutes,' Hitler said to Goebbels.

And Goebbels himself? He was having a rough time. That day he only managed two hours' sleep.

FRIDAY 9 DECEMBER

Goebbels Mocks Strasser
– *Vossische Zeitung*

We Demand the Right to Live for Working People!
Lift the Papen Emergency Decrees! National Socialists
Resist Intolerable Cuts to Wages and Pensions
– *Völkischer Beobachter*

Political Berlin was in turmoil. Newsboys on Wilhelmstrasse were announcing a sensational headline: 'Strasser Takes Over NSDAP!' – according to the *Tägliche Rundschau*, anyway. In the lobby of the Kaiserhof, people were conferring in groups. Excitement hung in the air. Upheaval. At Anhalter Bahnhof, a guard claimed to have seen Strasser boarding a train to Munich. What did Strasser want there?

Nobody could accuse Parliament of dragging its feet. The legislation regarding who would act on the president's behalf in case of illness had been passed on its third reading – it would now no longer be the chancellor but the President of the High Court. Thanks to the NSDAP's votes, the two-thirds majority required for a constitutional amendment had been far exceeded.

The proposed legislation for an amnesty had also been approved. Did that mean Carl von Ossietzky would be released?

The Nazi MP Hans Frank gave a speech in which he prophesied that 'within a few weeks Adolf Hitler will take power in Germany'. He was greeted with derisive laughter from large pockets of the assembly.

Abraham Plotkin met with an agricultural adviser from the SPD and the trade unions for a long conversation. Why were so many Germans starving, asked Plotkin. What was going wrong?

It wasn't a lack of food, replied the man, whose name was Bading. The problem was that people couldn't afford it. It simply rotted on the shelves.

Hitler was persevering.

In an effort to stall the break-up of his party, he had the NSDAP's press office circulate a statement: 'Party member Gregor Strasser has been given the Führer's permission to take three weeks' sick leave. All rumours and speculation on this subject are incorrect and utterly baseless.' Power was immediately redistributed among the leading party officials. Hitler himself took responsibility for organisation, while Goebbels was in charge of 'educating the people'. Strasser's allies were relieved of their posts, and each of the regional branch heads in Berlin were made to sign a declaration of loyalty. No arguments.

At the end of the day's session, the Reichstag decided to adjourn indefinitely, until the Presidium of the Reichstag and the Council of Elders – a special parliamentary committee of experienced if not necessarily elderly MPs responsible for internal affairs – decided to recall it. Only the SPD and the KPD voted against the motion.

Work in the various committees continued, but the Christmas lull descended sixteen days before the day itself.

The timing could not have been better for Kurt von Schleicher. Now he could read his government statement on the radio, rather than to the hooligans in the Reichstag.

NSDAP members of Parliament and various party functionaries gathered that evening in the palace of the President of the Reichstag, where Göring was staying.

Hitler gave an impassioned speech on Strasser and his betrayal.

'But if you want to leave me, then my life's work and my struggle no longer has any meaning, then the movement collapses,' he cried to the assembled men.

Every functionary shook hands with Hitler.

Every one of them pledged loyalty to the Führer of their party. It was a performance of solidarity. Imposed devotion.

Hans Frank met with the Führer at the Kaiserhof that evening. 'You're a bad lawyer,' said Hitler, alluding to Frank's prediction in the Reichstag that the NSDAP would soon take power. 'Your speech today was both accurate and realistic. It won't be long now.' Lawyers, Hitler believed, were rarely truth-tellers. Frank was Hitler's man when it came to big, attention-grabbing trials – he was in charge of the NSDAP's legal department.

Later, Hitler left the capital and travelled to Breslau, instructing Göring and Goebbels to deal with the Strasser affair. Goebbels made a note in his diary: 'Strasser is isolated. Dead man.'

Yet it was clear Hitler hadn't broken with Strasser for good. Instead, he waited, as he so often did, putting off an unpleasant decision. Perhaps he'd need Strasser one more time after all.

And, with that, another day was at an end: another day the National Socialist German Workers' Party didn't fall apart.

SATURDAY 10 DECEMBER

Check or Check Mate?
Gregor Strasser's Rebellion
– Vossische Zeitung

Gregor Strasser's leave of absence will be used by
the enemies of Germany to nourish the hope that
internal conflicts may drive National Socialism towards
self-destruction. The enemies of Germany hope in
vain! All have vowed loyalty to Adolf Hitler.
– Der Angriff

'It is winter,' wrote the poet and editor Oskar Loerke in his diary. 'Dreariness outside, the pines looking like silhouettes. The ground is frozen. The last chrysanthemum blossoms are still hanging colourfully from their stems.'

The chancellor called a meeting of his senior staff. He needed his war on unemployment to show results, and quickly. Günther Gereke, the new Commissioner for Work, had to deliver the goods.

He ordered the formation of a committee of cabinet members to focus on this issue and another on the hugely controversial policy of Eastern Aid and rural settlement. The question of how to help East Prussia's ailing agriculturalists was a delicate one. Prussia was the home of the influential landowners known as Junkers – political heavyweights, many of them friends of Hindenburg. Even the president had an estate there, a gift from industrialists and landowners.

Schleicher wanted to chair the committees himself, although he had to leave that particular meeting early.

Gereke, he instructed, please be present at all future cabinet meetings!

Gereke wasn't a minister, but he was the man who could help Schleicher draw the poison from Germany's veins.

Wedding was the classic Berlin working-class area, where it wasn't uncommon to find members of the SA and the Red Front living cheek by jowl. It was in Wedding that, on 1 May 1929, police working for the Social Democratic government of Prussia had shot at demonstrating workers, killing fifteen people in the street. 'Bloody May', they called it. It was still fresh in people's minds, still raw.

In Köslinerstrasse, it struck Abraham Plotkin how tightly packed the tall apartment blocks were – so tightly that barely any light filtered through into the narrow courtyards.

At No. 2 he was surrounded by a swarm of children. 'How many tenants in the house?'

'Eighty.'

'How many unemployed?'

'Five are working.'

His guide was a man named Hans from the local soup kitchen. He was twenty years old and looked like any American boy his age, only sadder and wiser, thought Plotkin. By the glow of a cigarette lighter, they navigated their way through the dark hallway. A rat darted aside. They knocked at a door. A woman opened; she recognised Hans. It was two in the afternoon, but inside it was pitch black.

Frau Schoner invited them in. Her daughter appeared and curtseyed. Eleven years old.

'The rats were becoming unbearable,' reported Plotkin. 'They were eating the little food they had.' The woman's husband was trying to find the janitor. Plotkin, noticing the damp on the walls, was overcome by a wave of nausea. The apartment smelled strongly of warm urine.

There were four of them in the family, and they paid 23 marks per month for two rooms. They received 60 marks from the government.

Cabbage soup made up the bulk of their diet, or sometimes potatoes with herring. On Sundays they ate meat: one pound of it between four. They rarely had milk. The children needed it, of course, but there wasn't any.

Their American guest and his companion left the apartment, the smell becoming unbearable. What on earth was causing such an awful stench? wondered Plotkin. 'We swung into the rear of the tenement house, and as we entered I saw two huge dung pits filled with fresh cow manure, and two men with pitchforks loading it on a dray cart. Behind the pits was a stable, and in the stable a number of cows.'

They climbed further up the stairs. First stop, the Gehrings. Then, above them, Frau Fluchalt and her seven children – five boys, two girls. Her husband was an ironworker, but had been out of work for four years.

As they left Köslinerstrasse, Hans remarked that there were other places in Berlin worse still.

Joseph Goebbels was preoccupied once again with an irksome topic: the finances of his branch of the NDSAP. 'We must introduce very rigorous cost-cutting measures and bring in an outside administrator,' he confided in his diary.

The lobbyists flocked from all sides. A letter from the Federation of German Unions of Workers, Salaried Employees and Civil Service Employees appeared on Schleicher's desk.

The most pressing tasks, they argued, were to take additional vigorous measures against unemployment, including adequate aid for the victims of the ongoing economic crisis, to prevent any further wage cuts for workers, and to pursue a fair taxation policy as well as a trade policy that would stimulate the economy and the job market.

Schleicher's answer was friendly but evasive. The usual stuff. He was constantly on the defensive, endlessly putting out fires. At some point, however, things had to change. At some point, he'd get the chance to breathe.

At the Kaiserhof, senior foreign press secretary Ernst Hanfstaengl was reporting that a certain Dr Martin had visited Strasser the day before. Strasser, calm and resigned, had apparently said the following:

> Dr Martin, I am a man marked for death. It will be a long time before we see each other again, and for your own sake I suggest you do not come here again. Whatever happens, know this: from now on, Germany is in the hands of an Austrian who is a liar of genius, a former officer who is a pervert and a club foot. The last is the worst of all. He is Satan in human form.

By the 'pervert' he meant Ernst Röhm, a former captain in the military who was now head of the SA, and whose homosexuality was an open secret. The 'club foot' was Goebbels, Strasser's old rival in the battle for Hitler's favour.

Bella Fromm had made herself unpopular on the right. The Nazis despised her anyway because she had Jewish roots, but now the leadership of the Stahlhelm were shunning her too. At a dinner given by the Hungarian ambassador, Theodor Duesterberg – deputy leader of the reactionary paramilitary group – gave her a dressing down. 'You are too leftist,' he barked at her. 'I will not have my name mentioned in your paper.'

Bella Fromm bowed her head and let him vent his wrath. 'I hope the Stahlhelm comes to its senses before it is too late,' she replied.

Duesterberg, it should be noted, was known as a virulent anti-Semite.

At the Ministry of Defence they were still determined to draw lessons from the devastating conclusion of the simulation they had run in late November.

Bredow wrote to Schleicher: 'There are still a few issues to clarify regarding a state of emergency in-house, both on the military and civilian sides.' He enclosed a note that went to various departments, inviting them to a meeting with the Minister of Defence.

They were now preparing for the worst-case scenario. This was no longer a simulation. This was a plan of action.

SUNDAY 11 DECEMBER

First Phase of Reichstag Debate Concluded: Nat-Socis Successful
in Battle Against Social Reactionaryism and Judicial Terror
We Demand the Release of Our Imprisoned SA and SS Comrades!
– *Völkische Beobachter*

Geneva's New Formula
Equal Rights for Peace Pact – France Has Agreed – What Says Berlin?
– *Vossische Zeitung*

By now the days were short, growing light late and dark early. The air
in Berlin was smeared and grey beneath an overcast sky; it was slightly
foggy and very cold.

The penultimate Sunday before Christmas, known in those days
in Germany as 'Silver Sunday', marked the opening of the Christmas
markets in Berlin, when sales of Christmas trees began. A sizeable
specimen cost between 1.50 and 2 marks, somewhat cheaper than the
previous year. Some good news before the holidays.

Schleicher, too, finally had some good news. A diplomatic breakthrough on the vexed question of disarmament had been made in
Geneva: the USA, Great Britain, France and Italy had agreed to grant
the German Reich equality of military rights, on the condition that
the security of all nations was guaranteed.

The message was unmistakeable: the Treaty of Versailles, having
shackled the Weimar Republic for so long, was slowly being watered
down. The radical right wing would soon have fewer arguments to
draw on, and the military might have a few more soldiers to defend
the Republic from its enemies on the home front.

On Saturday the Foreign Minister, Neurath, had spent nine hours in negotiations. Now the agreement was ready to be signed. It was the best they were likely to get, he assured Schleicher, who instructed him to sign. His other ministers were not consulted. In fact, they were not even informed.

Mascha Kaléko (née Engel), born in West Galicia in 1907, had attended the Jewish community's all-girls school in the heart of Berlin before training at the offices of the Workers' Welfare Agency of the Jewish Organisations of Germany. In 1928 she married the journalist Saul Aaron Kaléko, and the following year, aged twenty-two, she published her first poems. Now Rowohlt Verlag was going to be issuing her first volume of poetry in January: *The Book of Lyrical Shorthand: Everyday Verse*.

In the early 1930s she began appearing at literary cafés, earning her initial reputation. At the Romanisches Café, a well-known meeting place for artists, she was approached by an editor from Rowohlt who said that he'd been cutting out her poems from the newspaper for some time, putting together a collection. 'Show me everything you've got,' he told her at their first meeting. They agreed a 10 per cent royalty on the retail price and an advance of 200 marks.

Re: The First Snow

Light shines in the room one morning,
You're thinking, here we go again.
Snow and the barometer have fallen.
– Joy of joys, let sore-throat season reign.

[...]

Makes you wish you were fourteen once more:
Christmastime… let's bring out that sled!
No more sniffles, no colds, but somewhere
A small house you can stay instead.

Outside stand a few snow-covered firs,
It's a place that's many hours from town.
A place where there're no offices and no phones.
– Almost no commitments tie you down.

All we ask are days when nothing happens!
Just a few hours when no news comes in.
After all, you don't have much to lose if
You don't own a single thing.

Schleicher's most important man at the Ministry of Defence was hard at work. Bredow, preparing his boss's speech for the radio, wrote: 'I consider it necessary to advise these organisations that mil[itary] affairs are not a matter for the youth or for an organisation, but solely for the German armed forces.' Like his chancellor, Bredow was an officer to the core. The private armies maintained by parties and other organisations appalled him. But how could the SA be cut back? And could those well-drilled men be used to defend the nation and fight the good fight against the Communists? How could Schleicher phrase it in his speech without nettling the NSDAP? Bredow was happy to tweak the content, but the wording he left to others. A great wordsmith he was not. His boss, too, valued facts above emotional rhetoric. Would it be well received? Some of his advisers were worried that Schleicher's speech would go down badly with voters – but there were still four days to find the appropriate tone.

Abroad, too, people were listening very closely to what Schleicher had to say – especially in America. The US had around 4 billion dollars at stake in Germany, claimed Knickerbocker, who had a fondness for statistics. This enormous sum, he added, 'is equal to more than one per cent of our national wealth', far exceeding anything invested elsewhere in Europe. He went on to cite another statistic: 'America alone has thirty-eight per cent of the total direct foreign investments in Germany'. If the Republic collapsed and the country drifted into right-wing extremism or a Communist dictatorship, disaster would ensue. Propping up private capitalism in the Reich was thus, argued Knickerbocker, of paramount importance.

The British writer Christopher Isherwood, resident in Berlin, stood watching the crush of Christmas shoppers on one of the city's busiest streets. 'All along the Tauentzienstrasse,' he wrote, 'men, women, and boys are hawking postcards, flowers, song-books, hair-oil, bracelets. Christmas-trees are stacked for sale along the central path between the tram-lines. Uniformed SA men rattle their collecting-boxes. In the side-streets, lorry-loads of police are waiting; for any large crowd, nowadays, is capable of turning into a political riot.'

Abraham Plotkin had now been in Germany for several weeks, but still found himself wondering what sort of country it was. How to account for the rise of extremism? 'Everyone tells me that the middle class in Germany is ruined,' he noted pensively. 'But what I see with my own eyes is hard to contradict. [...] everywhere I go, the stores are occupied and the vacancies are rare and far between. I have seen far more store vacancies in the States in normal times than I see here when conditions are abnormal.'

KaDeWe – short for 'Kaufhaus des Westens', the Department Store of the West – was doing a roaring trade in Christmas presents. Children's skates were 3.50 marks, an electric toaster was 9.75, and a travel clock with an alarm and a luminous dial could be had for 12.50. The department store, hung with festive decorations, was open until seven o'clock in the evening. On the third floor was a winter-sports display, where KaDeWe had rallied various celebrities to boost sales. Leni Riefenstahl, the famous actress, was signing autographs. She had appeared in picture-houses nationwide that year, starring in *Das blaue Licht* (The

Blue Light), an early talkie. Riefenstahl, like so many other actresses of her era, was a chilly beauty, but she had also directed the film herself. With previous credits including *Der weisse Rausch* (The White Ecstasy) and *Die weisse Hölle vom Piz Palü* (The White Hell of Pitz Palu), she was a natural choice for this winter-themed event.

Otto Meissner, head of Hindenburg's office, met the American ambassador. He assured Sackett that the break between Hitler and Strasser was 'of really serious proportions'. Strasser and Frick were ready and willing to support Schleicher's government. Meisser expressed himself satisfied that 'the country at large' was behind the current administration, and that the Reichstag was proving 'malleable' – that it might even be persuaded to adjourn until after Easter.

For the Americans, the signals were unambiguous. Schleicher was firmly in the saddle, and there'd be a few weeks' peace. Their own staff problems, meanwhile, could be papered over. Or was Meissner merely lulling the nervous American creditors into a false sense of security? In a report to the State Department Sackett observed that the calm was made possible by 'the tact and skill with which Chancellor von Schleicher dealt with the situation, in striking contrast to the provocative methods of his predecessor'. That said, he added, it was 'premature to expect at this time an open split in the Nazi party'.

Osram, one of Germany's biggest lighting manufacturers, advertised its 'electric Christmas candles' in the newspaper. 'Non-drip, easy to attach, and cheap, because you only need to buy them once. Just as atmospheric as wax candles. Not a fire hazard.'

Rowohlt Verlag was trying to promote Hans Fallada's new book. Thirty-five thousand copies of *Little Man, What Now?* had been printed, retailing at 4.50 marks. Set during the international financial crisis, the novel depicted the hardships of ordinary people. Its hero was Johannes Pinneberg, an accountant who marries his sweetheart, Emma, when she falls pregnant by him. Both are happy until Pinneberg loses his job. A crisis.

Would people still buy books like that in such times as these?

Another crisis was playing out within the SPD. The party wanted to defend the Republic, but it didn't know how. It was under pressure from both left and right. The Communists were poaching their voters while the National Socialists were going after the Reichsbanner. And Schleicher? How ought they to deal with the new chancellor?

Gustav Noske, Governor of Hanover, advocated working with Schleicher. Otto Braun, the recently power-deprived Prime Minister of Prussia, was similarly in favour of cooperation. So were the Herrs Leipart and Grassmann from the trade unions; indeed, they were already in talks with the new government. Even Carl Severing, Interior Minister of Prussia – hounded out of office on 20 July by Papen's coup, he now used the title on a purely formal basis – was inclined to tolerate the new cabinet.

Yet the good old SPD, stalwarts of the Weimar Republic for so many years, could not settle on a course of action. They continued to debate.

Since June of 1932, Hindenburg had been living at the Chancellery, Wilhelmstrasse 77, in apartments formerly the official residence of Otto von Bismarck. Meanwhile, ex-Chancellor Papen was still ensconced in his official residence at Wilhelmstrasse 74, the Interior Ministry. He had declined the diplomatic post in Paris offered to him by Schleicher, in part because Hindenburg had asked him to. When urgent business summoned him to the president's side, all he had to do was pick up the keys to the garden gates and within a few metres – crossing the Foreign Ministry park – he would be outside the door to the private chambers of the head of state and the latter's son, Oskar.

For the new chancellor, Schleicher, the situation was insupportable. He could, of course, have ushered Papen out of the apartment and moved into it himself; but that would have caused a stir, and the press as well as his political opponents would have jumped at the chance to capitalise on it. Besides, Schleicher and his wife Elisabeth had only just made themselves comfortable at their official apartments in Bendlerstrasse, at the Ministry of Defence.

Bendlerstrasse was quite a stretch from Wilhelmstrasse, at least in terms of proximity to the old man. But to move again so soon, with Elisabeth's eleven-year-old daughter from her first marriage, as well as their long-serving cook Marie Güntel and their two dachshunds – it was out of the question.

Until recently Otto Meissner had been living with his family in the presidential palace, where he'd been perpetually on hand whenever Hindenburg wanted him. Now the renovation work had forced Meissner into apartments on Bendlerstrasse, and nobody could be expected to rush all that way simply to discuss a point or two, gossip about other politicians, air the odd concern, or pin down a few solutions. Hindenburg might have made Schleicher chancellor, but it was now Papen he turned to, not Meissner, when he wanted a political chat in the middle of the night.

Schleicher knew this – and it niggled at him. Once, in more comradely days, he'd playfully called Papen by the diminutive nickname 'Fränzchen'; now the former chancellor was supposed to be comfortably sidelined. So what was he playing at?

He instructed his people at the Ministry of Defence to tap the telephone lines at the Chancellery. Technically speaking this wasn't a problem for the specialists at the Ministry, and Schleicher, of course, was thinking only of the Fatherland. He was trying to shield it from disaster. Unfortunately, Hindenburg didn't use the telephone. When he had something to communicate he scribbled it on little scraps of paper, and the notebooks in which he confided his innermost thoughts were kept locked in a safe in his bedroom.

That evening, Goebbels boarded a train to Munich. All day long he'd been coaxing functionaries in his party district to swear allegiance to Hitler, travelling from place to place, and had given a two-hour speech in Brandenburg in which he railed bitterly against the apostates. Now, sitting in his compartment, he could finally put his feet up and read the newspaper – until, in the corridor outside, he heard a whispered conversation. His curiosity piqued, Goebbels flung open the door: and there before him was the Führer. Hitler was on his way back from Leipzig, where he'd been stirring up his party to combat the saboteurs. This display of gumption enchanted Goebbels.

MONDAY 12 DECEMBER

The New Basis for Disarmament
The Agreement: Recognition of Equal Rights.
European Peace Pact – Germany Returns to Conference
– *Vossische Zeitung*

Hindenburg had called an important meeting. Summoned were Hermann Göring, President of the Reichstag, and Hanns Kerrl, President of the Prussian State Assembly. Another Nazi. Schleicher and Meissner were also in the room.

The issue at hand was the Prussian Coup, a complicated topic that was keeping scores of lawyers in work. Göring argued that they urgently needed to form a government in Prussia, as the State Court had demanded in its verdict. Hindenburg replied that he would not allow another power struggle between Prussia and the Reich: any new prime minister in Prussia would also have to be a member of the national government. Was this his way of trying to tempt the NSDAP into supporting Schleicher?

The Nazis demanded that the post go to Göring. The national government, however, would only join if Hitler were chancellor – the Führer continued to insist on that.

The situation remained messy.

In the Dutch town of Doorn, in a stately home occupied by the former Kaiser Wilhelm II, servants overpowered an intruder. The man clambered over the wall that afternoon without anybody noticing and slunk into the building, where staff discovered him in one of the towers. Upon his arrest, the police confiscated a revolver as well as a knife. They assumed the man was planning to attack the exiled monarch.

The parliamentary budget committee convened to discuss a winter relief programme for people on the breadline, and how it could be financed. Reinhold Quaatz was observing the frantic manoeuvring of the Nazis, Social Democrats and Centre Party, all of whom were trying to disguise their backpedalling on the issue. Schleicher's government had the upper hand, noted Quaatz. All the parties were terrified that Parliament would be dissolved, because that would mean fresh elections. Even the Communists were being uncharacteristically meek.

At the Blohm + Voss shipyard in Hamburg, business was precarious. The company's operating surplus was half that of the previous year, and there were no dividends paid to shareholders. Worse still, not a single new order had come in, so next year's outlook was bleak. Meanwhile, workers were kept busy with what few projects the management had acquired. The *Savarona*, a luxury yacht built for a wealthy American had just been launched, and two motor vessels for the Hamburg–America line were under construction. But after that?

Members of the SPD were gathering in Stuttgart on Monday evening. Kurt Schumacher had made the journey from Berlin to convey his impressions of the last several days to his home-town allies. Schumacher, thirty-eight years old and unquestionably the party's up-and-comer, did not mince words: the German press was suffering from 'Schleicher psychosis'. The new chancellor advocated progress and de-escalation; but they should not let themselves be deceived – Schleicher, he said, was the 'office Bonaparte of Bendlerstrasse'. He wasn't Papen's opposite, he was 'an opportunist, despite all modernising impulses, a man of the authoritarian state, an anti-democrat, a monarchist, a prisoner of his ancestry and his caste'. The SPD, he went on, had to oppose him 100 per cent.

Schumacher, one of the youngest MPs in the Social Democratic faction, was considered an aggressive, hard-line politician. He had categorically disowned the SPD's tacit support of Papen's predecessor,

Brüning, and was continually locking horns with the National Socialists. Standing at the podium in the Reichstag, he had called the NSDAP's
agitation an 'appeal to the inner bastard in human beings'. The Nazis
had hated him ever since. But there was a price to pay for his courage:
even in his home town of Stuttgart, where he led the SPD, he could no
longer go anywhere without Reichsbanner bodyguards. He no longer
met his colleagues at the Schlossgarten Café or the Taverne, a popular
restaurant, but in private apartments. Better safe than sorry.

Meanwhile, a spirited SA get-together in the town of Gladbach-Rheydt
devolved into a brawl. Several members had started arguing about the
split between Hitler and Strasser. When one group called it a scandal
that Strasser had been forced out, a number of other men – supportive
of the Führer – pounced on their comrades. The senior SA officer on
scene tried in vain to stop the fighting. In the end, the police had to be
called.

TUESDAY 13 DECEMBER

German Plan of Action for Geneva
Security, Disarmament, Reorganisation of the Military
— *Vossische Zeitung*

Power or Struggle!
Führer's Uncompromising Politics Gets Tumultuous
Response at Party Meetings in Silesia and Saxony
— *Völkischer Beobachter*

At ten o'clock in the morning, the inaugural 'Brown Christmas Market' opened at Lehrter Bahnhof, one of Berlin's major railway stations. It was a point of honour for committed Nazis to buy Christmas presents there for their nearest and dearest. The market stayed open until ten o'clock at night for the next three days, and between six and seven the Kapelle Fuhsel – an SA-affiliated band – played military music. Entry cost 25 pfennigs, or 10 pfennigs for children and the unemployed.

General Franz von Hörauf, chief of the NSDAP's Defence Office at the Brown House in Munich, wrote to Crown Prince Wilhelm – a letter that fell into Schleicher's hands.

'After talking to Frick alone for more than two hours yesterday,' confided Hörauf, 'it's clear to me that in extremis he'll go with Strasser. Gregor Strasser has left the country, though – he telephoned yesterday from Rome. He'll be back on Christmas Eve to see his children.' How were things developing in the NSDAP? Franz von Hörauf had been mulling it over, pondering, too, how Hitler could be kept at bay: Strasser would have to step forward and unite the movement under his own leadership. That way Hitler would be forced to split the party, not Strasser. Hörauf concluded by offering to serve as go-between: 'If

Your Imperial Highness or Herr von Schleicher currently have anything to communicate to Gregor Strasser, I can do so at any time.'

In her column 'Berlin Diplomats', Bella Fromm reported on a reception given by the American ambassador and his wife, a lady of renowned elegance. Nearly the full complement of ambassadors and consuls were in attendance, as were various high-ranking staff from the Foreign Office. Freifrau von Neurath, married to the Foreign Minister, was among the guests, as was Otto Meissner's wife. Several senior officers appeared as well, including General Hammerstein and Colonel Bredow.

Fromm liked Bredow, and not only because she had a weakness for German military officers. He was an old friend, and a capable one. She met with him often, eventually becoming close friends with his boss, Kurt von Schleicher – and Schleicher she found delightful: such 'irresistible charm'. A 'courageous and farsighted man', he could be 'very sarcastic at times. His voice is well modulated and so is his laughter.' It was just a shame that Schleicher, the eternal bachelor, had got married the previous year. Still, he and Fromm remained on excellent terms. The general issued instructions that she be allowed to see him at any time, even without an appointment. 'You have been my faithful comrade all these years,' he told her once, touching her arm.

A meeting of group and military-district commanders had begun. Schleicher gave a short speech. It was imperative, he told them, that they obtain the cooperation of the Nazis under Strasser's leadership. If Hitler didn't give that his blessing, he'd have a fight on his hands – and 'not of the mosquito-bite variety!' Schleicher kept things vague but spoke of 'measures that the Nazis would use themselves, if they could'.

The officers, meanwhile, should not be surprised to see reports in the media that the Nazis were still being offered government positions: in order to be vulnerable, they had to be accountable.

All this doubtless reached Hitler's ears. After all, he had plenty of adherents in the military. Schleicher knew this, of course. People like him have a weakness for back-channel communication.

Goebbels was still in Munich when a piece of good news came in from Berlin – finally, a reason to celebrate. *Der Angriff*, his favourite tool of propaganda, had banked more than 60,000 marks that year. It would go some way towards clearing his local party district's debts.

A note that circulated among the SPD leadership listed infringements by the National Socialists:

> The Nazis are still terrorising the Altmark region to an extraordinary degree. Particularly striking in the last election was their intrusion into our meetings. Everywhere they make their voices heard by brute force. Our farm-worker colleagues are afraid of terrorisation by the Nazis, not least because it could result in them being dismissed from their jobs, and when they're in their home towns they submit to everything. When not, clashes are inevitable – we hear reports of these daily from the Altmark. Even our functionaries hardly dare venture out there because they continually have to deal with the most outrageous terrorisation.

The SPD leadership suggested using their own resources to increase security at such events.

WEDNESDAY 14 DECEMBER

Hitler's Star in Decline
— *Vossische Zeitung*

Two Cabinets Toppled!
In France and Belgium
— *Der Angriff*

No Truce with the Enemies of the People!
Rote Fahne Back in the Fray After Fiftieth Ban
— *Die Rote Fahne*

The morning editions announced that Chancellor Schleicher would be giving his maiden speech at seven o'clock on Thursday evening, when it would be broadcast across the Reich. The speech would last a whole hour. An abridged English version would be made available in the United States.

At the eleven o'clock ministerial meeting, Schleicher was naturally the first to speak. To begin with, a few admonishments: no writing articles for newspapers or magazines over Christmas and New Year! They'd caused nothing but trouble in the past. No leaving themselves open to attack – things were complicated enough as it was. And definitely no indiscretions! Indiscretions had been the bane of previous governments.

The problem was that Schleicher didn't trust all the ministers in his cabinet, not by a long shot. He'd have preferred to replace some of Papen's hand-picked barons, but Hindenburg refused to play along. Schleicher could only govern with those gentlemen the old man would accept.

Most pressing was the matter of a winter-relief programme. The Social Democrats were calling for two kilograms of bread and half a kilogram of meat per week, as well as twenty hundredweight of coal to be provided to all those who needed it between December and April – at the state's expense. It was going to cost 400 million marks: easy enough for an opposition party to demand, but unfeasible, Finance Minister Schwerin von Krosigk insisted, given the state of the national coffers. He'd been explicit during parliamentary debates that the government would only provide aid within the bounds of financial possibility. His suggestion? Measures had already been implemented to reduce the price of coal and meat – they ought simply to reduce them further still. This would mean an additional expenditure of only 20 million marks.

What about bread? What about milk? It would be too complicated for his civil servants to organise, the Interior Minister insisted. The meeting devolved into an argument.

Eventually, Schleicher cut the squabbling short. The relevant ministers, he said, were to decide among themselves what was possible in terms of bread and milk. Then he asked the cabinet to explore how the plight of needy pensioners could be alleviated. It was, he added, the president's wish. The Employment Minister promptly suggested making 1.8 million marks available.

For the cabinet, Hindenburg's word was law, and the president was always sticking his oar into day-to-day politics. Schleicher had no choice. Hindenburg commanded, he implemented.

In Munich, the NSDAP was censoring one of its own magazines. The *Illustrierter Beobachter* had been banned from publication after printing an article entitled 'Men and Characters: Gregor Strasser'. Four photographs depicted Strasser making determined gestures as he gave a speech: pointing index fingers, raised arms. Another image showed the Führer visiting Strasser in Oberstaufen, where the latter had suffered the skiing accident that still gave him trouble.

'We all know him,' gushed the article, 'the giant in the brown shirt, that oak made flesh amid the thunderstorm of political strife: Gregor Strasser, the archetypal Bavarian, mighty of figure, character and spirit, one of Hitler's most popular followers, before whom even his most hated adversaries cannot hide their respect.'

Now that's what you call bad timing.

German industry was still mourning the loss of Papen's government. The President of the Federation of German Industry, Gustav Krupp von Bohlen und Halbach, declared at a meeting of the federation's steering committee that 'our wish for the Schleicher government is that they be careful to ensure the basic agenda laid down by Papen is maintained, that they approach modifications requested by this or that group with all due caution, and above all that they prevent dangerous experiments with lending and monetary policy'. Krupp, one of the best-known businessmen in the Republic, continued, 'In this connection, I feel it is important to say that Herr von Papen deserves the most profound thanks for what he achieved during his time in office – not only for industry in the narrow sense of the word, but also for the people more broadly.'

The message was unmistakeable: Schleicher had better not abandon Papen's industry-friendly policies. It was these very policies, however, that Schleicher believed had driven Germany to the brink of civil war.

The president was throwing a party in honour of Ernst Lubitsch. Otto Meissner functioned as host, and naturally Bella Fromm was in attendance. She was sincerely fond of Lubitsch. A virtuoso of the comedy of manners, the forty-year-old director was already a Hollywood legend: that year alone, *Trouble in Paradise*, *One Hour with You* and *If I Had a Million* had all hit the cinemas. In her blunt way, Fromm asked Lubitsch why he no longer worked in Germany. '"That's finished," he said. "I'm going to the United States. Nothing good is going to happen here for a long time. The sun shines every day in Hollywood."'

The counterespionage was paying off. Schleicher was shown a telegram intercepted by his spies. Counterintelligence officers reporting directly to the Minister of Defence had long been monitoring
several leading Nazis, including Hermann Göring, then President of
the Reichstag. It would have been a huge scandal, of course, if the
operation ever came to light; but it didn't. Schleicher was tight-fisted
with his information, and very few people knew the full extent of the
surveillance. Even Heinrich Brüning, during his chancellorship, had
noticed something fishy – crackling telephones, wires poking out of
the chimney breast, strangers tampering with his desk – and suspected
the Ministry might be up to something. Wilhelm von Gayl, whom
Papen had appointed Minister of the Interior after Brüning's resignation, went so far as to hire a detective to prevent any surveillance.
Overwrought nerves – paranoia, maybe? Or healthy common sense?

The telegram that landed on Schleicher's desk had been sent
from the Italian embassy to the Foreign Ministry in Rome. Its subject? A meeting between Ambassador Vittorio Cerruti and Göring on
9 December regarding the supervision of Prussia and the Prussian
police.

Schleicher countersigned it after reading. He must have been
pleased with his intelligence network. Surely no military had ever
been better connected politically, better informed, more adroit at pulling strings ... He'd once scribbled on a Ministry employee's report:
'It's a shame I have no disposition for megalomania.'

Last year the intelligence service – still led by Colonel Bredow
– had uncovered a major scoop. Reading the contents of a telegram
Göring had sent Cerruti's predecessor, they had discovered the Nazis'
plans for a putsch.

THURSDAY 15 DECEMBER

DNVP Refusal
No Coalition Negotiations in Prussia
– Vossische Zeitung

Under Pressure from Hitler
Schleicher Dismantles Papen!
– Der Angriff

Unidentified miscreants had broken into a butcher's shop on Alexander-passage during the night. They knocked through three walls and forced their way into the meat locker, where they made off with a six-hundred-weight haul of sausages and ham. The next morning, a few kilometres away in Wedding, several perpetrators restrained the sales assistants at a grocer's while their accomplices snatched food off the shelves. They escaped with items worth 100 marks in total. In another shop, fifteen young men raided the display tables, stuffing their rucksacks full before fleeing on bicycles. In each case, the police arrived too late.

Once again, the civil servants at the Ministry of Defence had their hands full with the KPD. Bredow kept Schleicher regularly updated on Communist propaganda campaigns and military subversion. As early as 1930, they had tried to tackle the problem by distributing flyers in the barracks: 'You're a miserable scoundrel if you reveal military matters to a Communist agent for thirty pieces of silver. You will be committing treason and delivering your homeland into the power of its greatest enemy.' For some time, the 'watch directive' had been in force: anyone who identified a person disseminating Communist texts would be given a watch as a reward. But now the military was preparing to take a harder line.

Bredow announced in a 'short briefing' to his superior that the Department of the Wehrmacht had developed a contingency plan to deal with the KPD. 'The work has been carried out as a precaution. We await further developments in this situation. It will then be clear what measures to take.'

Beginning at seven o'clock that evening, Kurt von Schleicher's voice was broadcast into thousands of living-rooms and pubs across the German Reich. The new chancellor's radio address was a crowd-puller. In many cities various party get-togethers immediately debated his message: the SPD, KPD and NSDAP had all invited their supporters to listen to the speech en masse.

No audience, only the radio technicians: that was how Schleicher felt most comfortable. Yet as he sat stiffly in a pale suit in front of the large microphone, he looked strained, his expression anxious.

'I have had the greatest misgivings about accepting the office of chancellor,' he began, continuing:

> First, because I did not want to succeed my friend Papen, that bold and spotless knight whose influence – motivated by the purest desires and highest love of the Fatherland – will only be fully recognised in time; above all, however, because a defence minister who is simultaneously chancellor stinks of a military dictatorship, and because the danger cannot be denied that a connection between these two offices will involve the armed forces too closely in politics.

Schleicher's sentences were serpentine, his thoughts complex. Was this the language of a chancellor capable of winning over the nation? And had he really just called Papen a 'bold and spotless knight'?

'Only the consideration that such a step would throw the seriousness of the situation so sharply into relief and have such a chilling effect on certain troublemakers that it would prevent the military actually being deployed allowed me to put aside my misgivings.'

He wanted, continued Schleicher, to be viewed as 'the cross-party guardian of the interests of all social strata, hopefully only for a brief period in Germany's hour of need'. He denied any intention of establishing a military dictatorship: 'One cannot sit comfortably on the point of a bayonet. In other words, one cannot govern for long without broad public support.' His government would pursue one goal only: 'Job creation! All the measures the government will carry out over the coming months will, to a greater or lesser degree, serve this purpose.'

At the Ministry of Defence, representatives from all the various ministries and administrations had assembled. They were there to discuss the results of Eugen Ott's simulation. On the agenda were 'combatting political strikes' and 'preparatory measures for a state of emergency during a time of political tension'. It was Bredow, the second most important figure at the Ministry, who had called the meeting. They could confer uninterrupted: his boss was addressing the nation.

Chancellor Schleicher was now speaking in great detail about job creation. Were people across the country sitting eagerly by their wirelesses? Were they hissing at each other to be quiet? Or had many of them already switched him off?

A few of his comments were unexpected. Germany was divided, yet Schleicher claimed to be uninterested in division: 'I am heterodox enough to guarantee that I am a devotee of neither capitalism nor socialism, that for me terms like "private enterprise" or "planned economy" have lost their terror, quite simply because these terms do not exist in the economy in absolutely purity and can no longer exist.'

Then Kurt von Schleicher called himself a 'social general'.

Politics is partly the art of weaving a narrative around oneself. Perhaps the idea of a 'social general' would stick in the minds of a nation desperate for help and for leadership.

Joseph Goebbels had also been listening to the chancellor's speech. Very thin, flat, artificially matey – such was his verdict. Schleicher was simply promising too much. Within a few weeks, he predicted, all those illusions would be shattered.

And from Paul von Hindenburg? Not a peep. The president finally had some peace and quiet, now that the chancellor's first days were behind him.

Time to let Schleicher show what he could do.

SILENT NIGHT

16 DECEMBER 1932 TO 1 JANUARY 1933

FRIDAY 16 DECEMBER

Schleicher's Legal Threat to Communist Party!

– *Rote Fahne*

AN HOUR OF SCHLEICHER

Papen, relying on the military as a last resort, tried to govern despite opposition from 90 per cent of the population. Schleicher, who wants to avoid involving the military, knows that he won't simply be able to reverse that ratio.

– *Vossische Zeitung*

Lazy Political Compromises
Schleicher's Meagre Government Agenda

– *Der Angriff*

The morning editions were given over to a detailed analysis of the chancellor's radio address. Give him some leeway, argued many of the articles. Most newspapers printed extracts or even the full speech on the back pages. The sharpest criticism came, as expected, from the Communist and Nazi papers, but the SPD-orientated press was sceptical as well. A 'social general' – what was that supposed to mean?

Hitler returned to Berlin, summoning the NSDAP faction from the Prussian State Assembly to Göring's opulent apartment.

The style favoured by the President of the Reichstag (162 MPs represented the Nazis in Parliament) is easily summarised: Göring liked anything expensive and heavy. His study was decorated entirely in red, prompting more than one visitor to muse that Nero might have lived in similar style.

The discussion on this day was broad-brush. How should the

NSDAP deal with the chancellor? Hitler made one thing crystal clear: dissenters would no longer be tolerated in the party. The Strasser debacle was unpleasant enough. Schleicher's announcement that he hoped merely to be a political guardian during a brief period of transition seemed to indicate that he'd learned from the mistakes of his predecessors, said Hitler. Yet his speech had been weak. Feeble. It revealed that when Schleicher was thrust into the spotlight he lost much of the élan that made him so persuasive backstage. 'Our will and our way is clear,' he told his MPs. 'Never will we be dissuaded from our goal. We have the German youth, we have the greater courage, the stronger will and the greater tenacity. What else do we need for victory?'

For Schleicher's strategy to work, he needed the support of the 'Iron Front', which included the leftist unions, the Reichsbanner and the SPD. Senior representatives of all three convened for a discussion in Berlin. How ought they to approach Schleicher? The chancellor had been making overtures – there was no doubt about that. The Social Democrats, however, favoured an adversarial stance. Party Chairman Otto Wels urged them to bypass the 'ordeal of a debate' – there must be no chinks in the Iron Front.

Yet the trade unions wanted to keep cooperating with Schleicher. A row ensued.

The NSDAP was still mired in crisis. In Hamburg, the leader of the Nazi contingent in the local assembly was relieved of duty – he'd been openly backing Strasser. The next day, Hitler was expected in the city for a 'conversation with the Führer'.

In Hessen, meanwhile, Karl Lenz – head of the regional branch of the NSDAP – had resigned his post, giving up his seat in the State Assembly and the national Parliament. He did not do so willingly. He, too, was Strasser's man – now, on Hitler's orders, he was going on sick leave. Quite a number of high-ranking National Socialists seemed to be contracting sudden illnesses.

Then, abruptly, a fresh nuisance cropped up in the Strasser case: his brother, Otto, published an article in which he bemoaned the 'fear and cowardice in the NSDAP'. Hitler was beside himself. When an old supporter of Gregor Strasser came to visit, hoping to put in a good word for the movement's former second-in-command, he unleashed a torrent of abuse.

Goebbels, for his part, was in jubilant mood, mocking the 'wrath of the unsuccessful'. By this point Strasser would surely be out of favour with the majority of the party.

The new chancellor's speech had come as a shock to many industrialists. The director of the Hansa League for Commerce, Trade and Industry, Ernst Mosich, wrote to the Chancellery. 'Very broad segments of the business community [had] not received Herr von Schleicher's radio address yesterday with anything approaching the positive response generally apparent today in the bourgeois press.'

Schleicher, he continued, ought 'to be in no doubt as to the strong psychological obstacles in the way of reconstruction efforts and the readiness to rebuild the economy'. Schleicher's remarks about capitalism and socialism had gone down like a lead balloon among Germany's prominent industrialists. Such woolly-headed notions would never have been mooted under Papen.

If Schleicher was serious about his social policy, about currying favour with workers and their political representatives, then he must have been as pleased as Punch.

Abraham Plotkin was also out and about that evening. These days, whenever he mentioned his surprise that the Communists and Nazis should recently have taken up a common cause over the transport strike, the Germans laughed at him. It was obvious, they told him. They were both against social democracy!

Plotkin decided he had to see the Nazis for himself – at close quarters. Extraordinary things were said of their gatherings. He decided to arrive in good time, having heard these events were always packed when the charismatic politician Joseph Goebbels was speaking.

The meeting was set to begin at eight, doors opened at six, and Plotkin arrived at seven. When he got off the bus he saw dozens of police officers and Nazis in black trousers. He was cross with himself – was he too late? Apparently not. He bought a ticket for one mark, without issue.

The Sportpalast. A site of great battles, great speeches and inordinate pageantry. The stadium had opened in November 1910, at Potsdamer Strasse 172, in the area of Berlin known as Schöneberg, originally as an indoor ice-skating rink. This was where the boxer Max Schmeling had fought, where regular bock beer festivals were held, and where, above all, the stage hosted enormous political rallies.

Yet, as Plotkin entered the vast hall, he was disappointed. 'The building is shaped like an O. The rear was curtained off and a platform raised in front of the curtain for the orchestra and the speakers. The main floor, I judge, has a seating capacity of five thousand. Three balconies hold an additional seating capacity of ten thousand, about fifteen thousand in all.' For all this, there were only two thousand or so people in the hall. The young Nazis, thought Plotkin, 'in spite of their uniforms, looked disheartened and disappointed'. By eight the crowd had swelled to perhaps seven thousand, at least a thousand of those in uniform.

At eight on the dot, the orchestra – two hundred strong – 'broke into a martial air'. The applause was muted. Was it something to do with the NSDAP's internal squabbling? Or because political rallies were forbidden? Something wasn't right. Everything seemed so soulless. 'One felt as if the spirit had taken flight.'

The musicians played for half an hour, while Plotkin strolled around the hall and studied the audience. Slightly more than half the spectators were middle-aged women. About half past eight, people started craning their necks, and a fife-and-drum corps marched down the aisle, followed by two columns of uniformed men and enormous swastika flags. The audience raised their arms in a Hitler salute, most without much enthusiasm. The thought popped into Plotkin's head that 'the raising of the hand above the head [...] when done sloppily resembles very much an old lady signalling a streetcar'. When the corps reached the stage, the orchestra started playing so loudly that 'every rafter in the huge building' shook. 'It was the only moment in the entire evening when the audience was completely carried away.'

But where was the enthusiasm? Where were the rapturous masses? There was supposed to be plenty of both at the Nazis' infamous rallies. Not this tired performance. Plotkin couldn't understand it. The NSDAP reminded him of the Klu Klux Klan, whose popularity had also recently imploded.

The corps climbed onstage and played until nine, when a black-uniformed man stepped up to the microphone:

> There was something wrong [...] After a few preliminary remarks, during which he gathered his military courage, he finally announced that there was a political truce in Germany, a truce to which the Hitlerites had agreed. The Nazis, he went on, never break their word. The word of a Nazi was the most precious thing in Germany. This was met with some cheering, but mostly silence.

Soon Dr Goebbels would be speaking, he continued, although not about politics. A woman called out, 'That's not right!' Loud applause. They were charging one mark per ticket – for this?

Plotkin had seen enough. 'So this was the famous menace to Germany and to the world. [...] A prizefight would have been much more exciting.'

He left the Sportpalast before Goebbels even reached the stage.

So what *was* going on with the Nazis? Reinhold Quaatz of the DNVP had a meeting with Meissner. One of their clandestine little chats. Yes, admitted Meissner, Strasser had indeed left the country, but Schleicher was still expecting a split within the NSDAP. Unfortunately, Hindenburg and his inner circle viewed this tactic with a certain 'reserve'. The president had been fond of Papen.

So what were the president's feelings towards Schleicher, then? enquired Quaatz. 'Chilly,' was Meissner's reply.

That evening, finally, Franz von Papen made his grand return. The arch-conservative 'Gentlemen's Club' had invited him to its annual dinner, and the former chancellor was due to give the formal address. Seven hundred guests streamed into the Kroll Opera House near the Brandenburg Gate. Politicians, industrialists, military officers. The last piece to be performed at the theatre, one year earlier, had been *The Marriage of Figaro* – an opera thick with intrigue, deception and revenge – before spiralling costs had put paid to further cultural events. Now Papen was providing the entertainment. He defended his six-month government, praised the Gentlemen's Club and even had a few good words for the National Socialists. A cautious overture, perhaps? Yet Papen also had something friendly to say about Schleicher. After all, the chancellor had paid him a compliment in yesterday's radio address. His friend and successor in the office of chancellor, said Papen, had a clear agenda; its wisdom, as well as the energy and expertise of Schleicher's staff, deserved their full confidence.

Faint praise? Were Schleicher's staff the only ones with expertise? Worth listening carefully, perhaps.

One person was paying special attention that night: Cologne-based banker Kurt Freiherr von Schröder. After dinner he approached the guest of honour. Would it not be tempting to have a little chat with Adolf Hitler about the political situation? He'd be glad to arrange it, Schröder offered.

Why not? Papen was in.

Schröder was sympathetic to the Nazis, although he wasn't a member of the party. He was part of the 'Keppler Circle', an elite group of businessmen working to bring the NSDAP to power. In November he'd been among the signatories to a letter urging Hindenburg to give Hitler the reins.

While the Gentlemen's Club celebrated, Hitler was meeting with the faithful. Goebbels was among them. The Führer spoke of the good old days, although to be honest even then the movement had been bedevilled by traitors. Segestes, according to legend, was a German nobleman who betrayed his leader Arminius to the Romans; the Segestes of Nazism, Gregor Strasser, still had admirers within the NSDAP. Hitler and Goebbels knew it, although they claimed otherwise. They decided to go on a charm offensive. Every Saturday and every Sunday for the next few weeks they would address representatives from a different local branch of the party. If they didn't put out the fire soon, it might eat the party alive.

Erwin Planck, State Secretary under Schleicher, was given an urgent warning. Papen had revealed his enmity towards Schleicher, reported an informant – and not just at the Gentlemen's Club dinner. His intimacy with Hindenburg also posed a real threat to the new chancellor.

Yet Planck was unfazed by Papen. 'Let him talk, utterly insignificant,' he responded. 'Nobody takes him seriously any more. Herr von Papen is a puffed-up busybody. This speech is the swansong of a sore loser.'

The 'Foreign League of German Women' was throwing a ball. Bella Fromm was on the guest list, of course; attendance was a professional duty. Still, she found the increasing radicalism and extremist propaganda nauseating. 'You hear a great deal of talk there about *Lebensraum*, and about the abolition of the Treaty of Versailles.' The Nazis were similarly fond of such talk. Nevertheless, there were so many diplomats attending that Fromm had to be there, too. Crown Prince Wilhelm and his wife, Cecilie, were the stars of the evening. Graf Wolf-Heinrich von Helldorff, a boorish man who had turned up in his SA uniform, made a disagreeable impression. Head of the SA in Berlin, he was deeply loyal to Goebbels, and also acted as an intermediary between the NSDAP and Schleicher. Someone asked why he wasn't in evening dress. 'Because the SA uniform expresses my convictions. If the Hohenzollerns have any objections,' brayed Helldorff, 'let them kick me out of here.'

Fromm was deeply discouraged by how many friends the National Socialists had made among the old aristocracy. She got into an argument with a nobleman who earnestly insisted that Hitler wanted to restore the monarchy. Later she bumped into Prince August Wilhelm on his way to the dining room. Known as 'Auwi', he was the fourth son of the deposed Kaiser Wilhelm II. He, too, wore a brown SA uniform.

By now Fromm was genuinely exasperated. All of a sudden, Magda Goebbels hove around the corner. She had met industrialist Günther Quandt at the age of eighteen; they married, Magda was unfaithful, and they divorced – it was soon afterwards that she met Joseph Goebbels. Less than four months ago the couple had had their first child, a daughter. Magda was looking rather beautiful that evening, Fromm had to admit. 'No jewels except the string of pearls around her neck,' she noted. 'Her golden hair owes nothing to any drugstore or chemist. It, too, is real. Her big eyes, iridescent and ranging from dark blue to steel gray, radiate icy determination and inordinate ambition.'

André François-Poncet, the cultivated French ambassador, approached Fromm. 'How do you like her?' he asked. Then, without waiting for a response, he remarked: 'I never saw such ice-cold eyes in a woman.'

SATURDAY 17 DECEMBER

Schleicher Speech at Time of Hunger, Unrest
An Unsuccessful Attempt to Win Popular Trust
– Völkischer Beobachter

Terror Legislation Axed
No Renewal of Protection Act
– Vossische Zeitung

A hated government that had to be brought down. Conspirators prepared to stop at nothing. Weapons stockpiled.

Then: the bomb went off too early. The conspirators had tipped their hand.

It was a botched coup against the military junta in Argentina. Numerous members of the Unión Cívica Radical, the Radical Civic Union, who had used violence to force the return of democracy, were arrested, including two former presidents of Argentina. The government in Buenos Aires declared a state of siege, and civil rights were vastly restricted.

A dictatorship was defending itself against terrorists agitating for freedom.

Early that morning, members of the SA attacked a tram-conductor from Köpenick on his way to work, injuring him badly. One of the assailants had, until recently, been employed by the Berlin transport authority himself but had been let go following the strike at the beginning of November. The SA had already set upon another tram employee during the night, beating him so badly that the man was rushed to Weissensee Hospital with life-threatening head injuries.

Wilhelmstrasse, the Chancellery. An eleven o'clock cabinet meeting. First, some housekeeping: the ministers were going to have to postpone their Christmas break. They needed to meet one more time for a discussion on agricultural policy, and Schleicher had settled on the afternoon of 21 December. Nobody could accuse the government of idleness.

Next, on to the important business! Job creation. Schleicher had promised to tackle unemployment in his speech on the radio. Now he wanted to talk facts. The most effective form of aid, declared the chancellor, wasn't a state-subsidised winter allowance but new jobs for the unemployed. A state-owned corporation should lead the way. Yet, according to Schleicher's information, the German National Railway – the biggest public employer – left much to be desired in this regard. Urgent action was required.

Several emergency decrees limiting civil rights would also soon be lifted. All in the name of domestic harmony.

Did Hindenburg take this as a personal affront? General Litzmann, the Nazi MP who had savaged the president during his speech at the opening of Parliament, was doubling down. Recently he'd announced that the victory at Tannenberg had, in fact, been his – Litzmann's. Not Hindenburg's. On top of that, it was about time the president made Hitler chancellor.

Schleicher had sharply criticised Litzmann's comments in his radio address, and Litzmann wasn't about to take that lying down. Speaking to the Nazi press, he called the field marshal the 'bitterest disappointment' of his life.

If there was one thing Hindenburg despised, it was disloyalty. And now there was disloyalty in the Reichstag – faithless men commanded by a former junior soldier named Adolf Hitler.

In Karlsruhe, in Baden, the local Nazis were conferring. A meeting of leaders was set to begin on Saturday evening, and it would last until late afternoon on Sunday. Regional party boss Robert Wagner opened the proceedings:

> The decisions of Adolf Hitler have thus far always proved correct, even if an individual only realises this after six months or so. It is also not necessary for every single individual to understand the Führer's actions; this is, in fact, impossible, for nobody knows the reasons behind the decision – but it is necessary that every individual has unshakeable faith in the Führer!

Calls for perseverance. Oaths of allegiance. 'If our opponents believe', said Wagner, 'they can create division in this movement, then we say to them: our movement listens solely to the man who founded it and made it into the strongest political party in Germany.'

SUNDAY 18 DECEMBER

Adolf Hitler on the Struggle Ahead
Führer Offers Guidance to Prussian Faction
Schleicher Era a Passing Epoch
– Völkischer Beobachter

Time Is Working Against Hitler and for Schleicher
– Die Sonntags-Zeitung

Six days until Christmas, yet winter still felt far off. 'Glorious autumn day,' noted the poet Oskar Loerke. 'Sun in the garden. Festivities. Silence. A few violets blooming, although they give off no scent. The last weather-beaten chrysanthemums.'

Bella Fromm was headed for the Chancellery that morning. She wanted to say a brief hello to Schleicher and hand him a small present. The chancellor had instructed that she be allowed to visit him at any time – now she was going to make use of that privilege. Unfortunately, however, Schleicher already had a visitor. And Fromm couldn't wait long, because she'd arranged to meet someone for an early lunch.

Instead, she left the bouquet of lilies with Schleicher's subordinate, Bredow, asking him to give them to his boss. 'Who told you that these are his favorite flowers?' asked Bredow.

'I guess it must be love,' replied Fromm before she hurried off.

Meanwhile, on this sun-drenched day, Hitler was attending a party meeting in Magdeburg. Members of the NSDAP from the Altmark, Anhalt and the Magdeburg Börde region had gathered in the large assembly room in the municipal hall. Outside, in the main courtyard,

Hitler was marching past rows of Brownshirts, his arm outstretched in a salute. Later, in the assembly room, he used his speech to complain about his scheming adversaries before making everybody swear allegiance, then immediately setting off again on his travels. He was due to give a similar speech in Hamburg to members of the party, the SA and the SS, who were pouring in from across northern Germany.

Hitler was fighting tooth and nail for the survival of the NSDAP.

Goebbels, too, was on the road: Hagen, Münster, Essen. Within the span of twenty-four hours he addressed twenty thousand functionaries. Quite the grand tour.

In Tegel Prison, Carl von Ossietzky scribbled a few lines to Kurt Tucholsky. 'If I'm released in the near future and you travel north again, we'll have to meet up somewhere, if you don't want to come to Berlin.' Ossietzky was permitting himself a cautious ray of hope. It wouldn't be possible to visit Tucholsky in Switzerland straight after his release – his passport had been confiscated the day before he was taken to prison in May.

In Kassel, two divisions of the SA were mutinying. Sturm 5 and Sturm Bettenhausen had unanimously decided to withdraw from the NSDAP in protest against the expulsion of one of their commanders. The man had sold three hundredweight of potatoes donated by farmers and used the money to buy uniforms for his men, who had been waiting months for party funds to come through. Some members had even paid suppliers themselves. Yet the purchase had not been approved, the man had been slung out on his elbow, and now there was trouble brewing in the Kassel SA. All in all, a third of the indignant Brownshirts took back their oaths of allegiance.

Local elections took place in Ostritz, a small town near Dresden. Fewer than two thousand people voted; under ordinary circumstances it would barely have registered in Berlin. What caught people's attention this time, however, was the National Socialists were yet again haemorrhaging votes. The Centre Party had emerged victorious, ahead of a conservative-leaning coalition. And so it was that the small-town election made front-page news in the *Vossische Zeitung*: Nazi fever, it announced, had broken.

Abraham Plotkin was settling in. He spent that Sunday playing cards with Furtwängler and Eggert, two trade unionists he'd befriended. They drank beer and toasted to a Merry Christmas and a Happy New Year. The conversation then turned to Theodor Leipart, chairman of the Federation of German Trade Unions, who had invited Plotkin for a chat. Plotkin was flattered, but hadn't yet taken him up on the offer. 'Furtwängler looked surprised,' wrote Plotkin, 'and then said that in Germany an invitation from Leipart is equivalent to a command.'

He decided to write to Leipart the very next morning.

Advertising in the *Arbeiter Illustrierte Zeitung*, Intotourist GmbH – a company headquartered at Unter den Linden 62–3 – was offering readers 'Cheap winter getaways to Soviet Russia 1932/33. For workers and salaried employees, 28 January to 18 March, 6 days from Berlin from 160 marks. Study trip for German teachers 23.12, 9 days, 225–.'

Christmas in the USSR?

It was a wonderfully mild day, nearly 8 or 9 degrees, but Oskar Loerke was tossing and turning in bed. He woke to find his nerves jangling. He had dreamed of a vast, sinking ship. 'Water seeped in through cracks beneath the benches on deck,' he wrote. 'Soon a dreadful rocking back and forth. Woke up at the moment of being swept overboard.' Loerke was feeling the effects of a society in crisis, of political turbulence. He felt excluded. He felt like he didn't belong.

MONDAY 19 DECEMBER

Führer in Halle, Magdeburg and Hamburg
Hitler on Saturday Evening: 1932 Has Seen NDSAP
Rise to 'Germany's Most Pivotal Movement'
National Socialists Have Right to Leadership
– Der Angriff

No Reichstag before Christmas
Majority in Reichsrat Pro Amnesty
– Vossische Zeitung

It must have seemed impossibly fast: a train that could cover the 287 kilometres from Lehrter Bahnhof in Berlin to the main railway station in Hamburg in just two hours and twenty-two minutes! At 8 a.m. the new DR 877 set off on a test run from Berlin, and by 10.22 it had reached its destination. A new record for rail travel, the train reached speeds of up to 160 kilometres per hour, a feat made possible by the twin 420-horsepower diesel motors coupled to a direct-current generator and the electric nose-suspended traction motor. The express, painted cream and violet, had been tested and optimised in a wind tunnel, and it tapered at the front. There was space for ninety-eight passengers in its two large cabins and another four in the refreshment room.

Colloquially known as the Flying Hamburger, the DR 877 couldn't maintain that pace across the route, as the line wasn't designed for such high speeds. All the signals had to be replaced: the 'Motor Lightning Train', as the press dubbed it, took much longer than any other locomotive to brake to a complete stop.

Agents working to bring the Communists to power may have come and gone through the Soviet embassy in Berlin, but senior politicians were on highly civilised terms – they were seeking common ground.

Kurt von Schleicher was meeting with Maxim Maximovich Litvinov, the People's Commissar of Foreign Affairs – the equivalent of a foreign minister. He was determined to forge closer bonds with the West, so it suited him that Schleicher was pursuing a new course when it came to the government in Moscow. Papen had not only combatted Communists in Germany but had considered the Soviet Union a prospective adversary. Schleicher, as ever, was more pragmatic. He could certainly use the Soviet Union's help to boost the German economy – in fact, he had his eye on a trade deal, although Parliament wasn't yet playing ball.

Litvinov knew all this, of course. Even so, he must have been glad to hear that Schleicher had another trick up his sleeve: he was going to find out, explained the chancellor, whether he actually needed the Reichstag's agreement to implement a deal.

A demonstration was forming outside Aschinger's head office. Germany's largest restaurant company, with nearly thirty eateries and beer halls in Berlin as well as bakeries and hotels, Aschinger was an institution. In *Berlin Alexanderplatz*, Alfred Döblin had described one of its branches in detail, while one of Erich Kästner's main characters made a pit-stop there in *Fabian*.

Aschinger sold cheap food and reasonably priced beer. Now there were twenty youths on its doorstep demanding food and drink for free. The management invited a delegation for a chat. The youths demanded a loaf of bread, a pound of lard and a sausage each.

The management requested the demonstrators submit their demands in writing. It would then be decided whether they could help. The delegation reacted indignantly; one of them threatened violence. Then they all decamped to Alexanderplatz.

To the restaurant Döblin had described.

Demanding lunch for every member of their hungry procession.

We're sorry, came the reply. We can't distribute free food unless we have permission from head office.

One of the group gave an off-the-cuff speech to the restaurant guests, describing how bitter it felt to go hungry while watching other people eat their fill. That didn't help their case.

The youths moved on, and nowhere did they find anything to eat. At last they broke into a grocer's on Alte Schönhauser Strasse in central Berlin, then scattered.

The police investigated. Their working theory? Communists had planned the hunger march to stir up trouble.

Frau Löwenstein was the most endearing woman he had met in Germany. As they sat in her apartment by the tiled stove, Plotkin felt immediately at home. He was enchanted. It would be a long time before he forgot her 'warmth and charm'. But it was Dr Löwenstein he had come to see, head of the Berlin-Lichtenberg Health Department.

Plotkin pulled himself together. He told Löwenstein what he'd seen in Wedding – the hunger, the sickness – and asked the doctor what was going on. Löwenstein was in his late thirties, with thinning hair and sunken cheeks. A lean man, with eyes large, dark and keen.

Löwenstein spoke for an hour. 'Fact after fact, analysis after analysis, pyramided themselves into a story of the physical and mental decay of a nation,' noted Plotkin dejectedly in his diary afterwards.

Infectious diseases were on the rise in Germany. Public baths had lost two-thirds of their customers because people could no longer spare the few pfennigs for a wash. Consumption of alcohol had vastly increased – the Germans were drinking to forget. There were a million abortions a year, and thirty thousand women died during botched procedures.

One apparently trivial question had long been bothering Plotkin. He'd wondered about it at the Reichstag, when he'd nearly been assaulted by the police. He'd wondered about it as he strolled through the city. Why were there so many people out on the streets?

'You need not wonder,' said the doctor. 'The crowds on the streets are not there because they enjoy walking. Most of them, particularly the single people, have no money for either lighting or coal. It is pleasanter on the streets than in their miserably cold, dark rooms.'

After the lecture, Plotkin was exhausted. It felt like a nightmare. He realised now that in Wedding he'd only scratched 'the ulcers on the surface, not the cancers hidden deep within'.

Löwenstein must have understood the effect on his American visitor. 'I tell you this as a medical man and not as a propagandist,' he said. 'The first epidemic that will come will wipe out huge sections of the population as if they were flies.'

What then? asked Plotkin. Communism?

'Impossible. It would mean war,' came the answer. 'Hitler has lost 40 per cent of his following. [...] A monarchy is possible, much more probable than any other form – it will be fought hard and bitterly, but I think it will come.' For the first time in their oven-side chat, Löwenstein betrayed emotion. 'More chaos in Europe. More prewar conditions that many of us had hoped were gone forever, and, who knows, perhaps more battlefields for our young to die on. I can hope – but I cannot see the way out.'

The Council of Elders convened at the Reichstag, the Communists having forced a meeting. They were demanding a full parliamentary vote before Christmas on the winter-relief package and pushing for a motion of no confidence against Schleicher's cabinet. If the motion passed, there would be new elections. Since nearly every party except the KPD had lost votes last time around – on 6 November – nobody else showed much enthusiasm. Parliament was adjourned.

Reinhold Quaatz had got wind of a new rumour about the National Socialists. The movement was now in dire straits: apparently another eight units of the SA were mutinying in Berlin, and money was increasingly short. Meissner had told him recently that the NSDAP was 14 million marks in debt.

Wilhelm Keppler, a prominent businessman and economic adviser to the NSDAP, paid a call on Hitler. He'd recently been in Cologne, he said, where he had met with Hjalmar Schacht, the financier Kurt Baron von Schröder and the former chancellor, Franz von Papen. Papen wanted to talk.

Really? Papen? During his chancellorship he'd been the Nazis' sworn enemy.

Yet he could rely on Keppler, Hitler was certain. He'd drawn together numerous other businessmen – the so-called Keppler Circle – who were sympathetic to the cause, and had joined the party way back in 1927. Membership number 62424. In those days the Nazis had been far from power; they were still considered a fringe movement.

Keppler had exciting news. According to Papen, Hindenburg's relationship with Schleicher was on the rocks, possibly because Papen had explained to Hindenburg how Schleicher had forced him out. Papen still had the president's ear.

How about an exchange of views? No obligation. Baron Schröder had offered to host proceedings at his house in Cologne.

6.45 p.m.: the Reich Governmental Committee for Job Creation convened for a discussion. In the room were Schleicher, Finance Minister Graf Schwerin von Krosigk, several other cabinet members and, of course, Commissioner Gereke. In future, Gereke would be chairing the meetings. It was the Commissioner's responsibility, added Schleicher, to speed things along as firmly as possible. He, meanwhile, would make himself available at any time to settle any important, fundamental questions that arose.

The chancellor wanted results. Fast.

The Hotel Esplanade was hosting a charity ball for the Cecilienwerk, and, for the first time, tickets were available to anyone. Previously the event had been held under the patronage of Crown Princess Cecilie of Mecklenburg, but now it admitted a 'crowd more colorful than actually distinguished', as Bella Fromm described it. The fallen empire was embodied by representatives from the House of Hohenzollern: Crown Prince Wilhelm of Prussia wore his old regimental uniform, the 'First Leibhusaren', a cavalry regiment in the Prussian army. The uniform included a fur cap with a silver skull and crossbones – a symbol that no quarter would be given. The crown prince had been given command of the regiment in 1911. His brother Oskar, the former Kaiser's fifth son, was also in attendance.

The ailing republic was represented by the former chancellor, Papen, and his wife, as well as Alfred Hugenberg, Chairman of the DNVP. How absurd Hugenberg always looked, thought Fromm, 'with his military haircut, full-spreading mustache, small eyes hidden in rolls of fat, and a perpetual leer on his face'.

It wasn't long before her smile vanished. She spotted Viktoria von Dirksen, a Berlin socialite who idolised Adolf Hitler. Dirksen had brought a special guest: Magda Goebbels. Fromm's mood took a nosedive. 'It is stomach-turning to see how people abase themselves to enter her good graces.'

That evening, Schleicher's orderly tracked Fromm down. The flowers! He'd brought a short note of thanks from the chancellor: 'It was lovely of you, please do come again!' Fromm was glad Schleicher had understood her small gesture. He knew how highly she thought of him – and she knew how rough a time he was having these days.

TUESDAY 20 DECEMBER

Christmas Truce Secured
– *Tägliche Rundschau*

Amnesty! Reichsrat Decision Today
– *Der Angriff*

The Reichsrat, a legislative body composed of representatives from the various constitutive states in the Weimar Republic, functioned as a counterpart to the elected Parliament. Today, it was voting on whether to object to the amnesty proposed by Schleicher and passed by the Reichstag. By forty-four votes to nineteen, it decided to let the amnesty stand.

This meant that the legislation could be finalised the very same day – by Christmas, whole wings of Germany's prisons would be standing empty.

The National Rural League was playing go-between, setting up a confidential chat between Hitler and Hugenberg. The DNVP chairman was at pains to diffuse the tension.

The president addressed the German nation. 'These hard times must trump all that divides us. Those who heed the call – "we want to help" – and contribute to Winter Relief are creating new hope and new faith in the people and the Fatherland.'

Hindenburg said nothing about strengthening the Republic. Perhaps it wasn't the time for a Christmas miracle.

WEDNESDAY 21 DECEMBER

New Smear Campaign Against NSDAP Fails
Jewish Press's Lies Too Blatant!
The 'SA Beatings' and 'Mass Exodus From NSDAP' and the Truth
– *Völkischer Beobachter*

47 Million for Winter Relief
20 pfg. Allowance Per Capita Per Day for Young People
– *Vossische Zeitung*

The Christmas amnesty came into force, and the first prisoners were set free. Had Carl von Ossietzky already packed his suitcase? Was he grateful? After all, several members of the SPD – although they were often on the receiving end of his criticism – had pushed hard for his release.

The DNVP hosted a breakfast for American journalists, Hugenberg and Quaatz representing the party. The conversation turned to the crisis in the NSDAP – apparently the SA was in a shambles. Even though the men were going hungry, they were still being asked to pay their membership fees.

The NSDAP reacted to the various reports of internal conflict in the party and the SA with a stout rebuttal:

The united adversaries of the National Socialist movement have launched a new large-scale offensive of lies and slander against the NSDAP. As part of this campaign of lies, the Social Democrat *Vorwärts* and the Jewish *Frankfurter Zeitung* have published so-called 'reports' on the NSDAP branch meeting in Halle and the speech given there by the Führer, which were then disseminated by dozens of 'bourgeois' newspapers. Their claims include that hostile members of the SA and SS were involved in a 'punch-up' with those loyal to Hitler at this meeting. Furthermore, Adolf Hitler is alleged to have made a series of remarks on the 'Strasser case'. We strenuously deny every word of these slanderous reports.

Chancellor Schleicher was meeting with the venerable British ambassador, Sir Horace Rumbold. The two of them chatted about this and that before the conversation turned to more important political matters. Even then, the mood remained cordial throughout, and they parted on excellent terms. For Schleicher, it made for a pleasant change – although they still hadn't settled the debate about disarmament and the payment of Germany's war debts, of course.

Paul von Hindenburg didn't give many interviews. The journalist and writer Rolf Brandt, however, was a familiar face – Brandt had been a war correspondent – and so the president granted him an audience. 'Look,' he blurted, 'all I can do is repeat it over and over again: be united, united, united! Damn it, it's better if men who are sincere offer their hand rather than waving it about under the other fellow's nose.'

Finally, Hindenburg added: 'One must elevate the Fatherland so high, so high that one forgets oneself.'

At five o'clock, Schleicher had a meeting with his cabinet. On the agenda was the usual day-to-day business of government. The atmosphere was gloriously calm.

Was this the glimmerings of a routine?

Schleicher's former mentor, Wilhelm Groener, wrote to a friend:

More and more, general opinion on the Nazis is drifting towards my own point of view, even among old Hugenberg's stubborn lot. I hear similar things from Schleicher; at any rate, from the military side they seem to be conspicuously buttering me up. Schleicher wants to make peace with me. I haven't turned him down. He sent me a telegram about it, saying that when he entered office he thought of his old friend and master, and in reply I expressed my wishes in the spirit of our old intellectual fellowship. Now I'm waiting to see what he does as chancellor.

After all these years, Groener had lost his appetite for politicking. He smelled conspiracies and plotting everywhere, perhaps correctly. 'My impression', he wrote, 'is that both Brüning and Schleicher have been putting on a Punch and Judy show with the Nazis.'

In Munich, Franz von Hörauf, head of the SA training schools and one of the organisation's most senior commanders, was still keeping 'Your Imperial Highness' Crown Prince Wilhelm in the loop on affairs within the NSDAP.

He considered the split between Hitler and Strasser irreparable. 'As far as I can tell, H. has misjudged the situation once more, this time within his party, completely.' Then: 'In point of fact the thing has done him tremendous damage and is far from concluded.' A substantial number of party members, he went on, especially the younger ones, were sick of the eternal standing on the sidelines and the flat rejections, sick of waiting for the day that Hitler would sweep to power. They just wanted to be part of the government at long last. 'If it were possible to find Strasser – who I consider a really exceptionally competent, organisationally gifted and immensely energetic man – a position of responsibility within the government, [...] it's my view that the party would inevitably unite behind him, with or without Hitler.'

This letter ended up on Schleicher's desk, too.

THURSDAY 22 DECEMBER

Unemployment Still Rising
– Tägliche Rundschau

Gereke's Emergency Scheme
Additional 500 Million Earmarked for Job Creation
– Vossische Zeitung

A telegram arrived at Tegel Prison from the Public Prosecutor's office. It concerned Ossietzky's treason case. 'In view of the amnesty, immediate release ordered for […] the editor Karl von Ossietzky. Confirmation requested.'

Shortly before Christmas, indefatigable American journalist Edgar Ansel Mowrer bumped into the former President of the National Bank, Hjalmar Schacht. What plans did he have over Christmas? asked Mowrer. 'I am going to Munich to talk with Adolf Hitler,' replied Schacht.

'You, too, my fine Democrat!' said Mowrer.

'Ach, you understand nothing,' answered Schacht. 'You are a stupid American.'

'Granted. But tell me what you expect from Hitler in words of one syllable and I'll try to understand.'

Schacht, with his centre parting, his stern gaze and his downturned mouth, replied: 'Germany will have no peace until we bring Hitler to power.'

Bella Fromm was attending a reception given by US Consul General George Messersmith, who had been stationed in Berlin for two years and kept a close eye on the Nazis. While Ambassador Sackett was increasingly convinced that Schleicher had contained the threat, Mess-ersmith disagreed. 'The German government', he told Fromm, 'had better act quickly, and strongly. It's really upsetting to find so many people of importance in the National Socialist party. There are going to be fireworks here pretty soon, unless I'm badly mistaken.'

Fromm remarked dryly in her diary: 'I do not think that my friend Messersmith is mistaken.'

One person in particular was finding it difficult to get into the Christmas spirit: Joseph Goebbels. Despite a few unexpected injections of cash, it looked like party employees would have to take a pay cut. There was no getting around it. So close to Christmas, at that. Goebbels cursed fate for keeping the movement from power.

There was one consolation: his staff were all showing such self-sacrifice that it filled him with pride. Even so, the situation was tense in the extreme.

Christmas. A celebration of love. He was already feeling sick.

The chancellor was seeking a negotiator for a crucial mission. He had a plan. Schleicher wanted to adjourn the Reichstag yet again, tem-porarily bringing Parliament to a standstill without risking new elec-tions. His main priority, meanwhile, was to fuse the Reichsbanner and the reactionary Stahlhelm into a single 'Reich Warrior League' while banning all other paramilitary organisations – including the SA.

It was a controversial plan, and the SPD would need to play ball. Bredow, Schleicher's confidant, would conduct the negotiations.

Suddenly a call came in from Rome: Gregor Strasser. Lovely weather, remarked Strasser down the crackling telephone line.

An appalling story was doing the rounds. A father had strangled his twelve-year-old son then hanged himself at the Old Cemetery. A widower out of work since 1930. Desperate.

Suicides were increasingly common in Berlin. They plunged into the River Spree or turned on the gas, asphyxiated, hanged or poisoned themselves. The newspapers ran articles. People swapped stories, furrowing their brows and softly shaking their heads, with shoulders hunched and fear in their hearts.

The heavy gate, like something out of a medieval fortress, swung open at six o'clock. Carl von Ossietzky walked out of Tegel Prison a free man at last, emerging from that 'sequestered world that looms among us, walled-in, and of which we know less than of Tibet or the Easter Islands'.

Since 10 May he'd been behind bars: 227 days. Ossietzky wanted to retch. He was ashamed to be going home so soon before Christmas while other inmates had to stay, and his conscience was urging him to write about his incarceration. The next issue of the *Weltbühne* was out in a week, so he should have time. Back to work so soon? Ossietzky knew nothing else. He went straight from prison to the editorial office.

Oughtn't he to see his wife first, though? He'd written Maud countless anxious letters from Tegel. She was ill – very ill, in fact. An alcoholic. Ossietzky was perpetually worrying she might collapse one day. From prison he'd asked his friend Tucholsky to look after her when he could, but, of course, Tucholsky was in Zurich. Ossietzky was now free to take care of Maud himself – but, then again, he'd always been more the intrepid journalist than the conscientious husband.

Theodor Leipart, now chairman of the Federation of German Trade Unions but originally apprenticed as a turner, was almost as old as the Social Democrats. Sixty-five. He gave a Christmas speech on the radio that focused, inevitably, on the current crisis. For a man with his responsibilities there could be no other topic. 'Ladies and gentlemen,' he began, 'for many of you, my fellow Germans, there will be little cheer this Christmas. The privations of our age are weighing heavily upon the whole nation but especially upon the great masses of its working people.'

Leipart was not in an uplifting mood. 'Given this situation, which has destroyed the happiness of so many families, it is understandable that a feeling of profound bitterness has crept in, and that there is a mood in the country that threatens both Volk and state. Yet matters cannot be improved with radical slogans.'

'Adolf Hitler's first and only record makes a wonderful Christmas present and will be an abiding source of enjoyment for any National Socialist. Price 5 marks. Available at any book or music shop. Musikverlag Frz. Eher Nachf., Munich.'

An advert in the *Völkischer Beobachter*.

Strings of fairy lights glowed in the dusk. Billboards illuminated the shopping streets, where festive windows displayed their colourful wares. 'The whole city is in a ferment of Christmas shopping,' observed Plotkin as he wandered through Berlin, 'and every wurst shop window is filled with delicatessen enough to make the mouth water. Roast *Gans* seems to be the favourite.'

FRIDAY 23 DECEMBER

Only ½ Billion for Job Creation
Huge Disappointment / Gereke Explains
Scheme (Originally 1.5 Bn. Planned)
– Tägliche Rundschau

Gereke's Tragi-Comedy
Ambitious Plans – Execution Flops
When Capitalists Do Socialism
– Der Angriff

Joseph Goebbels' telephone rang. Adolf Hitler on the line, a note of alarm in his voice. It had come to his attention that Gottfried Feder, an economic theorist and founding member of the NSDAP, was apparently conspiring with Schleicher. He'd come to Berlin – so close to Christmas! – for that express purpose.

Yet another prominent traitor, then?

Hitler demanded an investigation, so Goebbels sent an ally to the Hotel Excelsior, where Feder had booked a room. Strasser had often stayed there, too. Then, relief: Feder wasn't in talks with Schleicher. He'd come to the capital for personal reasons. Hitler would be pleased.

The Goebbels were attending a Christmas party for the local branch of the NSDAP, held in the ballroom on Vossstrasse. Joseph gave a short speech in which he declared that the new year would sweep the movement to victory once and for all. Back in their apartment on Reichskanzlerplatz, Magda – who was pregnant again – suddenly complained of feeling unwell.

Joseph Goebbels sent for Magda's gynaecologist, Professor Walter Stoeckel, who ordered her immediate admission to a private clinic established by the Ida Simons Foundation at the University Women's Hospital, where Magda had given birth to their daughter Helga in

September. The doctor seemed deeply worried. When she learned she'd have to spend Christmas at the clinic, Magda Goebbels cried.

Her husband ended up spending Christmas by himself. How lifeless their apartment seemed, he thought. Goebbels brooded. He suffered. They'd only been married for a year, since late 1931.

They fought often and they made love often. He accepted that Magda worshipped Hitler in her own special way. Once, after the two of them had been brazenly flirting, Goebbels poured out his troubles in his diary. 'Magda embarrasses herself in front of the boss. I suffer greatly. She is not altogether a lady. Not a wink of sleep all night. Must do something about it. Fear I can't rely on her fidelity. That would be dreadful.' And Hitler? Any reproaches? 'I don't begrudge the boss a little warmth and loveliness. He gets so little of it.'

Goebbels was feeling deeply lonely. Elsewhere in his diary he'd written: 'I have few friends in the party. Only Hitler, almost. They all envy my success and my popularity.' A while back, the SS, under Heinrich Himmler, had actually set up an intelligence office in Berlin for the sole purpose of spying on him – until the Führer intervened.

So many people were leaving Berlin! 'Everyone is going home,' noted Plotkin.

The Germans were scattering to their home towns over Christmas.

Edgar Mowrer, correspondent for the *Chicago Daily News*, was jotting down his thoughts on the Christmas trade. 'The third depression Christmas, but not so bad as last year. Quite unexpectedly the pessimists have had to admit that the Christmas trade is fairly satisfactory.' And yet Germany was looking poorer than ever: even the parties were out with their begging bowls. Some of them were young men carrying swastika flags, but others were in Communist and nationalist colours, 'shaking tinware in one's face'.

And everywhere, more visible than ever before, were 'beggars and persons who hide their beggary under the pretense of selling something, real peddlers, street musicians and little children, badly clothed, with blue fingers'. Mowrer was moved, especially by the neglected children. Girls of eleven or twelve had been left to roam the streets.

President Hindenburg had retreated to East Prussia for the holidays. Writing from his residence at Neudeck, far from the teeming city, he sent Schleicher a message in Berlin: 'Thank you for this calm, peaceful Christmas, the calmest I have experienced during my time in office,' he wrote, 'it is a pleasure to tell you, my dear young friend, how deeply satisfied I am with the way you are leading the government.'

There was an astonishing new warmth in his tone. Had Hindenburg forgotten he was nursing a grudge? Or was he simply overcome with the Christmas cheer?

The chancellor, on the other hand, had an excruciating festive season. He toiled and toiled, despite a painful issue with his gall bladder. A few months earlier, before he was made chancellor, he'd remarked of Hindenburg that 'men of such advanced age are beyond feeling camaraderie towards their staff. Only the influence of family is lasting. When the old gentleman no longer needs me, he'll cast me aside as unhesitatingly as he did with Brüning.'

Bella Fromm had received her first present – one day before Christmas Eve, when gifts are traditionally opened in Germany. The Rotter brothers had invited her to their Christmas show, the premiere of *Catherine I*, starring Gitta Alpár and Gustav Fröhlich.

Alfred and Fritz Rotter owned nine theatres in Berlin, including the Theater des Westens, the Lustspielhaus, the Lessingtheater and the Metropol. Their company, the German Dramatic Corporation, was so complexly structured that they could never be held personally liable for any financial problems. Their premieres, whether operettas or Shakespeare plays, were always a major event on the Berlin social scene, so the Christmas performance was inevitably sold out. Fromm was pleased to find herself seated near the Schleichers, who were in the neighbouring box. The chancellor had two military acquaintances in tow: a Captain Noeldechen and Commander Hans Langsdorff, both in uniform. 'It is our private demonstration against "private armies",' said Langsdorff.

Their boss, in civilian clothes, kissed Fromm's hand. 'Kurt, you promised me you would always wear your uniform,' chided Fromm. 'You know mufti is most unbecoming to you.'

Schleicher's wife nodded in agreement. 'He won't listen to me.' She explained that he was overworked, sitting at his desk every night until two a.m. or even later. Tonight's trip to the theatre was his first in a long time without papers and telephone calls.

After the premiere, the Rotters threw a reception at their villa in Grunewald. 'A bit super-elaborate,' commented Fromm, who loved sumptuous parties. 'Floods of champagne, gigantic lobsters, a fantastic cold buffet.'

The Meissners had been invited, too, of course – Frau Meissner never missed these events. She sat at a table with Bella Fromm, as well as the French ambassador, François-Poncet, and his elegant wife. Otto Meissner was in his element. He kept scurrying to the buffet and returning with lobster. Fromm had heard countless tales of Meissner's gluttony on such occasions, but she was still awestruck. André François-Poncet, grinning, gave his wife a surreptitious nudge. The Meissners seemed not to notice. Dismantling a lobster does, after all, require a degree of concentration.

Why was the head of the DNVP so unpopular? So much would have been easier if Alfred Hugenberg hadn't been Alfred Hugenberg. Writing in his diary, Reinhold Quaatz had a sobering realisation: 'He has no sex appeal.'

The doctors' concerns had proved well founded – Magda Goebbels was going from bad to worse. Was she going to have a miscarriage? That evening Joseph Goebbels sat at home, brooding dismally.

'The year 1932,' he confided in his diary, 'has been one long streak of bad luck. It should be smashed to smithereens.'

SATURDAY 24 DECEMBER
CHRISTMAS EVE

KPD Stirring Up Trouble
Police on Red Alert
1932: A Christmas Catastrophe
– *Der Angriff*

Another Appeal to Hitler?
Reichstag on 9 January?
Dissolution and New Elections?
– *Tägliche Rundschau*

Christmas Eve. Five degrees. Rain. So much for a white Christmas in Berlin.

Members of the SS were putting up the Goebbels' Christmas tree. Helga, their four-month-old, smiled as she watched. Joseph Goebbels envied his daughter her childish ignorance: he'd just heard from the hospital that his wife's condition was critical. Magda was fighting for her life. Elsewhere, the world was settling down for a peaceful Christmas, and Goebbels just wanted to be alone, somewhere high among the mountains. Seeing nothing, hearing nothing.

A poem by Mascha Kaléko. Her book would soon be on the market. This poem she'd entitled 'Single Man on 24 December', and it began thus:

There is no other room as bare
As mine now. The last shopgirls are

walking home
– Christmas lunges, I'm caught unaware.

Not everybody had shut up shop, however. The ever-industrious Quaatz had gone to see Meissner, reckoning that a quick chat couldn't hurt. Later that day he reported to Hugenberg: 'Today I dropped by my friend, since he'll be travelling for a few days after Christmas, and I read him your letter. In response he said again that there is a willingness to appoint DNVP party members to leading roles. We then discussed the situation, and I hinted that the mood against Schleicher within our party is darkening.'

So much for goodwill to all men.

The birth of Christ had no spiritual significance for Abraham Plotkin, who was Jewish, but he'd observed that many German Jews put up trees in their homes and celebrated the day in their own style. That year, Christmas Eve also happened to fall on the first day of Hanukkah, the Jewish festival of light.

Yet Plotkin was not in a celebratory mood. Despite the mizzle, he took a walk through one of Berlin's working-class neighbourhoods then spent the next few hours helping at a community kitchen in Wedding. They were handing out double portions in honour of the season. Taking the opportunity to nose around, he found that the unemployed locals had set up a library that included books by Goethe and Schiller, Dostoyevsky, Dickens and Upton Sinclair. On his way home, he saw a boy no older than five playing in the street – wearing slippers. Another boy was standing outside a bakery, gazing through the window. Plotkin, who had noticed him there on the way to the kitchens, asked why the child had lingered so long.

No answer. 'Either he couldn't tell or was frightened,' Plotkin speculated. 'Or was it that the sight of cookies was too tempting to leave?'

The American literary power couple Dorothy Thompson and Sinclair Lewis had also deserted Berlin over Christmas. They were celebrating the holidays in Semmering, a resort town not far from Vienna, where they were joined by numerous friends, including the Mowrers. They were going to spend ten days in the unspoiled countryside, toboganning, breathing fresh air and generally enjoying life. They also hoped to save their rocky marriage.

Yet the rain and mist offered scant opportunity for winter pursuits, and they quickly got on each other's nerves. At a Christmas party for American and British expats there was an orchestra, dancing and far too much wine. For Thompson these were days of reflection; in her diary she described lesbian experiences and wrote about her unfulfilled longing for love. She was a woman on the verge of forty, searching for a scrap of happiness.

Günther Gereke had been given the honour of delivering the government's Christmas speech. Or had been strong-armed into it, more likely. The entire cabinet, he assured his listeners, was making every effort to reduce unemployment that winter in a way that people would actually feel.

The *Allgemeine Illustrierte Zeitung,* a Communist newspaper, splashed a photomontage across the front page. It depicted a member of the SA with a collection bag and sign in his hands, and beneath it ran the headline: 'Give for the Führer's Travel Expenses'. They also printed a poem that made fun of Strasser's 'sabbatical':

> Little SA man, what next?
> Oh poor Hitler man,
> Little Hitler man,
> Wants to go on 'holiday'
> Like the grand old gentlefolk,
> At each other's Aryan throats

Silly German!
You're just 'vermin'
And you're going to find out soon
That dancing to your Führer's tune
Will lead you wrong if you persist
Better join the Communists.

By five o'clock most shops were closed. The streets emptied swiftly, and the trams glided virtually unoccupied through the city.

Magda Goebbels was in a bad way. Professor Walter Stoeckel, an expert in gynaecology, warned Joseph Goebbels that his wife's case was 'more serious than I thought'. She was experiencing heart spasms and cramps.

Still, Goebbels had arranged a little Christmas party at the clinic. He and Harald, Magda's preteen son from her first marriage, lit the candles on a tree in the corridor outside her room.

Hitler sent a get-well telegram. Presents, flowers and cards poured in from other members of the party. Yet nothing lifted Goebbels' mood. 'A sad Christmas!' he remarked. 'The heart is heavy and anxious.'

He would be spending the evening with his bodyguards, faithful companions who'd stuck by him all year long. Goebbels was now itching to get back to work.

The country was preparing for a silent night. As soon as darkness fell, candles were lit. Tinsel hung from decorated firs and spruces. The churches were crowded with people hoping for salvation. There was peace in the hearts of those disposed to such emotions.

It was a German Christmas. Hushed conversations about days long past, memories of those long gone. Ancient family traditions. Sausages and sauerkraut dished up in Silesia. In many households the rituals were ones that people had learned as children, when the Kaiser was still on his throne. Before everything had gone to rack and ruin.

At Neudeck in East Prussia, the aging President of Germany was recharging his batteries, grateful for a temporary respite from the hysterical wheeling and dealing in Berlin. Perhaps he was thinking of the Kaiser in exile; certainly he was consulting God.

Franz von Papen had gone to stay with his family in Wallerfangen in Saarland, near the French border; but he'd taken Berlin with him. Berlin! He was bent on revenge, desperate to get rid of Schleicher. The coming days could easily see a reversal of their fortunes.

Hitler was in the Bavarian mountainside retreat of Obersalzberg. Did his eyes, too, light up as he gazed into the flames of the Christmas candles? Was it Wagner he listened to for edification? Or the sound of his own voice? Goebbels had recorded a speech or two onto gramophone records, so now Hitler could wallow in his own rhetorical gifts whenever he felt so inclined.

'Christmas is kitsch – but what's to be done?'

Alfred Kerr, theatre critic for the *Berliner Tageblatt*. Tomorrow was his birthday. He'd be sixty-five years old, but retirement was still a distant prospect.

SUNDAY 25 DECEMBER
CHRISTMAS DAY

There's no shortage of things to buy. Thousands of
people and machines are waiting to produce even more.
Yet everywhere there is hunger and hardship.
— *Die Sonntags-Zeitung*

No Christmas without National Socialism!
Our Struggle for Germany Has Restored Faith in the Light
— *Völkischer Beobachter*

A day for families. Many Berliners went to church again, to mass, ora-
torios, organ concerts. It was a contemplative day.

'Peace on Earth: Observations on Military Politics'. Wilhelm Groener
had contributed an article to the *Vossische Zeitung* in which he referred
to the recently concluded Five Powers Conference in Geneva as a 'gift
to all peoples'. He praised the diplomatic expertise of the new government, which was treading in the footsteps of Heinrich Brüning. A
half-compliment to Schleicher, then.

Christmas Day went too quietly for Joseph Goebbels. He was preparing for the upcoming election campaign in the small German district
of Lippe – a form of therapy to ward off his depression. From the
clinic he had hopeful news: his wife was doing somewhat better.

MONDAY 26 DECEMBER

[No newspapers were published on this date]

Tens of thousands of Berliners were out on the streets, modelling their Christmas presents. Jewellery, new coats, new hats, chic boots. Restaurants and cafés were heaving. Yes, there was a crisis; still, people wanted to live their lives.

The local football cup final between Hertha BSC and the Berliner Sport-Verein attracted twenty thousand fans. Hertha – the favourites – came away with a 3–1 victory; the players seemed nervous initially, but soon began to dominate.

A Christmas cabaret – primarily a grab bag of comedic sketches – was staged at the Volksbühne. It featured several star performers, including Werner Finck.

Finck was perhaps the most popular cabaret artist in Berlin. He'd found a group called the Catacombs a few years earlier, based at Bellevuestrasse 3, for which he acted as master of ceremonies. He wasn't considered a particularly acerbic political commentator, but that autumn he'd declaimed the following lines onstage:

> The way it rained last night
> I thought at once: Ah, right!
> Looks like the summer's gone.
> Prophetic was the warning!
> How chill the air this morning
> Autumnal, pale and wan.
> The sun still cheerfully beams

But that's just how it seems
It's barely clinging on.
The summer's gone, I fear,
So now the fields are clear
For troops that march through crisply.
How quickly past that slipped!
Don't think dictatorship
Will vanish quite so briskly.

Kurt von Schleicher, too, had eased his foot off the pedal, although he wasn't spending time with his family. He and his wife had no children, although Lonny – Elisabeth's daughter from her first marriage – lived with them. No, Schleicher was networking behind the scenes. Off-the-record tête-à-têtes, messages flying back and forth. He went for dinner with Louis Paul Lochner, head of the Associated Press's Berlin office, who had lived and worked in Germany since 1921. They discussed the political situation. Germany had entered a phase of 'Quiet, quiet, quiet,' said Schleicher. 'As you see, I have succeeded. Germany has for a long time not been as quiet as now. Even the Communists and the Nazis are behaving. The longer this quiet continues, the more certain is the present government to reestablish internal peace.'

Lochner was confused. Did the chancellor really believe the Christmas lull augured better times ahead?

Kurt Schumacher of the SPD saw no good news on the horizon. He spent much of the time between Christmas and New Year talking to his fiancée, Maria Seibold, whom he nicknamed Miga. They discussed the wedding – surely it was about time they set a date? Then Schumacher grew serious. 'For the moment I cannot bind another human life to mine,' he told her. 'The Nazis must come to power now or not at all. I don't know what they'll do; whatever they do with me when they fight me, I've come to terms with that, but I don't want them doing anything to you.'

What exactly did happen in August of that year? Hitler had believed that power was virtually within his grasp when President Hindenburg rebuffed him. So what was going on behind the scenes?

There were plenty of ambitious men eager to know – men probing for a way to bring Hitler to power. Wilhelm Keppler wrote to Kurt Freiherr von Schröder, the financier who had approached Papen at the Gentlemen's Club, about a meeting between Hitler and Papen. 'I hope the conversation will lead to a thorough explanation of the political events of the past months; I suspect we have Herr v. Schl. to thank for 13 August; in which case an explanation of this would be especially gratifying.'

It was on 13 August 1932 that Hitler had heard from the president that he would not be made chancellor. A traumatic moment for the Führer, even now; it had unleashed fury, disappointment and bitterness within the party. Had Schleicher been the one pulling the strings? Maybe Papen – then still in office – had been relatively innocent? Naturally Hitler wanted to know. It would take the pressure off their upcoming conversation, because he'd been fuming about what he believed was Papen's subterfuge. In his letter to Schröder, Keppler added:

As a consequence of 13 August, which the Führer always took as a personal defeat, his feelings towards Herr v. P. were very negative for a long time. I have always spoken up for v. P. and against v. Schl. in his presence; his feelings have gradually improved, and it seems he is happy to oblige us; I hope it is within your power to dispel his final reservations during their conversation.

The theatres were open that night, and Harry Graf Kessler saw *Liliom*. The play was the talk of Berlin: Hans Albers, a famously commanding actor, was playing the main role. Yet Kessler was unimpressed. 'Silly, sentimental kitsch, seasoned with brutality by Albers.'

TUESDAY 27 DECEMBER

Emergency Decrees Intended to Destroy NSDAP Abolished
Decree to Maintain Domestic Order
– Völkischer Beobachter

Murder Among Comrades Exposed
Body of SA Man Found Near Dam
Nazi Vigilante Killing in Dresden
– Vossische Zeitung

The final days of 1932 were spent in the fundamentally human hope that better times lay ahead. Children played with their fathers. Mothers were glad to see the back of relatives. Tax returns were prepared. People picked up books they'd been meaning to read for ages.

The citizens of Berlin reflected on the trials of 1932, met with friends, made trips out of the city and ignored the newspapers; they were still in the kind of mood that only Christmas can reliably conjure in the German soul. Introspective. Misty-eyed and warm-hearted. The atmosphere was peaceful – despite all the animosity there had been no war in Germany for fifteen years, almost a generation, and the nation would probably survive this crisis, too.

Carl von Ossietzky's first issue of the *Weltbühne* since his release – previously he'd been issuing instructions from his cell – reached its subscribers. Ossietzky presented himself neither as a hero of press freedoms nor a martyr for free speech. He wrote seventeen lines about his time in Tegel Prison in which the word 'I' appeared only twice. 'Return' was the succinct headline. 'Having been in prison is an immense experience that no political person can erase from their existence,' wrote Ossietzky. 'I came to know the prison not as a place of intentional harshness and the traditional cruelties, yet nonetheless as a house of sorrow, where behind each iron door another melancholy globe revolved, held in orbit by the entanglements of fate. Guilt? In this building the word was never spoken; here there were only victims.'

Gregor Strasser had left Rome! He was on his way back to Germany. Finally. The chancellor would have his opportunity to get Strasser on board.

Franz von Hörauf was still sending SA gossip to Crown Prince Wilhelm. In a letter from Munich he wrote: 'In Berlin a Stülpnagel–Papen–Hitler front seems to be forming, with the aim of using the president to topple the chancellor ahead of fresh elections.'

Joachim von Stülpnagel, a general of the infantry who had retired voluntarily from military service, was another of Schleicher's adversaries.

'How it can be countered', continued Hörauf, 'is beyond my ability to judge. I only wish to say one thing, even at the risk of contradicting the views of Your Imperial Highness: at the moment it would be inappropriate to raise the question of the monarchy.'

And what about Hitler's greatest rival? Hörauf knew him well. 'I had a very long discussion with Strasser today,' he wrote. 'I found him in a good frame of mind and with a very cool, clear appraisal of how things stand. This man's role is not yet played out.'

The *Vossische Zeitung* reported a planned meeting between Hitler and Strasser. The evening edition ran the headline 'Strasser's Demands: Must Hitler Give In?', and the article argued that 'If Strasser comes back, it won't be as a supplicant to the Führer, cowed and remorseful, but as a decisive force.' Gregor Strasser, they continued, wanted to be Secretary General of the NSDAP, assuming total control. The question was – would Hitler agree? Could their relationship be repaired? And, if not, who stood to lose the most?

The Theater des Westens was staging *The Good Soldier Švejk* by Jaroslav Hašek. Alfred Kerr, often a harsh critic, found it a heartening experience. 'The evening made up for the ordeals of recent times,' he wrote in his column for the *Berliner Tageblatt*. 'All else may be going haywire, but there is still exquisite theatre being performed.'

His new book was coming out in the next few days: *An Island Named Corsica*. A travel journal.

WEDNESDAY 28 DECEMBER

SA Attrition
Central German Units Refusing to Play Ball
Crisis and Decay Within NSDAP Goes Deeper Than It Seems
— *Vossische Zeitung*

Wrestle Back Stolen Wages!
Price Regulation for Margarine Today/Mobilise All
Workforces/Give Surplus to Unemployed
— *Die Rote Fahne*

The days between Christmas and New Year – drowsy, un-urgent – came as a welcome lull for many Germans. Others, meanwhile, were already trying to steal a march on 1933.

Joseph Goebbels visited his wife in hospital before setting off for the mountains: Hitler had invited him and his little 'travelling companion', Magda's eleven-year-old son Harald, to spend a few days in Obersalzberg. Goebbels hurriedly packed a suitcase, and the two boarded a train to Munich. There he met Martin Mutschmann, head of the Saxony branch of the NSDAP, who announced that Strasser was negotiating with Schleicher for a cabinet role. The final betrayal! Goebbels, Harald, Mutschmann and his wife then travelled to the town of Berchtesgaden before piling into a sledge for the final stretch to Obersalzberg. It was there, amid the idyllic, snow-capped mountains, that Adolf Hitler awaited his guests.

It must have been harrowing.

Hugenberg wrote to Hitler. He was deeply concerned 'about the ultimate success of the whole national movement, for which I feel partly responsible', he said. 'You will not be happy if the Centre Party ends up holding the balance of power again, and the Marxism we have long since put behind us is given fresh impetus.' Hugenberg, keen to form a nationalist movement, was probably worried Hitler would do a deal with the Centre Party, and he wanted to get the DNVP involved. He suggested 'negotiating again to see whether we can reach an agreement after all'.

As yet, Gregor Strasser's plans weren't quite as sinister as imagined. Mutschmann had promised to put in a good word for him with Hitler, but only on the condition that he broke off his relationship with Schleicher – by the time Mutschmann visited Hitler in Obersalzberg, he wanted something concrete. Yet they parted having come to no agreement, Strasser travelling onwards to Berlin and Mutschmann to Bavaria with his wife.

When he got to the capital, Strasser checked into the Hotel Excelsior. A few minutes later, his telephone rang.

It was the Chancellery on the line. Schleicher wanted to speak to him. Immediately.

Strasser refused but said he would be willing to meet soon.

Hitler chewed things over with Mutschmann that evening. When Mutschmann tried to bring the topic around to Strasser, however, he got the sense Hitler was no longer interested in the whole affair. Old news.

Chancellor Schleicher was throwing a dinner party, an intimate gathering of only twelve guests. Among this exclusive circle was Bella Fromm, Schleicher's old 'comrade', as he'd once called her.

Fromm was worried about her friend. After all, everybody on the political scene knew that Papen and his Gentlemen's Club clique were scheming to bring the Nazis to power. Now, at last, she had a chance to speak to Schleicher undisturbed, and she described her conversation with Karl von Wiegand. The American correspondent believed that Hitler's time was near at hand. If Schleicher wouldn't take her concerns seriously, maybe he'd listen to the 'dear old alarm signal'.

But Schleicher only laughed. 'You journalists are all alike. You make a living out of professional pessimism.'

Fromm insisted that Papen would cooperate with Hitler and was planning to make a comeback as chancellor. 'I think I can hold them off,' said Schleicher.

'As long as the Old Gentleman sticks to you,' was Fromm's reply.

Later they spoke more openly still, when she and the chancellor were alone in his study.

'In confidence, Bella, I think a lot of Gregor Strasser,' Schleicher remarked. 'National Socialist, but far over on the Leftist side of it. Maybe, if I had him in the cabinet …'

Fromm didn't think much of that idea. 'How about the church and Jew-phobia of the party?'

Schleicher did his best to reassure her. 'You ought to know me better than that, Bella,' he said. 'All that will be dropped entirely. I'd like to have your friend Brüning back, sooner or later.'

Strasser in government? Brüning back? Did Schleicher really believe there was a realistic chance of that – or was he merely saying what he thought a chancellor ought to say? By now it was obvious that Strasser had lost whatever clout he'd had in the NSDAP, and Brüning spent more time taking rest cures than talking politics.

The lines of communication were open. Schröder telephoned Franz von Papen: Hitler would meet with him whenever convenient. They agreed on 4 January, one week from today.

THURSDAY 29 DECEMBER

ESCAPE TO ITALY

DRESDEN KILLERS SEEK ASYLUM

The murder of Dresden SA unit leader Herbert Hentsch, whose
body was found in the Malter Dam in the Ore Mountains
on 26 December, has increasingly broad implications.

– *Vossische Zeitung*

Price Hike Campaign!
Schleicher's New Emergency Decree / Prices Raised on
Key Foodstuffs / SPD Agitating for 'Social' General /
Fight for Higher Wages and Subsidies!

– *Die Rote Fahne*

In Berchtesgaden, Hitler was dictating his New Year's address. It was
an impassioned call for solidarity within the NSDAP, in which he
argued that any hint of compromise would threaten to destroy the
party and the future of Germany:

> We know our adversaries, and we know their thoughts. 'Give
> the party a share in government, overburden them with respon-
> sibility and prevent them from having any real say' … For when
> our adversaries invite us to take part in such a government,
> they do so not with the intention of slowly but surely giving
> us power but in the conviction that they are thereby wresting it
> from us forever.

Hitler was in the throes of what he would probably have termed
a 'vast defensive battle'. Strasser's tactics had made one thing clear to
everybody: there was an alternative to Hitler's strategy. And to Hitler
himself.

Goebbels received alarming news from Berlin. Magda was getting worse. She'd had a miscarriage. He was packing his bags when a friend telephoned to report that, actually, she was getting better after all. Goebbels, wavering, chose Hitler above his wife. He remained at Obersalzberg.

A tenants' meeting was taking place at Ackerstrasse 132, in Wedding, in a six-courtyard complex known as Meyer's Hof. The occupants decided they would stop paying rent as of 1 January 1933 until the following demands were met: 1. there was a complete renovation of the entire building; 2. clean drinking water was provided; 3. all evictions in progress were withdrawn; 4. outstanding rent was written off; and 5. the rent was lowered by 25 per cent.

Two hundred and twenty-seven of the tenants backed the decision, with only three – supporters of the National Socialists – refusing to fall in line.

It was a cold day in the capital. For the first time in weeks, the temperature dropped below zero.

That evening Hitler and Goebbels had a conversation. It revolved primarily around the Strasser danger. Mutschmann's impression was way off the mark – Hitler had simply been playing it cool. Presumably he had not forgotten that Mutschmann was formerly one of Strasser's closest allies; he'd even named his district headquarters 'Gregor Strasser House' and not, like everybody else, 'Adolf Hitler House'.

Yet there was light on the horizon. In a few days, probably on 4 January, Hitler would be meeting Franz von Papen, who was still thick as thieves with President Hindenburg. Negotiators on both sides were scribbling letters and meeting behind closed doors, including Werner von Alvensleben, a notorious right-leaning power broker and a leading member of the reactionary Gentlemen's Club. While sympathetic to Schleicher, Alvensleben was also on excellent terms with prominent National Socialists. It was he who'd arranged the crucial meeting between Schleicher and Hitler's people that spring, a meeting that had brought down Brüning's government. Now it seemed a new opportunity was up for grabs.

FRIDAY 30 DECEMBER

A Mother's Accusation
'Protect Your Children From the NSDAP'
– Vossische Zeitung

Westphalian Farmers Organise Campaign Against Schleicher
– Der Angriff

People in Germany were shopping for the last big bash of 1932. Those fond of sparkling wine could pick up a Henkell – making the Ribbentrops happy – while those who could afford it treated themselves to champagne.

Henkell, the drinks company, was advertising its sparkling wine in the newspapers.

In Berchtesgaden, Goebbels' mood had brightened. Encouraging news from the clinic in Berlin: Magda was on the mend. Goebbels telephoned Professor Stoeckel, who reassured him. Hitler and Magda's son, Harald, who was also staying at Obersalzberg, wrote a joint letter to the patient. The political situation in Berlin remained unchanged, so Goebbels remained in the winter sun, enjoying the panoramic view over the Alps and the opportunity to spend some time with a more unbuttoned Führer. In the evening, Hitler showed him the finished New Year's speech, in which he railed against all the naysayers, dismissed any prospect of reconciliation with Strasser and swore he would fight until his dying breath.

His radicalism alone, thought Goebbels, would sweep them to victory. 'Hitler is fantastic,' he wrote in his diary.

The KPD was preparing for a mass rally in the Lustgarten, a park in central Berlin. 'Show Schleicher your strength!' urged *Die Rote Fahne*.

If Joseph Goebbels had read the Munich Political Police's analysis of the NSDAP, the view would have been the last thing on his mind. 'Not only have the new admissions almost all failed to appear, but an increasing lack of enthusiasm is palpable among the members; there are frequent departures, fees are paid only intermittently, and membership cancellations due to outstanding fees are increasingly common.' The party, the SA and the SS were looking embattled. The officers, whose information came from various senior sources in the NSDAP, continued: 'It is now a widespread view among National Socialists that they are past their peak and that their once favourable prospects are behind them.'

The 'Political Police' – the Republic was far from defenceless. This division of the police force, which included numerous informants and was estimated at up to a thousand strong, had been set up to protect the state from its more radical adversaries. Its agents stirred up trouble, set traps, reported on illegal demonstrations. Some were exposed in their turn by KPD or NSDAP counterintelligence units.

Since the previous year, the Political Division at headquarters in Berlin had been designated the 'central authority to observe and combat the undermining of the military and police in Prussia and the Reich as a whole'. Suspected enemies of the Republic had been systematically arrested ever since. By now the agency's card index contained more than half a million names – and those were just the ones living in Prussia.

SATURDAY 31 DECEMBER
NEW YEAR'S EVE

They're Hunting Communists!
Proletarian Mass Organisations Threatened with Dissolution
– Expulsions Prelude to Escalating Suppression of KPD
– Die Rote Fahne

Göring Snubs Hindenburg
President's New Year's Reception
– Vossische Zeitung

A thin, slowly melting layer of ice covered the streets and pavements. It was extremely slippery: Berlin was literally frozen stiff. Cars and buses slowed to a crawl, yet there were still constant accidents; paramedics were called out thirty times before noon. Broken bones, sprains, concussions.

Hitler had issued invitations to a party, so almost every senior Nazi was converging on Berchtesgaden. Hitler's residence, the Berghof, had been decorated in grand style.

Hermann Göring was the Führers' eyes and ears, and Hitler trusted him more than almost anyone else in the movement. Yet he had not accepted his invitation. This year he would be celebrating with friends at Rockelstad Castle in Sweden, the birthland of Göring's first wife, Carin, who had died unexpectedly in 1931.

With him he'd brought a radio given to him as a Christmas present by Emmy, his new girlfriend. Göring wrote to her: 'Your gift is currently playing songs on Swedish radio. You've given me such pleasure with it! And now, my darling, I give you my deepest thanks for all your love, your sacrifice and everything you have done for me. May the coming year continue to be good to us.'

Recently Abraham Plotkin had been spending his Saturdays with a fellow trade unionist, Martin Plettl. They would hop on a train out of Berlin and take a walk through the forest. He and Plettl, a nature-loving Bavarian, would usually end the afternoon in animated discussion at the pub.

Theodor Leipart was defending his relationship with Chancellor Schleicher in the *Gewerkschafts-Zeitung*. Above his article ran the words 'Against the Accusation of Betrayal. To the German Workers', and in it he bemoaned the litany of slander. 'We have been accused of negotiating with Chancellor Schleicher. We are suspected of collaborating with reactionary groups. It is believed we have given up our greatest goal, the realisation of a socialist economy.'

The opposite, he argued, was the case. Schleicher's government would never make socialism a reality, but it had agreed to a number of the unions' demands. 'In a situation such as this, can we afford to turn down the government's invitation to participate in their efforts to create jobs?'

More than a few people in Leipart's circle would have answered: yes, definitely, or we're betraying ourselves!

Berlin's hotels, theatres, cabarets, restaurants and pubs were expecting significantly more trade this time around than two years earlier. The Institute for Business Research even declared that 'With the year 1932 Germany virtually overcame the crisis which had shaken its business structure to the foundations.' Certainly something worth toasting. 'Today,' reported Edgar Mowrer, 'German economists are convinced that things cannot and will not get worse, that this country has descended to the valley's bottom and is crossing a level area beyond which Germany is bound to rise.'

It's worth remembering that none of the expected political catastrophes had actually taken place. Hitler had not seized power and Communism had not spread as widely as anticipated. The Weimar Republic was still limping on. Mowrer concluded, hopefully, that 1933 would probably be an improvement on 1932.

Theodor Haubach, a prominent member of the Reichsbanner, reflected on the past year in the organisation's newsletter. 'It has been battered and trampled, yet the Reichsbanner has claimed the field of battle and arrayed its forces for a new campaign. We step forward once again, still in the twilight of doubt and despair. [...] We have nothing but the certainty that the army that could withstand 1932 cannot be beaten in 1933.'

What comforted the SPD and its allies was their unshakeable certainty that there was simply no way around them.

President Hindenburg had a message for his soldiers: 'I send my most heartfelt best wishes for the New Year to all members of the armed forces. The old soldierly virtues of loyalty, obedience and duty must remain your guiding principles.' Kurt von Schleicher had signed the statement as well – in his capacity as Defence Minister.

Sir Horace Rumbold conveyed the British Prime Minister's greetings to Schleicher, adding that Sir Ramsay MacDonald was 'looking forward to nothing with more hope than warm cooperation between our two countries in all that makes for European friendship, neighbourness and cooperation'.

Harry Graf Kessler saw in the New Year quietly. Kessler – a fixture at receptions and dinner parties – was usually eager to seek out the company of interesting people, but he spent New Year at his house in Weimar. All alone.

Schleicher sent a New Year's telegram to Franz von Papen in Waller-fangen. 'All best wishes for 33 and heartfelt thanks to the standard-bearer in the decisive battles of the previous year. Much love to my dear Fränzchen and his family. Schleicher.'

Who would send a telegram like that to a revenge-plotting rival? 'My dear Fränzchen?'

Schleicher, evidently.

In the villa belonging to the George family at Bismarckstrasse 34 in Wannsee, raucous festivities were underway. Heinrich George, one of the most famous, popular and brilliant actors of his era, was celebrat-ing with friends and family, having arrived at the villa a couple of days earlier.

As they set off fireworks outside, the family's German mastiff, Fellow, crept behind an armchair in the hall. Berta Drews, George's future wife and the mother of his son, Jan, stroked the dog to reassure it, while Jan squealed in his cot, eager to return to the fun of the party. Just after midnight, the guests watched spellbound as George per-formed his 'pyrotechnic stunts' in the garden. After the fireworks he brought out a bowl of flaming punch, giving himself a generous help-ing. Later, dressed up as an oriental beauty with a head of black curls and a fluttering veil, he told his guests' fortunes.

He and Berta already knew theirs. They were getting married.

Midnight. Zero hour, 1933.

In Obersalzberg, Joseph Goebbels shook the Führers' hand. He gazed at him and said: 'I wish you power.'

Firecrackers were exploding in the valley below, their reddish glow flickering across the mountaintops. The bells began to toll. 'The old year smashed!' thought Goebbels.

Later, while the other Hitlerites were celebrating, drinking and talking, he was glued to the telephone. A call from Berlin. Magda was suddenly much worse. She was being fed through a tube. The situation was dire – his wife was in serious danger. Before he heard any more, the line went dead.

Not the most auspicious of starts for Goebbels.

SUNDAY 1 JANUARY 1933
NEW YEAR'S DAY

Full-Scale Nazi Attack on Democratic State Defeated
— Frankfurter Zeitung

NEW YEAR — NEW STRUGGLE!
A difficult year lies behind us. One no less difficult lies
ahead. In order to survive it, we must summon the full
force of the strongest workers' party in Germany.
— Vorwärts

Everywhere, all across the world, people were talking about …
what's his first name again? Adalbert Hitler? And then? He vanished!
— Berliner Tageblatt

New Year's Day. Germany awoke to a hangover.

At 1 a.m. in Utrechter Strasse, sixteen-year-old Walter Wagnitz of the
Hitler Youth had been knifed in the gut. Communists, probably. A
man by the name of Sarow was suspected of his murder. Wagnitz had
been celebrating New Year at a pub with his local branch of the Hitler
Youth, and the stabbing took place on the street outside.

Joseph Goebbels was headed back to Berlin. Would Magda still be
alive when he got there? These days Goebbels often found his mind
turning to God.

At the French embassy's traditional New Year's reception, André

François-Poncet gave a generous-spirited speech. 'When it comes to the relationship between Germany and France, we can at least say with satisfaction that it is entering into a calmer and more relaxed phase.'

Yet the disarmament negotiations in Geneva – rearmament negotiations for the Germans, strictly speaking – had increasingly come to reflect French mistrust and German defiance. During Papen's chancellorship, at least according to the Americans, the delegation had changed tack, becoming less humble.

New Year's messages of all stripes appeared in the newspapers. Fritz Demuth, an adviser with the Berlin Chamber of Commerce and Industry, radiated optimism: 'By the end of the year, even a cautious appraisal will conclude that the German economy has pulled through the worst of the crisis. We hope to maintain the status quo in the winter but improve in the spring.'

Meanwhile, the president's reception at twelve o'clock was obligatory for all those invited. Everybody knew that – and yet the senior members of the NSDAP were nowhere to be seen. Nor were the leadership of the Prussian SPD government, who, athough disempowered, were still technically in office.

The event began with a reception for the diplomatic corps. Hindenburg and Schleicher both advocated a softly-softly approach, reported journalists, allowing Germany to make peace with itself. 'It has indeed taken immense effort,' said Hindenburg, 'necessitating recourse to exceptional measures, to protect the life of our state and economy from dangerous internal destabilising forces. But the crisis is not yet overcome.'

Then, it was Schleicher's turn. He spoke directly to Hindenburg:

When you appointed me only a few weeks ago to the head of
the national government, Herr President, you told me to create

jobs and seek to alleviate the tensions within our nation by addressing social disparities. The government will be guided by these principles, for only in this way can we succeed in giving back the German people hope and purpose. The path will, however, be long and difficult – let us be in no doubt about that.

Schleicher concluded by thanking his predecessor. The current administration, he said, was building its programme of job creation 'on the commitment and valuable work of the Papen government'.

A kind word never hurts.

In the small Bavarian town of Partenkirchen, the now traditional New Year's ski jumping event was in full swing, and the young German athlete Toni Eisgruber took first place. It would be the last jump off this particular hill – a larger, wooden structure would soon be built at Gudiberg Mountain for the 1936 Winter Olympics.

Representatives of the Communist parties of Germany, France, England, Italy, Poland, Belgium, Austria, Czechoslovakia and Luxembourg convened for a secret summit in Essen. Had they come to discuss the imminent revolution, perhaps? Sadly the agenda was a secret, too.

The KPD was torn between feelings of triumph and self-castigation. After the last parliamentary elections in November, the Central Committee had announced that 'the most important feature of the whole proletarian shift is the fact that the Communists are winning while the Social Democrats and National Socialists cannot hold back the masses nor harness them any longer in the service of the bourgeois dictatorship'.

The results of the election had entirely validated the party's approach, hadn't it? Six weeks previously, on 17 September, the Secretariat of the Central Committee had announced 'that the struggle to bring down the Papen government and against the establishment of a Fascist dictatorship demands the primary attack be against the SPD as the main pillar propping up society among the working class and against the NSDAP as the Fascist terrorist and paramilitary organisation of financial capital'. There was, however, one problem with this struggle: the party's own dubious fitness for combat. 'Our party organisation,' admitted the Secretariat, 'is still severely deficient in its role as organiser and leader of all forms and methods of the mass struggle'.

The Weimar Republic may not have been entirely ready to defend itself, but it seemed the KPD didn't believe its members were entirely ready to attack.

For Kurt von Schleicher, the situation at the beginning of the year looked bright. The president seemed content and the economy would soon be perking up. In its quarterly report, the Institute for Business Research concluded that 'the recession is over and the bottom of the valley has been reached. Once crossed, there will be new growth and we will see an economic upswing.'

Not to mention that the price of bonds and shares on the Frankfurt Stock Exchange had risen by more than 30 per cent since the previous spring.

In his New Year's address, Ludwig Kaas spoke of 'struggle or coalition', and called for a solution 'from the leadership'. 'Where Germany's saviour will come from, God alone knows,' he declared, but his party would 'gratefully and unbegrudgingly' support such an individual. A person 'distinguished by true greatness, with a record of achievement, who would inspire allegiance and satisfy the longing of the masses. [...] It's a matter of supreme indifference who leads Germany. It's not important what he is, only what he can do.'

Hearing these words from the mouth of a moderate, Catholic party chairman ought to have been deeply concerning. He seemed to be suggesting there were no values or standards of behaviour a future leader of the German nation necessarily had to possess. That the political messiah might come from anywhere.

Hans Zehrer was the owner and editor-in-chief of the *Tägliche Rundschau*, a newspaper with close ties to Schleicher. In August 1932 it had been bought by a group of intellectuals around Zehrer who were also involved in publishing the monthly journal *Die Tat* (The Act), and it was rumoured Schleicher had given financial assistance. *Die Tat*, which Zehrer also edited, had a reputation in younger conservative circles for being particularly insightful on important issues of the day – Zehrer represented a kind of right-wing Ossietzky. A Nazi, however, he was not.

In Sunday's *Die Tat*, he wrote that

> If General Schleicher hopes to prevail, he can do so only by making up his mind to restructure things once and for all. In other words, if he incorporates the will of the people – currently incapacitated – into his government. This is all the more crucial as General von Schleicher is the last remaining man of the generation qualified to oversee a coherent transition into the new era, and there is no obvious candidate to replace him. If the General fails, we will most likely slide into a brief and varied phase of experimentation followed by a civil war that will seriously endanger the survival of the nation.

Hans Zehrer was indeed angling for an influential post in Schleicher's administration, just as rumoured in Wilhelmstrasse. These articles can, of course, be read in that light, but, in fact, the authoritarian state of Zehrer's imagination had nothing to do with democracy.

After their trouncing by the Netherlands, Otto Nerz's football squad lost another match to Italy. In front of thirty thousand spectators in Bologna's half-empty Stadio Littoriale, Oskar Rohr put the Germans ahead early before Italian star Giuseppe Meazza countered, and the eventual score was three one to the hosts.

Under manager Vittorio Pozzo, Italy was one of the dominant teams of its age. Cost had prevented them from participating in the

1930 World Cup in Uruguay, but they won the European Cup that year, came second to Austria's 'Wunderteam' the year after that, and were considered frontrunners for the upcoming 1934 World Cup, which they would also be hosting. This had been confirmed in October, thanks to the lavish sums Benito Mussolini had committed to spending.

Speaking of Austria: in 1931 their squad – anchored by Viennese pro and advertising star Matthias Sindelar – had beaten Germany 6–0 and 5–0. The team promised great things. Germany, on the other hand, was still trying to break into the international elite.

A majority of the tenants in buildings operated by the Roland and Primus housing associations were going on strike. Of the 2,800 residents, many spent half their income on rent. They had previously demanded it be lowered by 10 per cent, but their protests had fallen on deaf ears.

An official statistic: there were 166,152 housing blocks made up of 1,357,812 apartments registered in Berlin. Two-thirds of them had only one or two rooms.

According to the 1931 census, the city was home to 4,288,700 people.

At the Bonbonnière cabaret in Munich, only four hundred metres from the Royal Court and National Theatre on Max Joseph Platz, the Pepper Mill cabaret group was performing that evening.

The names of its founders were familiar to many German intellectuals: actress Therese Giehse, the daughter of Jewish parents, and the Mann twins, Erika and Klaus, children of the Nobel Prize-winning Thomas Mann. Although not actually twins, they seemed to be joined at the hip, and they marketed themselves as a twosome, publishing books and series of articles about their travels.

The Bonbonnière was next door to a beer hall called the

Hofbräuhaus, formerly one of Hitler's favourite haunts. Which seems appropriate, somehow, because when the cabaret act performed there in 1933 they set their sights squarely on Hitler and Fascism: the founders' stated aim was to be 'militantly anti-Nazi'. Their name, meanwhile, had been Thomas Mann's idea. Erika had been complaining at the dinner table that her group still didn't have a name when her father held up the pepper mill and said: 'How about this, then?'

As master of ceremonies, Erika Mann's job was to greet the guests and introduce the programme. She described Hitler as a man of lowbrow intellect whose character was subject to the most unpredictable fluctuations. As for his body? Most unfortunate. The National Socialists weren't exactly fans of the free-thinking, free-living feminist, but Giehse's participation in their act must have really hurt. Hitler had once said he thought she was 'excellent', declaring – clearly he knew nothing about her Jewish parents – that she was 'an artist of the people, the kind found only in Germany'.

It would not be long before he changed his tune.

In Berlin, Kurt von Schleicher went to see Offenbach's operetta *La princesse de Trébizonde*, which was set in the East. Afterwards, other members of the audience reported that one of the actresses asked at the climax of the plot: 'What are we doing now?' to which another replied: 'We're forming a new government and dissolving Parliament.'

Commotion in the audience.

The chancellor apparently gave a broad grin.

Hitler was also taking in a show: Wagner, at the Royal Court and National Theatre in Munich. He could always rely on Richard Wagner to tug at his heartstrings. *Die Meistersinger von Nürnberg* did so for more than four hours – certainly when it was conducted by the famous Hans Knappertsbusch, Music Director of the Bavarian State Opera. Hitler had close ties to the Wagner family; he was always welcome in Bayreuth.

Accompanying him was the blonde assistant to Heinrich Hoff-mann, Hitler's photographer. The name of the outspoken young Fräulein was Eva Braun. By now she and Hitler were involved. In what, exactly, his friends weren't sure; but they couldn't allow him to be seen with a woman at his side – it might cost them votes. Specifi-cally, women's votes. Ernst Hanfstaengl was also attending the opera, as were his wife Helene, a friend of Hitler's from the early days in Munich, and Rudolf Hess and his wife Ilse.

After the performance the group went back to Pienzernauer Strasse, where the Hanfstaengls were staying. They listened to one of Rachmaninov's piano concertos on the gramophone while sipping coffee by the fireplace and chatting, then Hanfstaengl played some Wagner. They all forgot the time. Hitler hadn't liked Knappertsbusch's interpretation, but he was cheerful, almost merry. When he wrote his final entry in the guestbook, it seemed to Hanfstaengl that Hitler had to suppress his excitement. 'This year belongs to us,' the Führer told him. 'I'll give it to you in writing.'

IN THE MAELSTROM

2 TO 29 JANUARY 1933

MONDAY 2 JANUARY

Time to say goodbye to Christmas trees and stollen.
Germany's obligatory year-end political lull is over.
— *Vossische Zeitung*

In many German cities, the Communists were preparing for a series of rallies. They painted signs and practised slogans. 'Out with Schleicher's government and every Fascist regime!' 'Down with wage dumping, welfare cuts and price-hike campaigns!' And, of course: 'No more Brownshirts death and terror!'

Kurt von Schleicher was complaining to a friend how stressful it was dealing with complex financial questions in such detail, especially when all the parties were digging their heels in. The economy wasn't exactly Schleicher's forte, but if it didn't pick up then Germany was in for a rough ride – and so was he.

That morning, the intelligence division of the SS went back to work. Their office was located near the end of a cul-de-sac in the elegant Munich neighbourhood of Bogenhausen, not far from where the Hanfstaengls lived, in a building belonging to Reinhard Heydrich and his family.

Like the NSDAP, which financed the SS, Heydrich's organisation was running out of funds to pay its members, and many employees simply didn't show up for work on 2 January. They were already out looking for other sources of income.

Lina Heydrich cooked for the men who'd come to work, as well as for other party members. She made soups from dehydrated vegetables and prepared a herring salad (sans herring). Spirits were low. Some of the men were probably eyeing the door as they spooned down their soup.

TUESDAY 3 JANUARY

SCHLEICHER PUSHES FOR CLARITY

The holidays are over. Yesterday the truce elapsed, and
tomorrow the Council of Elders will meet at the Reichstag
to decide when Parliament should reconvene.

– *Vossische Zeitung*

To the Streets!
Mass Red March against Schleicher Dictatorship and Brown Terror
– *Die Rote Fahne*

The parliamentary truce, imposed on 7 November by emergency
decree, was at an end. And as of 3 January, rallies, demonstrations and
political gatherings were also permissible once more.

What did Carl von Ossietzky do, now that he had free rein? He wrote
and wrote and wrote, working from the offices of the *Weltbühne*
at Kantstrasse 152 in Charlottenburg. 'At the beginning of 1932,' he
declared, 'the Nazis seemed on the verge of a dictatorship, and the
air was full of the stench of blood. By the end of it, Hitler's party had
been shaken by a major crisis, and the long knives were put quietly
back in their box while all the Führer kept out was a wary ear. Germany is developing rapidly, if not smoothly.'

And Schleicher? 'An ambitious politician who got what he wanted.
If he brings the same unswerving approach to bettering the Fatherland as he did to his own career, then we have our golden age ahead of
us.' Ossietzky kept a remorselessly observant eye on Germany's politicians. He remained unimpressed by Schleicher, although many people
were pinning their hopes on him. Why *was* that?

Germany has proved itself as incapable of a counterrevolution this summer as it was of a revolution in 1918, and there is now a certain surprise on the left that those on the right are no more brilliant or energetic than they are. Schleicher has this confusion to thank for much of his recent authority.

Given the lack of any civilian counterweight worth mentioning, Schleicher will probably stick it out for quite a while, even if there's a revolving door of advisers, assistants and dogsbodies. One thing is certain: he has established a line of Praetorian chancellors.

It was a strange and powerful term, 'Praetorian chancellors'. By referring to the Praetorian Guard – assigned to protect the Emperor in ancient Rome – Ossietzky was reducing Schleicher to his military role. And did he really picture Hindenburg as the de facto German emperor?

An election campaign in the small district of Lippe was just beginning. Hitler had declared it the 'breakthrough campaign' a few days earlier, making it clear that the financially challenged party would be throwing everything it had into electioneering. Hitler announced that he would be visiting Lippe in person, yet when he boarded a train from Munich that evening it was the one headed to Cologne. Not even his chief press officer knew why.

Ossietzky despised many party politicians, but he reserved particular contempt for the NSDAP: 'The Nazis' crisis is primarily financial. Those members of the party with an interest in theory have always been vanishingly few in number; the majority are the stupidest of the stupid. The cadres of Brownshirts were held together by cash and not by conviction.'

Not even Gregor Strasser was immune:

Precisely because Gregor possesses sympathetic traits, one is inclined to examine him with an objectivity that would be wasted on a hysterical cheese mite like Goebbels, but this examination reveals nothing except empty air.

It's a special kind of drama, of course, to watch a party which a few months back was demanding everything – and, given its size, seemed entitled to demand anything – already in spasms. Yet here we must warn against expecting too much. Only a new general economic boom would be enough to fully strip National Fascism bare.

'Hysterical cheese mite'… Goebbels had always been sensitive to taunts: he once dispatched an SS thug to the offices of a journalist who had written disrespectfully about his wife. Or was that just a story he told to show off?

That night in Hamburg, an attempt was made to assassinate the editor of the *Israelitisches Familienblatt*, Ezriel Carlebach, who had gone out around midnight to post some letters when a young man fired several shots at him. Luckily they missed, but one of the bullets went through Carlebach's hat; he fell, hit his head on the ground and was knocked unconscious.

Carlebach had incurred the wrath of the KPD the previous summer when, after a visit to the USSR, he wrote a series of condemnatory articles about the experiences of Jews living in Soviet Russia. The Communists had been regularly harassing him ever since; now they'd made good on their threats.

WEDNESDAY 4 JANUARY

Reichstag Waiting for Lippe
Smallest Local Election Key Barometer of Public Mood
— *Vossische Zeitung*

VALUED COMRADES!
Comrades! Make sure our enemies' organisations
don't get ahead of us and absorb our youth – try to
induct indifferent young people into our ranks.
Freedom!
— *Reichsbanner*

The National Socialists had cooked up a few ideas to shake off anybody who might be tailing the Führer. Early that morning, Hitler and
other members of the NSDAP also bound for Lippe arrived in Bonn,
having taken the night train from Munich. The entourage was picked
up at the station in a six-seater car before being driven to the Hotel
Dresden in Bad Godesberg, a district of Bonn gloriously located on
the Rhine.

Hitler instructed his chief press officer, Otto Dietrich, to head in
the direction of Düsseldorf in a second vehicle, keeping the curtains
closed, then wait three miles outside Cologne. Dietrich was supposed
to sit next to the driver – Hitler's usual spot – with his cap drawn down.

Hitler and his companions, meanwhile, would set off in the first
car. At the wheel was Wilhelm Keppler, the businessman who had
founded a group of advisers to help the Nazis build relationships with
powerful financiers and industrialists.

Plotkin was still in Berlin, reading the headlines. The papers announced
mass demonstrations by the Communists and National Socialists,

while the police were offering 500 marks for information leading to the arrest of 'young Hitlerite' Walter Wagnitz's murderer. The Nazis claimed it as the first political murder of the year. Others described it as the regrettable result of a drunken brawl.

The police in Berlin had been on high alert since two o'clock. The KPD had announced a rally in the Lustgarten that afternoon – on 3 January the ban on demonstrations, in place since 31 October 1931, had been lifted.

Hitler was, in fact, headed to Cologne – to a villa owned by banker Kurt von Schröder, a striking man with a receding hairline and a duelling scar across his left cheek.

As he and his companions pulled outside at Stadtwaldgürtel 35, Hitler was annoyed. Why was there a photographer at the door? Hadn't they agreed on strict secrecy?

For two hours they talked in Schröder's study: Adolf Hitler and Franz von Papen, formerly chancellor and now Hindenburg's right-hand man. Papen had actually left a hunting trip early in order to arrive punctually in Cologne. He told Hitler he thought it would be best to form a government in which the conservative and nationalist elements that had supported him were represented alongside the Nazis. Why not lead such a government together, the two of them?

Hitler responded in typical fashion: he gave a speech. If he were chancellor he would certainly appoint many of Papen's allies to ministerial posts, assuming they supported his policies.

It was a beginning. *The* beginning, even.

So far 6,074 political prisoners had been released under the amnesty, but few would lobby as hard for the Weimar Republic over the coming days as Carl von Ossietzky.

Was that a political scandal in the offing?

Neudeck, Hindenburg's ancestral estate in East Prussia, was suddenly a hot topic. The property had been mired in debt when a group of industrialists and landowners bought the deed in 1927 and presented it to Hindenburg to mark his eightieth birthday – it had long been in his family, and his ancestors were still buried there.

General Erich Ludendorff had sharply criticised the gift in his weekly magazine *Ludendorffs Volkswarte* (Ludendorff's Watchtower of the People), implying that Hindenburg had accepted it in exchange for his support of *Osthilfe*, or Eastern Aid. Eastern Aid was a conglomeration of up to sixty-one laws and decrees with which various governments had sought to boost agriculture and prevent mass migration to cities.

The estate had also been transferred to the name of Oskar von Hindenburg, the president's son; by doing so, Hindenburg hoped to avoid death duties when he finally reached the end of his days. Was it legal? Was it a morally appropriate thing for a president to do?

Schleicher did not leap to the president's defence, much to the displeasure of the Hindenburgs.

Noticing the Communists on their way towards the Lustgarten, Abraham Plotkin was gripped with curiosity. Thousands of people, mainly young men, streamed towards the demonstration, and meanwhile the police were out in force. Did he remember his earlier warning to steer clear of crowds? That day he'd come within a whisker of being beaten up by a German officer. But Plotkin couldn't resist.

The Lustgarten is a park on an island in the River Spree – about the size of Washington Square, thought Plotkin. It was bordered by the cathedral, the Imperial Palace, and a number of Berlin's most magnificent museums. The Communists opened the demonstration with a raw and full-throated performance of 'The Internationale'. Then, speeches. A cheer went up for the 'Rote Front' – the Red Front: 'every right fist moved upward in unison, three times repeated until the cry was thunderous'. The crowd was one hundred thousand strong.

It was a cold, dull winter's day, engulfed in fog. Plotkin glanced around. 'I became aware of the strange lighting. In the fog, the lights of Berlin are different from any other city I have ever been in.'

'Red Front!'

He mused for a while, intrigued.

'Red Front!'

'The lamps are a light yellow with some pink, and the result is a rose-colored light that accentuates and marks every approaching face and figure.'

'Red Front!'

The day's main speaker was Wilhelm Florin, a KPD Politburo member of four years' standing, as well as an MP. Florin was an experienced orator, and what he said must have enthralled the massed crowd. He called on all proletarians to 'forge a united front in the struggle against the capitalist system', before concluding: 'We must put an end to national and social oppression, uniting ever more firmly the front in the international class war under the leadership of international Communism.'

They sang 'La Marseillaise', the French anthem to freedom.

Arise, children of the Fatherland
The day of glory has arrived!
Against us, tyranny's
Bloody standard is raised.

Yet something was missing. Some inner spark, enthusiasm, conviction, whatever one might call it. Plotkin was surprised. And yet, he thought, these people were as disciplined as soldiers, having marched for hours in an orderly fashion from every corner of Berlin.

As the crowd began to disperse, Plotkin was still baffled. The Communists formed neat lines and sang songs in unison as they left the Lustgarten, pausing obediently on the street when it was blocked by the police. 'Is this the real Germany?' wondered Plotkin. 'The Germany that can ritualize itself into a revolution?'

No, he thought. 'I know that within their hands today there is nothing resembling real power.'

This wasn't the Communists flexing their muscles; it was a masquerade.

The parties' campaign schedules for the Lippe elections were made public. Hitler would speak at sixteen meetings within ten days, each in a different town or village. At his side would be allies like Göring, Goebbels and Kerrl, all participating in a campaign that would include 150 such gatherings.

The Communists, under Ernst Thälmann, announced 160, while Hugenberg and the DNVP were organising a hundred meetings. The Social Democrats, who had been in power in the tiny state since 1918, were planning 150 campaign appearances.

All this to woo just over 117,000 registered voters. Under different circumstances one might be tempted to call it a triumph of democracy.

In the Prussian State Assembly, the Nazis proposed that in future the Central Authority for Thoroughbred Breeding and Racing should deny foreigners 'the licence to practise the professions of trainer or jockey'.

The moment he realised there was a photographer lurking outside Schröder's villa, Papen knew someone had spilled the beans. He'd have to act quickly if he didn't want to fall out with Schleicher, so he went straight to Düsseldorf – where his mother lived – and wrote the chancellor a letter in which he defended his parley with Hitler.

The Council of Elders was meeting to decide when to recall Parliament. Chancellor Schleicher dispatched State Secretary Erwin Planck to inform them that the government was ready to appear before the Reichstag and explain its policies. After heated debate, the Council took a vote and settled on 24 January for the first session, securing the agreement of the Social Democrats, Communists, Centre Party, DNVP and DVP. The Nazis had abstained. The Council would meet one more time, on 20 January, to confirm the date.

Otto Dietrich had been waiting for hours at the rendezvous point. It was getting dark by the time Hitler's limousine finally appeared. The Führer, heading to Lippe at last, told the driver to put his foot down, although the roads were slippery as glass.

So who had sent that photographer? Was it a detective, as Papen suspected? After all, he knew Schleicher's spies were watching him. Or one of Strasser's agents, as Schleicher would later claim?

As it turned out, the photographer had been hired by a Berlin-based dentist whose patients included former chancellor Heinrich Brüning as well as Gregor Strasser and Kurt von Schleicher. His name was Hellmuth Elbrechter, and he moonlighted as a journalist, writing for Hans Zehrer's *Tat* and *Tägliche Rundschau*. As a fighter pilot during the First World War, he'd been shot down twice and survived; then, in the 1920s, he came to know Gregor Strasser and Joseph Goebbels. Some people considered him an adviser to Strasser, but also to Schleicher, especially when it came to economic questions. Certainly he made himself available to both politicians for clandestine meetings at his apartment at Schaperstrasse 29.

The photographer was a retired army captain by the name of Hans Johannesson, a man with ties to Strasser. His images reached the *Tägliche Rundschau* in Berlin just in time to be splashed across the front page of the morning edition.

Zehrer had a scoop.

That evening, Hitler gave his first speech of the Lippe campaign. The icy roads meant he reached the small town of Bösingfeld two hours late, but the audience was still waiting patiently in the cold marquee.

Although by now it was ten o'clock, he spoke for more than an hour to thunderous applause before travelling onwards to the regional capital at Detmold, where he gave his second speech around midnight.

By the end of a day like that Hitler was drenched in sweat, exhausted and drained; he might listlessly eat a bowl of soup before falling into bed. Success took its toll.

Yet their chances looked good. The campaign seemed tailor-made to extricate the Nazis from their current crisis. Lippe, situated northeast of the Teutoburg Forest, was the smallest of the Weimar Republic's seventeen states, making up only 0.25 per cent of the nation in terms of both population and area. A rural, Protestant region, it was particularly receptive to the Nazis' message. Large-scale industry and mining were virtually non-existent, although there were small factories producing furniture or meerschaum pipes.

Lippe was also surrounded by densely populated states, and that made it easy for the movement to bring in help – and crowds. For Hitler's initial speeches the NSDAP chartered six trains as well as buses and lorries to transport its sympathisers, and hundreds of Brownshirts arrived on bicycle; yet while the Führer spent the night at a magnificent moated castle, they sought shelter from the biting frost in barns and attics.

Still, their hustings weren't boring like those of the equally hard-working Social Democrats: they hired bands and played marches. Anybody who stood out was immediately removed from the hall.

Lastly, at the previous local elections in 1929, the National Socialists had won only a single seat out of the total twenty-one.

The only way was up.

THURSDAY 5 JANUARY

Workers' Army of Victory Marches Against Schleicher Dictatorship
More Than 100,000 in Lustgarten
– Die Rote Fahne

Hitler and Papen Versus Schleicher
– Tägliche Rundschau

The report in the *Tägliche Rundschau* dropped like a bombshell. The newspaper described the not-so-secret secret meeting between Hitler and Papen at Schröder's villa, and an account also appeared in the SPD's *Vorwärts*, never exactly pro-Schleicher. It seemed a coalition was forming in Cologne against the chancellor – or was it?

Franz von Papen saw the headlines, too. He was certain his nemesis, Schleicher, was using his connections in the press to outmanoeuvre him.

Every journalist in Berlin pounced on the story immediately. The revolving doors at the Kaiserhof hardly stopped spinning, and the switchboards couldn't cope with all the calls.

Had Schleicher and Strasser met yesterday? Such was the rumour doing the rounds at Wilhelmstrasse. Was this an anti-Hitler coalition? 'Nothing from Papen,' noted Bredow in his diary.

Abraham Plotkin was still puzzling over the demonstration. The Communists handled their meetings, he wrote, 'with an iron discipline'. Yet Florin hadn't been able to generate much enthusiasm – 'it struck me', added Plotkin, 'that he didn't particularly want to'. Nor was he sure why the Social Democrats were keeping so quiet. They still hadn't called any rallies. 'Perhaps', he mused, 'they are waiting for the others to shoot their guns.'

Exactly. Perhaps the Social Democrats were waiting. And when the time was right, they would strike.

More news on the political grapevine. Hans Zehrer, it was rumoured, had paid one of Hitler's security guards an astronomical bribe for information about the cloak-and-dagger meeting with Papen.

The year had begun rather tamely. The only bad omens were the political killings – five people had been murdered since 1 January. In Breslau a young Social Democrat had been stabbed by Nazis, and there were altercations reported between Communists and members of the NSDAP in Hamburg, Erfurt and Aachen.

For many Germans, the KPD were the real threat to society. Controlled by an aggressive new world power, the Soviet Union, they weren't afraid to use violence against the state, and this seemed significantly more threatening than the nationalist rantings of the Nazis.

A year and a half earlier, in the summer of 1931, Communists had murdered several police officers in Berlin – malicious attacks that deeply unsettled the public. Between January 1928 and the end of October 1932, eleven members of the Prussian force were killed and 1,155 injured. Eight of the dead and 870 of the wounded had been assaulted by Communists; the other three murders had never been solved.

Officially the KPD distanced itself from crimes like these, but the Chancellery was perpetually on the verge of banning the party. Doing so would also have radically adjusted the balance of majorities in the Reichstag.

Kurt von Schleicher, too, discussed this option with his staff. The only question was whether outlawing the KPD might be playing with fire. What if the Communists actually followed through on their rhetoric? There could be a general strike – maybe even a revolution.

That evening Plotkin went to the Sportpalast. This time he wanted to hear Goebbels speak, and today the atmosphere was different right from the outset. No longer so … insipid. He found a seat at the top of the gallery. Once again the rally began with a parade, which included a man and a woman dressed in black. Those were the parents of Walter Wagnitz, whispered his neighbours, the murdered member of the Hitler Youth. Onstage, a man stood up and greeted the woman. *Goebbels*, Plotkin was told.

There was a slow drumroll, then the 'March of the Dead'.

Although Plotkin had brought opera glasses, he couldn't see Goebbels' face properly. 'Dark hair, dark features, strong features, never in repose' – that much he could tell, but it was impossible 'to get a good mental image of him'. Yet Goebbels' voice was impressive, so powerful Plotkin thought it might be audible even in Madison Square Garden.

'The political truce, he started, is over. The *Kampf*, he announced, is starting all over again. [...] Schleicher, he reminded them, says that he is neither socialist nor capitalist, neither Catholic nor Protestant. The man isn't anything. He has no principles. He is ruling by force and force only.'

Plotkin felt the applause growing warmer, as though the crowd was surging closer to the stage. 'At the head of each movement there is an individual who symbolises the entire movement. Remove Hitler and you destroy the whole Nazi movement.'

Goebbels was hitting his stride. He must have sensed what Plotkin sensed: the packed arena was enthralled. Endless, roaring *heils*.

'We will go on even if it takes a century. We have the strength of the old Romans who year after year fought their battles against Carthage until Carthage was destroyed. We will not stop working day and night until our battle is won. To that end we consecrate our lives.'

The storm of hails greeting this declaration of war swept the hall. I looked down on a mass of cheering men and women whose hands were in the air, and the lights danced before my eyes with the intensity of the excitement.

Goebbels continued to fan the flames. 'And who is responsible for the death of young Wagnitz?' he demanded. 'Who? Who? None other than the Jews. None but the Jews. Read their press. You will [find] nothing in it about the murder. Why? When anyone has nothing to say it means they have something they want to keep to themselves.'

The atmosphere was 'charged with electricity,' wrote Plotkin. 'Men and women were cheering themselves hoarse,' while others rained curses on the Jews.

For a moment Plotkin thought Goebbels would lose control and the rabble might splinter into different, contentious groups, but he swiftly brought them back into the palm of his hand. His voice crescendoed. 'The Jews have dominated our national life, our national economy, newspapers and our politics until we no longer have a German people. We have a nation of slaves dominated by a handful of Jews. It is to rescue Germany from the hands of the Jews that the National Socialist Party was organised, and until we do we are slaves!'

Plotkin was stunned. He could scarcely believe how callously Goebbels had exploited the boy's death to whip up the crowd. How he'd painted the Jews as the culprits. This, he realised, was the true mood of a Nazi rally. The sheer intensity of the emotion, the hatred at its root – such a movement could brook no patience nor any obstacle to its momentum. If it didn't sweep to power soon, it would collapse.

And if it did? Hatred would reign.

FRIDAY 6 JANUARY

The purpose of the discussion was presumably to ensure that Herr Papen would use his good relationship with the president and his son to advocate for a Hitler chancellorship, in return for which Herr von Papen will probably be given a cabinet post of some kind.

– *Tägliche Rundschau*

After reading the papers, Abraham Plotkin asked around and discovered a certain exhilaration on the left. Trade unionists and Social Democrats alike were already deriding the prospect of an alliance between Hitler and Papen. Didn't the Nazis make it clear what they thought of Papen while he was chancellor?

On the other hand, he was also told that prominent figures within heavy industry were dissatisfied; they found Schleicher's worker-orientated policies disconcerting.

Speculation was becoming increasingly wild, the pressure accordingly high. Papen and Hitler, who was still in Lippe, issued a joint statement: 'Contrary to the incorrect assumptions widely disseminated in the press about the meeting between Adolf Hitler and former Chancellor v. Papen, the undersigned can confirm that their conversation dealt solely with the possibility of a broad national united front, and that their views on the current cabinet were not mentioned during this general conversation.'

Was anybody going to believe that?

The gardens at Wilhelmstrasse were hibernating, the branches bare of leaves. Yet there were still signs of life. Kurt von Schleicher ushered a visitor through the back entrance of the Chancellery: Gregor Strasser.

Afterwards, Hindenburg spoke approvingly of Hitler's former right-hand man.

We can be sure their meeting came to Hitler's attention.

That afternoon the German chancellor called on the French ambassador for tea and an informal chat. The two men, who liked as well as respected each other, sketched out a spectacular future in a more peaceful world, one where 'Germany and France worked together step by step to build European economic contentment and accord'. Only a few days earlier, the two countries had resolved several contentious issues regarding trade and industrial policy, but it was still an audacious vision in an era when the Treaty of Versailles remained hotly disputed, farmers were demanding tariffs and the Nazis were out and on the march.

Naturally their discussion turned to the events of the past few days. Hindenburg, said Schleicher, had been 'deeply shocked' by the Hitler–Papen encounter. Papen, he continued, had made a serious mistake but not a malicious one. 'He's thoughtless,' said the chancellor. 'He probably imagined he'd pull off a masterstroke and serve us Hitler on a platter. As if Hitler hasn't shown us often enough already that he can't be trusted! Papen's embarrassed now. He's worried what we'll accuse him of. I'm not going to scold him. I'll simply say, "Well, my little Fränzchen, you've put your foot in it again."'

The Social Democrats were making their move. Otto Braun, the de jure Prime Minister of Prussia, had a proposal for Kurt von Schleicher.

If Schleicher could get President Hindenburg to reinstate his cabinet in Prussia, he would do his best to get the Reichstag and the Prussian assembly dissolved. Then Schleicher could rule by emergency decree – with Braun's support and using his influence with the Social Democrats. They could tackle the Nazis together.

It was an attractive offer, perhaps Schleicher's only chance to ally himself with the SPD. Yet he was still hoping Strasser would cooperate.

Schleicher was non-committal.

At almost exactly the same moment, other influential Social Democrats were mobilising. Rudolf Breitscheid, head of the SPD parliamentary group in the Reichstag, had asked Theodor Leipart to report to the party executive.

The Social Democrats hadn't failed to notice Leipart's apparent willingness to engage with Schleicher, and they were alarmed. Now they were hauling Leipart in to account for himself. For hours. How could he? What was he thinking? They had to stick together – on and on and on.

At last, Leipart cracked. From now on he would give Schleicher's cabinet a scrupulously wide berth.

If only the left had worked together. But with Ernst Thälmann at the head of the KPD, it was unthinkable. During the last presidential election, in spring 1932, he had run against Hindenburg and Hitler. 'A vote for Hindenburg is a vote for Hitler,' he'd insisted at the time. 'A vote for Hitler is a vote for war!' Clairvoyance, perhaps? Or a Stalinist smear campaign?

Originally from Hamburg, in Berlin Thälmann had been living with a family called the Kowalskis in Charlottenburg, at Bismarckstrasse 24, where he was registered with the police. Now he was moving to stay with another family, the Kluczynskis, at Lützower Strasse 9, which was also in Charlottenburg. The move was no secret; he regularly received visitors there.

As the highest-ranking German Communist, Thälmann was the voice of the movement.

Many Germans were afraid of the Communists. Some felt an almost physical distaste; Franz von Papen, for instance. The party had been gaining ground at national elections year on year, swelling from 4.5 million to 6.9 million votes between 1930 and 1932. A sixth of the ballot had gone to the KPD at the most recent election.

The Communists preached revolution. In flyers, at rallies, in the *Rote Fahne* – day in and day out. In Germany's regional legislatures, too. Only recently, a Communist MP by the name of Franz Böning had stood up in the Bavarian State Assembly and proclaimed: 'We Communists know that this state can only be toppled by force of arms. The workers can rest easy knowing that, come crunch time, they will have the weapons to fight these battles.'

This was the rhetoric of their politicians. It was ultra-leftist Ernst Thälmann's rhetoric, too.

At the age of ten he'd witnessed the Hamburg dockworkers' strike of 1896–7. In school he'd read Schiller's *William Tell*, which he once wrote had banished 'all my previous doubts at a single stroke' and 'allowed my ideas to develop much more freely and confidently towards Socialism, without me knowing what Socialism really meant or what it could do'.

Later, long before the war, Thälmann served in the Ninth Artillery Regiment in Cologne, but was thrown out as a 'Vaterlandsloser Geselle'. A derogatory term for a person 'without a Fatherland' – somebody unpatriotic – it was often used for Communists and other left-leaning Germans. He then worked as a coal trimmer on the *Amerika*, doing the voyage between Hamburg and New York three times. On 13 January 1915, by which time he already had his trademark bald patch and protruding ears, he got married, and was conscripted the very next day.

His wife, Rosa, ironed clothes at a laundry where Thälmann had worked as a driver. He was a man who liked a good debate. She'd never known him any other way. Ernst was a man who argued, who fought his corner, who wanted to remake the world for the working class, who would never abandon his principles.

Now, under the Weimar Republic, he was fighting on two fronts: against capitalism and against Fascism. But Thälmann was a well-schooled Marxist, who knew his dialectical materialism; he understood that capitalism had to reach a point of crisis before Communism could triumph. So it might be no bad thing if the Nazis came to power – it would shift them forward to the next phase of history, even though the Communists would initially be a target.

Thälmann did realise that. When members of the SPD and the Reichsbanner asked him in July 1931 whether his party was serious about forming a united workers' front, he had replied:

> Hitler's mob of officers and princes has stated that it wants to exterminate, hang, decapitate and break upon the wheel the Communist movement, which consists of many millions of revolutionary men and women; in view of this fact, in view of the imminent danger that Germany will become a land of the gallows and the pyre, how could we Communists not be serious about the united anti-Fascist proletarian front?

SATURDAY 7 JANUARY

Caught!
Hitler and Papen in Cahoots!
— *Vorwärts*

We have been reliably informed that part of the meeting's
purpose was to negotiate a ceasefire between the NSDAP
and the forces behind Papen. This was an effort to rebuild
the old 'Harzburg Front' on a new, broader basis.

— *Tägliche Rundschau*

At half past one in a Berlin funeral home, Nazis gathered to com-
memorate Walter Wagnitz. Among them were Joseph Goebbels and
Baldur von Schirach, head of the Hitler Youth. The boy's former unit
had kept watch over his body.

After the brief memorial service, the procession made its way to
the Luisenstädtische Cemetery. Tens of thousands of people fell in
line behind the hearse. The cavalcade took two hours. At the cemetery, they sang the first verse of the 'Horst Wessel Lied' before the
speeches, and wreathes and flowers were laid on the boy's grave. As
dusk fell, the crowd continued towards the Lustgarten.

Plotkin, meanwhile, was mingling with the spectators, watching the uniformed Nazis file past. His companion asked one of the
passers-by what the men were singing.

'I do not speak to Jews,' the woman replied.

By half past seven it was dark, and a hundred thousand people
had massed in the Lustgarten. More speeches. Plotkin found a spot on
the steps of a statue, giving him a view over the sea of hats. There was
a song for the dead. Then Joseph Goebbels took the stand.

'We know the names of the murderers,' he cried.

'The effect,' said Plotkin,

was a bombshell. From every part of the Lustgarten came cries as of madmen. Name them! Name them! He stood silent. He stood silent. When he started again his voice was loud but slow, and the same trick that he used in the Sportpalast meeting was brought into play, the repetition of the word or the phrase until it would leave an indelible print on the mind.

Standing on the raised terrace outside the palace, Goebbels continued. His words were subsequently printed in *Der Angriff*:

We raise our hearts and hands and cry: so far and no further. Our patience is at an end. The Jews are guilty, that is our accusation.

They have besmirched our honour. They take our work and our bread, they agitate for civil war. They do not want peace for Germany, but now they see a front of twelve million people marching towards them they are trembling; now the anxiety of the parasite has crept into their bones. They know Adolf Hitler is on their doorstep. They babble about division, disintegration and mutiny. This is wishful thinking.

They know we stand together, and, if we were to splinter, Judah would hold dominion.

The horde of a hundred thousand sang the 'Horst Wessel Lied':

Clear the streets
For the brown battalions
Clear the streets
For the Sturmabteilung!
Millions, full of hope, gaze upon the swastika,
The day of freedom
And of bread is dawning!

The Nazis didn't need facts, realised Plotkin. They didn't need truth to goad the mob into a rage, or to play on its emotions however they pleased. The narrow-minded crowd was easily seduced.

For the last time
The call to arms is sounded!
We stand prepared
For battle!
Hitler's banners fly on every street
The time of servitude
Is nearly at an end!

Later, when the rally was over, Plotkin watched younger members of the SA waiting for their orders 'like a bunch of schoolboys, and like a bunch of schoolboys bought hot dogs when the hot-dog men started to circulate among them'.

Sarow, the Communist suspected of killing Walter Wagnitz, was a free man. He'd been released for lack of evidence.

Joseph Goebbels' treason case was dropped, thanks to the general amnesty for political criminals. The senior prosecutor had started proceedings the previous April on the grounds of several inflammatory speeches and articles in which Goebbels called for a putsch.

SUNDAY 8 JANUARY

The games being played for power by a small number
of actors are taking increasingly peculiar forms, and it's
now abundantly clear that something must be done.
– Tägliche Rundschau

Do you remember how good butter tastes, proletarian
housewives? How long is it since you could put it on the table?
– Allgemeine Illustrierte Zeitung

Erich Sagasser, a member of the SA, died following complications
from a stab wound inflicted by a Communist the previous December. Another 'blood sacrifice' for the National Socialist movement, as
Joseph Goebbels liked to put it.

The work of young poet Mascha Kaléko wasn't exactly upbeat,
although she was usually cheerful and occasionally coquettish when
socialising with other artists at the Romanisches Café near the Kaiser
Wilhelm Memorial Church. The seed of confidence within her poetic
melancholy, however, leavened the reading experience.

Pale Days

All our days are pale and mounting
In the silence of the night
High into a greyish wall as
Stone is ever joined to stone.
All the empty hours of mourning
Shut themselves inside the soul.

Dreams come and dissolve away like
Ghosts that melt when daylight breaks.
In us the eternal timid
Grasping after coloured shards.
In the shadow of the pale days
We live because we do not die.

On the front page of the *Allgemeine Illustrierte Zeitung* was a photograph of two SA men duelling. 'SA Practising Assaults' ran the caption. 'All fun and games: the Brownshirts training with revolvers, rubber truncheons, spades and knives in a suburb of Berlin.'

The British author Christopher Isherwood had been living in Berlin since 1929, most recently at Nollendorfstrasse 17, not far from the Cosy Corner and other gay bars popular with him and his friends. Since November he'd been sleeping in the large front room, which was brighter during the winter months and easier to heat. He was only thirty-two, but the season affected him badly. 'I get uglier and more shrivelled every day. My hair is scurfy and drops out, my teeth are bad, my breath smells. However, I do see that it's absolutely necessary for me to stay on here at present. The last part of my novel requires a lot more research to document it.'

Like many other good writers, he drew closely on reality to invent a believable world. Isherwood took long walks through the city, calling it a 'dream', a place where the police were tolerant, the people cosmopolitan and the international nightlife incomparably risqué. It was a fascinating city – and an occasionally mournful one.

'The real heart of Berlin,' wrote Isherwood,

is a small damp black wood – the Tiergarten. At this time of the year, the cold begins to drive the peasant boys out of their tiny unprotected villages into the city, to look for food, and work. But the city, which glowed so brightly and invitingly in the night sky above the plains, is cold and cruel and dead. Its warmth is an illusion, a mirage of the winter desert. It will not receive these boys. It has nothing to give. The cold drives them out of its streets, into the wood which is its cruel heart. And there they cower on benches, to starve and freeze, and dream of their far-away cottage stoves.

Joseph Goebbels was having trouble sleeping. His wife's condition was still very unstable. 'This terrible agony and fear,' he confided in his diary. 'It's driving me to despair.'

Hitler had just telephoned; he, too, was worried about Magda. Tomorrow, he said, he and Goebbels ought to drive up to Berlin for a visit. 'I'm so grateful to him,' Goebbels wrote.

MONDAY 9 JANUARY

Papen Visits Schleicher
Talk Lasts Several Hours
– *Vossische Zeitung*

Franz von Papen was back in Berlin, and the first thing he did was visit Schleicher. Was he feeling chastened, now that he'd been caught out? Did he want to make amends? In any case, their conversation lasted hours. Papen told the chancellor that he'd been hashing out the terms under which the Führer would support Schleicher's government. Schleicher listened attentively. Was he suspicious? No more than usual. He'd known Papen for a long time – little Fränzchen would never try to hoodwink him. He didn't have the gumption.

Papen shared some intriguing information. Apparently Hitler no longer believed he would ever be chancellor. Instead, he had his eye on two cabinet posts: Defence Minister and Interior Minister, which he would occupy simultaneously.

Excellent news. Giving a Nazi command of both the police and the military was a risible notion, obviously, but it was encouraging to hear that Hitler was losing patience at long last.

Joseph Goebbels heard a different version. Papen, said Hitler, had put forward the offer unprompted: if the Führer agreed to let Papen be chancellor, he was welcome to take the two most important ministerial posts.

Hitler also described how 'sharply' Papen was opposed to Schleicher. He had the old man's ear; he lived in the same building as Hindenburg. Schleicher, noted Goebbels gleefully, was on his last legs. Best of all, he didn't have carte blanche to dissolve Parliament – Papen had confirmed it.

All this was great news, but Goebbels was still anxious. The Lippe election *had* to go well.

After his visit to Schleicher, Papen crossed the few metres to the Chancellery and went to see the president. He knew the way; he knew the building staff.

Hindenburg – eyes tired, face furrowed – was palpably on edge. After all, hadn't he been 'deeply shocked' to learn about the Papen–Hitler meeting, as Schleicher had told the French ambassador?

Yet Papen wasn't given a dressing-down. In fact, Hindenburg seemed open to what he had to say.

Schleicher, said the president, had asked him to stop seeing Papen alone. But he'd been convinced from the start that Schleicher's negative account of Papen's behaviour was wrong.

Hitler, reported Papen, had backed down: he was no longer demanding a presidential cabinet and full plenary powers. For the first time, the Führer had agreed to join a conservative coalition.

Good, good.

Paul von Hindenburg bowed towards Otto Meissner, who was also in the room. In that case they would need a new chancellor, said the president. And there was only one man for the job: Franz von Papen.

If it hadn't been clear before, it was now. The president and the former chancellor were ganging up on the chancellor currently in office. This was a conspiracy. So – how to proceed?

First, Papen wanted to keep the lines of communication open with Hitler. Personally, and in strict confidence.

Hindenburg agreed.

Then he turned to Meissner: not a word to Schleicher that he'd given his approval!

Dramatic reports were reaching Germany about an attempted anarchist coup in Barcelona and Catalonia. There was apparently fierce fighting at a train station in the city. No news yet on the number of dead or wounded.

In London, actress Elisabeth Bergner and director Paul Czinner were getting married. Both originally from Austria-Hungary, they had just filmed *Dreaming Lips* together, and were popular with audiences and critics alike. Until recently Bergner had been living in Berlin, at Faradayweg 15 in Dahlem, but the political situation in Germany had grown too precarious. She wanted a fresh start. Somewhere, she hoped, where it wouldn't matter that she was Jewish.

TUESDAY 10 JANUARY

A conversation lasting an hour and a half took
place on Monday between General von Schleicher
and Herr von Papen, at Papen's request.
In this conversation, Papen was at pains to establish his loyalty.
– Tägliche Rundschau

The Leader of the World Proletariat Speaks
Comrade Stalin Addresses Bolshevik General Staff:
'The entire capitalist world is pregnant with
the proletarian revolution – the party of Lenin
remains undaunted by any difficulties!'
– Die Rote Fahne

News hit Lippe that Strasser was gaining popularity in Hamburg. The
information unnerved the Nazis still on the campaign trail, although
Hitler himself was already elsewhere. Berlin had summoned him.
Early that morning he'd taken the night train from Bielefeld to the
capital – his first visit of 1933.

Chancellor Schleicher thought he had the upper hand. In a conversation with Josef Reiner at Ullstein, the company that published the
Vossische Zeitung, he described Hitler as 'frankly in a state of despair',
and said he could feel 'the party crumbling beneath him without it
ever having achieved any position of authority'. Hitler would never
wash with the president, because for Hindenburg the Führer was
'almost as bad as a Communist'.

Did he really believe that? Or was his optimism forced, mere whis-
tling in the dark? Time was running out for the chancellor to bring
the Nazis into the fold, yet that was the task before him. Soon the

Reichstag would reconvene, and they were bound to pass a motion of no confidence. He would have to see Hindenburg beforehand and ask for the authority to dissolve Parliament – and that would be the moment of truth. Would the president stand behind his chancellor?

So far, admittedly, Hitler had kept his nerve. But what if Schleicher struck where he was most vulnerable?

As usual, the chancellor had a plan. Over the coming days he would leak the news that he was 'underpinning' his cabinet by appointing three new ministers: first, Adam Stegerwald, a Centre Party MP and leading figure in the Christian Trade Union Movement; second – a political bombshell – Alfred Hugenberg, head of the DNVP, who would be offered a post as Minister for Agriculture and the Economy.

The third man on Schleicher's list would be made Vice-Chancellor and Minister of the Interior, as well as Prime Minister of Prussia. His name was Gregor Strasser.

It was a bluff.

Schleicher had come to no agreement with Hugenberg, nor with Stegerwald – and Strasser was an iron still very much in the fire.

The success of any bluff depends on its target's credulity. This one was directed primarily at one man: Adolf Hitler.

Schleicher let it be known that his door was always open to the Führer.

What would Hitler's next move be? How would he react?

As it turned out, he wouldn't.

No phone call. No visit. Not even a letter.

The Führer was silent.

A press conference at the Chancellery. What was the state of the president's relationship with the chancellor? Was it true that Hindenburg's relationship with Schleicher was less close than the one he'd had with Papen?

It was true, replied a press officer, but it was also clear 'that Schleicher would absolutely be given authority to dissolve Parliament'.

So. That meant the chancellor didn't have presidential authority to defend himself against a vote of no confidence.

Or didn't *yet*? That was the question.

Less than a week after their not-so-covert conversation in Cologne, Papen and Hitler met for a second time – again under the strictest secrecy. This time it took place in Berlin, in the elegant neighbourhood of Dahlem, formerly home to Elisabeth Bergner and Paul Czinner. Lentzeallee 7–9 was barely three kilometres from Faradayweg.

Joachim and Annelies von Ribbentrop, hosting the evening, had their driver collect Papen around nine o'clock. All the servants bar two trusted retainers had been given the night off. At ten, a car drew up by the side of the house, and Hitler slipped in through his usual garden entrance. In Joachim von Ribbentrop's study, Papen and Hitler talked late into the night.

WEDNESDAY 11 JANUARY

Onward, Red Army of Freedom
The World Is Listening!
Stalin Heralds Victory for Socialism
– Die Rote Fahne

Hitler's Berlin Detour
No Meeting with Chancellor
– Vossische Zeitung

Commissioner Gereke was explaining his job-creation scheme to the Reichstag Social Committee. Five hundred million marks were being made available from public funds to improve infrastructure, with the contracts being awarded primarily to private companies. 'We've already had more requests come in than can be satisfied under the scheme,' he assured them.

If there was one person in the room Schleicher pinned his hopes on, it was Gereke. His contacts on the right as well as with the unions might prove very helpful. If he managed to reduce unemployment, if Germans had more money again, more to eat, if they were more content – that would be a triumph for Kurt von Schleicher. Problem was, it had to happen quickly.

Gereke knew that, and he was doing everything he could. Before Christmas, Gereke had written a cabinet bill, Schleicher had endorsed it and Hindenburg had waved it through; now the scheme was up and running. Many of the projects proposed were approved without much checking – building new roads, repairing bridges, laying drains. Construction was beginning across the country; the unemployed were being paid wages collectively agreed.

Since the beginning of December, Gereke had been working sixteen- or seventeen-hour days. He had to build a whole department from scratch, although he was, at least, given carte blanche to poach hard-working, trustworthy civil servants from other ministries, whom the chancellor promptly transferred across with minimal red tape. Every morning at seven o'clock he was picked up and driven to Wilhelmstrasse, usually not returning until after midnight.

It was a lot to expect from anybody. Schleicher once grinned, 'That's what I like to see! You're keeping two drivers, two personal aides and twice the number of typists in employment.'

The chancellor needed men like that.

The Prussian Coup of 20 July 1932, when the regional assembly had been deposed by the state, had angered Social Democrats and leftist trade unions alike, but Otto Braun's offer was still on the table. The chancellor confided to Gereke that he'd be happy to reverse the emergency decrees, bringing Leipart and the unions on side – it was the president, he said, who refused to play ball.

It was long since dark by half past five, when a group of politicians convened for a tense meeting chaired by Hindenburg himself. Schleicher was in the room, as were the Minister for Food and Agriculture and the Economics Minister. So were representatives of the National Rural League.

The National Rural League – the *Reichslandbund*. You'd be hard pressed to find a more influential group of lobbyists in the whole Weimar Republic. The President of the League had even been appointed Minister for Food and Agriculture under Brüning two years earlier, thanks to pressure from Hindenburg. As minister he'd made little pretence of neutrality, shamelessly pushing through tariffs on foreign goods. The league was an association of wealthy landowners, agrarian businessmen and East Prussian Junkers, and they had little time for the supposed merits of democracy. At the last presidential elections they'd sided with Hitler, while Hindenburg had sided with the Social Democrats; by now, various Nazis had assumed key positions within the league. At its head – and present at the meeting – was Eberhard Graf von Kalckreuth, a fifty-one-year-old landowner and aristocrat who had signed the petition submitted to Hindenburg in November, in which numerous businessmen had backed Hitler as chancellor. Hindenburg thought very highly of Kalckreuth.

The president evidently bore the league no ill-will. He himself was from landowning stock; could it be he was acting in self-interest? Surely not.

Kalckreuth and the other agriculturalists were complaining. Hadn't Schleicher agreed to continue Papen's policies? To introduce tariffs, trade barriers and all sorts of other measures to make importing cheap food harder? And what about agricultural enterprises that went bankrupt – under Papen, foreclosures had been delayed. Schleicher had to do the same!

Well, said Schleicher, there were several measures in the pipeline, but even creditors were entitled to protection.

Eventually the president waded in, instructing Schleicher to confer with the relevant minsters. He expected a solution on his desk the very next day.

It was an insult – not to mention a violation of the constitution. Hindenburg was overstepping his authority, there was no doubt about that. Article 56 of the constitution averred that 'the Chancellor of the Reich determines the overall direction of government policy'.

Before they got up from the table, one of the representatives from the league pressed a sheet of paper into Schleicher's hand. It was a resolution they had also sent to the media. The accusation it contained was devastating: Schleicher, they claimed, was pursuing a policy of agrarian Bolshevism.

The meeting ended in a row. Schleicher was aghast.

He swiftly issued his own statement. As a result of this 'unfounded demagogic attack' and 'disloyal conduct', the government would cease to negotiate with representatives of the National Rural League.

Hindenburg had approved Schleicher's statement. He, too, declared himself outraged by the landowners' underhanded methods.

THURSDAY 12 JANUARY

Unemployment Still Soaring
More Than 400,000 Left Jobless in December
And Yet – More Reckless Spin and 'Silver Lining' Politics
– *Völkischer Beobachter*

Soviets Changing the Face of the Earth
Stalin's Speech at Conclusion of First Five Year Plan
– *Die Rote Fahne*

Another commotion at the Ribbentrops' villa. Hitler and Papen were coming to lunch – precautions must be taken, absolute secrecy ensured. It was possible this meeting would alter the course of German politics. If so, it could hardly fail to benefit the host's future career.

Papen arrived as agreed; Ribbentrop had known him to be reliable ever since their days in the military, when both officers had served on assignment in the Ottoman Empire. But then a message arrived: Hitler sent his apologies. The Führer was still in Lippe.

They had lunch anyway, of course. As they ate, Papen and the Ribbentrops discussed the upcoming election, although it didn't really interest Papen. He hadn't come to twiddle his thumbs and eat soup with his ambitious host while the others were out pulling strings, hatching plans and making good use of their time.

More and more tenants in working-class areas of Berlin were going on strike. There were no exact figures, but it must have amounted to several thousand citywide.

The residents of Ackerstrasse 132 had decided to stop paying rent as of 1 January. Abraham Plotkin didn't realise it, but this Thursday he was visiting Berlin's most notorious tenement complex: Meyer's Hof in Wedding. Journalists loved visiting these buildings, describing holes in the cobbled courtyards so big you could trip and break your leg, the words 'We want to live like people!' scrawled on one of the bare walls, rotting window frames, leaking toilets, roofs that didn't keep the rain out. 'In Ackerstrasse, birth is a curse,' the *Weltbühne* columnist Kurt Tucholsky had recently observed.

The complex at 132 included the street-facing block and five blocks behind, arranged around courtyards. At one point, up to 2,100 residents had been packed in like sardines. The complex had been built in the 1870s, and desperate homeless people had started squatting in it before it was even finished. Small businesses later sprang up in the courtyards: printers, roofers, cobblers. In 1929 the *Berliner Morgenpost* had calculated that more than a thousand couples had been married there and five hundred children born, while 150 people had died at the complex.

Access to Meyer's Hof was through a vaulted gateway, where a guardsman appointed by the strikers only let Plotkin through because he knew the password: 'Turmarkin'.

Alexander Turmarkin was the name of the most hated man at Meyer's Hof: the new Russian owner, who invested absolutely nothing in building maintenance.

Plotkin showed his passport. An American? He was ushered inside.

The tall blocks were like narrow gorges, dark and chilly. Nearly every window had the red flag of the Communists flying. The complex dated from before the city had a modern water supply, which probably explained the sludge leaking from the pipes. A tenant on the second floor showed Plotkin a bottle of muddy water filled from the tap. 'It is dirt from the pipes,' he said, which turned the water rusty and red-brown.

Today the complex housed 355 families – 1,301 people in all.

'You have the exact figure right at your fingertips?' asked Plotkin.

'Sure,' was the answer. 'We have to. Now and then the police arrest one of us, and that is the way we have a daily check-up if there is anyone missing.'

Plotkin was then given a tour of the basement, where people were also living. He met one of them, a woman called Martha, whose room was 'freshly painted, although the dampness has already created whitish splotches through the green paint'. Plotkin judged her no older than forty, but her face was 'heavy with bloat' and her hands were calloused and hard. Plotkin was fascinated. He asked the woman what she did for work.

'I am not working. There is no work.'

Martha had been paying 18 marks a month for her apartment, which she called a 'hole'. She almost cried as she told him this. Twelve marks on top of that for heating and light – meanwhile, she received 36 per month from the local authority.

'This leaves me 6 marks a month for food!'

Plotkin took her hand and turned it palm up; he felt her trembling, but noted in surprise that the hand itself was hard and firm. 'As if suffering had steeled it with a purpose,' he thought.

The Italian football club AS Roma signed Argentinian striker and World Cup veteran Alejandro Scopelli, paying an estimated transfer fee of 80,000 marks to Scopelli's former club, Estudiantes de La Plata.

Would this soon be common practice in Germany, too? For years the German Football Association had fought the professionalisation of the sport, even banning fourteen FC Schalke 04 players in 1930 because they had charged 10 marks' expenses per match instead of the permitted 5.

A few weeks earlier, however, in October, the National Conference of the Football Association had approved a 'Reichsliga' that would allow professional players: their top clubs had to be able to compete on the world stage.

At NSDAP headquarters in Lippe, news arrived that President Hindenburg had recently met with Gregor Strasser. So Schleicher had been serious. Writing in his diary, Joseph Goebbels noted: 'Strasser stirring the pot. Met with Hindenburg ...! That's what I call a traitor. I've always seen through him. Hitler is very upset.'

Sunday was the election. The battle for Lippe was still raging, and it was uphill work. Hitler was occasionally dipping into his royalties from *Mein Kampf* to fund the campaign, something he'd otherwise been loath to do. Now he had little choice. For one event an organiser had asked Otto Dietrich to lend him money to cover the advance on renting the hall, while at another a bailiff had shown up and confiscated the night's takings.

The Executive Committee of the National Rural League was still gunning for Schleicher. They broadcast their deep dissatisfaction with his administration, claiming it was 'utterly blind to the miserable condition of German agriculture'.

In an open letter, the league asked Paul von Hindenburg for help. There had been no breach of trust, they argued – on the contrary, it was explicitly the league's duty to lobby on behalf of struggling farmers. Word on the presidential grapevine was that Hindenburg agreed.

It looked like Schleicher had bitten off more than he could chew.

Reinhold Quaatz was still keeping his ear to the ground. He'd heard from Wilhelm von Gayl, former Interior Minister, that Schleicher's fall ought not to be forced – as though his fall was a done deal. 'The egg's been cracked,' said Gayl, referring to the relationship between Schleicher and Hindenburg. Quaatz noted with some satisfaction that the parties loyal to the Republic were getting nervy. That said, Gayl didn't much like Schleicher – the chancellor had booted him out of the cabinet only a few weeks earlier, replacing him with Franz Bracht.

A local newspaper in Lippe printed the resignation letter of a doctor and long-serving regional party leader with the NSDAP. In it the man called the senior leaders 'little political charlatans, Cagliostros, sorcerers' apprentices and windbags' and claimed the organisation was 'rife with sycophants'. Local branches, he said, were constantly poaching employees from each other. He finished his letter with a flourish: 'One cannot fight the battle for freedom with the souls of slaves.'

Oskar von Hindenburg – the president's son, adjutant, adviser and co-occupant – was still a useful source of information. Gereke, who'd got to know him well during the previous year's elections, heard from Oskar that Schleicher still hadn't been granted the authority to dissolve the Reichstag – and he never would be.

In other words, he would be hopelessly vulnerable to his political opponents' attacks. They could unseat him if they chose to.

It was true Schleicher had once been his friend, added Oskar. But now he despised the man.

What had happened between them? Oskar didn't specify.

That evening at the Kammerspiele, a theatre at Schumannstrasse 13, the 'Ensemble of Out-of-Work Actors' was putting on a comedy by the German writer Joachim Ringelnatz. The title of the play was *The Bottle and Its Travels*.

FRIDAY 13 JANUARY

Minister for Food and Agriculture Must Go
Rural League Demands
— *Vossische Zeitung*

Brownshirt Terror Benefitting Wealthy
Industrialists and Agriculturalists
United Front against Plundering by Fascist
Dictatorship and Its Henchmen
— *Die Rote Fahne*

The American diplomats in Berlin had heeded Washington's sledge-hammer hints to send more analyses back to HQ, but Christmas had been a peaceful period for the embassy. The political calm gave them time to teach their younger staff the ropes – and everybody's allowed a day or two off.

Ambassador Sackett was still missing Chancellor Brüning, but since Herbert Hoover's recent electoral defeat in the USA he'd been concentrating on preparations for the World Economic Conference in Geneva. Friday saw him back in Switzerland. The conference was due to take place in April or May, with the aim of boosting international trade. If only the new president, Roosevelt, would stop stalling!

German domestic politics? Nothing much was currently happening in Germany – that was the diplomats' assessment. True, there'd been that meeting between Papen and Hitler on 4 January. The papers had been all over it. At the US embassy, however, the general consensus was that it must have been prompted by the Nazis' dwindling funds. The party was still spiralling into debt – they'd now hit 12 million marks, sources suggested – and the NSDAP's creditors were probably pressuring the Führer to join the government at last. This was most likely all Papen had conveyed.

Nothing very exciting, then. Nevertheless, George Gordon, a high-ranking member of Sackett's diplomatic corps, conveyed news of the meeting to Washington on 13 January, nine days after it had taken place. If the gentlemen in the White House wanted proof that the embassy was keeping busy, then proof they would get.

The Führer, still in Lippe, had another piece of bad news: there was trouble brewing in the Franconian branch of the NSDAP. Wilhelm Ferdinand Stegmann, an MP and senior officer in the SA, would have to resign his seat in the Reichstag – Hitler had already personally instructed he be stripped of his rank in the Brownshirts. Stegmann was embroiled in an ongoing dispute with Julius Streicher, the Franconian Gauleiter, whom he believed was withholding money that rightfully belonged to the SA.

Streicher's lawyers painted a different picture. And they did so publicly. Stegmann had already received 6,000 marks, and he'd still produced no evidence that he'd used the money for SA purposes, as he claimed.

Stegmann said he'd given 1,500 marks to the Lower Franconian SA, but the money wasn't there. It was also common knowledge that he'd accrued massive personal debts by renting a country estate he couldn't afford.

All told, it was an unpleasant business.

Abraham Plotkin was still obsessively gathering statistics. He wanted to know everything, understand everything; he wrote everything down. Maybe, he thought, he could sell his account to the newspapers when he got home.

He went to see Dr Haertel, head of the Berlin employment office, who had agreed to explain the thorny concept of unemployment insurance – Plotkin didn't understand it, and he found the literature on the topic 'as muddy as the waters of the Mississippi'.

In recent years, said Haertel, unemployment insurance and

emergency welfare programmes had been repeatedly slashed. Claimants now received roughly a third less than in 1927, simply because there was so much more demand. They also had to have worked longer to be eligible.

Haertel seemed worried but wouldn't offer any open criticism – a typical German civil servant. In parting he gave Plotkin a set of blank forms, 'in the hope, I suppose, that eventually we will have use for them in America'.

Edgar Ansel Mowrer had recently published his book *Germany Puts the Clock Back*, and he was now in the running for a Pulitzer Prize. In January he was named President of the Foreign Press Association in Berlin, where he'd been living for several years with his wife, Lilian Thomson, and their daughter, Diana.

Three weeks after their last meeting, Mowrer once more bumped into Hjalmar Schacht, and he enquired how things had gone with Hitler in Munich.

'Brilliantly,' answered Schacht. 'I've got that man right in my pocket.'

Mowrer was aghast. 'From that moment,' he observed dryly in his memoirs, 'I expected the worst.' Germany was a country he knew well. He would often ride along with the Berlin police in their armoured vehicles – going to 'the front', as Lilian put it – to report on Nazi attacks on Jews and foreigners, visiting the cafés and beer halls where brown-shirted thugs hung swastika flags.

On one occasion, Mowrer asked one of them what he had against the Jews.

'Jews are not people like the rest of us,' came the reply.

Mowrer persisted, wondering whether the young man was thinking for himself or echoing the party line.

'We are sick of thinking,' said the man. 'Thinking gets you nowhere. The Führer himself says true Nazis think with their blood.'

One day not long afterwards, Mowrer's daughter came home from school and asked her mother: 'Mutti, am I a Jew or a Christian?'

Apparently they'd been discussing the issue in class. Her mother tried to explain that faith was personal.

'It isn't good to be a Jew,' her daughter had decided.

Alfred Hugenberg and the DNVP favoured a dramatic increase in the authority afforded to the president. This was why they'd supported Chancellor Papen in the autumn, and why the Nazis had launched a vicious smear campaign against them at the previous elections, causing a scuffle between the two right-wing parties. Giving those swastika-waving ruffians the responsibility of government? Giving them command of the police and the military? For the DNVP it was unthinkable.

Hugenberg went first to Hindenburg and then to Schleicher. During their conversation, the chancellor raised the idea of giving Hugenberg two ministerial posts in his cabinet: Agriculture and the Economy. A tempting offer. In Hugenberg's opinion there was only one person in Germany competent to undertake those roles: Alfred Hugenberg. Still, he insisted, he would only join the cabinet if the government adopted a radically authoritarian new course, bypassing the Reichstag for a whole year.

Schleicher refused. The cost was too high. Hugenberg's industry-friendly tack would isolate him politically, because both the Strasser wing of the NSDAP as well as the SDP and the unions would fight them tooth and nail.

He'd come to the end of the road with the DNVP.

Erich Marcks – a government press officer – had invited journalists to an informal dinner at the Chancellery that evening. Schleicher turned up early, in civilian dress, which no longer surprised anybody. It had been a long time since the General had worn his uniform. He was looking pale and thinner than before taking office. His cheeks were sunken. After dinner the group withdrew to an adjoining room for an informal chat. Josef Reiner, who was supposed to be writing a report on the evening, was among the journalists present.

Schleicher had switched his charm to full-beam. His tone was comradely. He was banking on the journalists' promises to keep this part of the evening off the record, and as they leapt from topic to topic he was happy to follow. Indeed, he seemed hugely optimistic.

How was he dealing with the National Socialists? 'I'll soon bring them into line,' he assured the reporters. 'They'll be eating out of the palm of my hand.' Schleicher smiled, giving a dismissive wave. He would disabuse the Nazis of their 'exaggerated messianic faith', he said, declaring that 'Hitler shrinks from the responsibility of government'. The Führer saw the word 'national' as interchangeable with 'National Socialist', and if he were Defence Minister he would want to turn 'the independent national army into a National Socialist force'.

Schleicher talked and talked. Rarely were journalists granted such an insight into his reasoning. Hitler had told Papen, confided the chancellor, that as Defence Minister he would start by visiting every base in the country, speaking to officers, non-commissioned officers and other ranks separately. This proved that Hitler had no understanding of how soldiers thought, argued Schleicher. All that speechifying and lobbying was anathema to the military mind.

Why was Papen no longer chancellor? The question prompted a tirade about Papen's 'romantic figures of speech', before Schleicher outlined what he called the 'dangerous situation' at the end of November. It had developed into a 'positive psychosis against Papen'; if he 'hadn't been willing to accept the chancellorship then three days later the military would have been out on the streets with machine guns'.

Strong words. Schleicher wasn't pulling any punches that night.

Of course, he wanted to get his own messages across, too. Military training was one major issue. Earlier that week he'd invited students to the Chancellery for a 'beer evening', and only the socialists had declined. It had been an enjoyable event. Schleicher said he'd sensed 'huge enthusiasm for compulsory military service as well as more generally for fitness and training among young people and for military camps'.

By 'military camps' Schleicher meant a training camp designed to prepare young people for military service. It was not a term he could have used in public – the issue was far too sensitive. But the journalists would soon see for themselves. Once they started running 'youth camps', young men currently in the Reichsbanner or the NSDAP would start signing up in droves. They were laying the foundations, explained Schleicher. The moment Germany was granted permission to rebuild its armed forces, the immediate task would be to establish a military loyal to the Republic. Then, probably as early as 1934, they would introduce compulsory military service.

Then, the big question: how was Schleicher planning to govern long-term? What was going to happen when the Reichstag reconvened?

Well, said the chancellor, in principle the work of government need not be obstructed by Parliament; and right now that was all the Reichstag was: an obstacle. Best to dissolve it and keep a steady hand on the tiller until the crisis was behind them.

It was a typical, run-of-the-mill event in the political calendar. Yet something unusual happened – something strange. Two of the chancellor's allies contradicted each other, fundamentally and completely independently. On a crucial point.

Commissioner Günther Gereke blurted out during a discussion that Schleicher would be gone within six weeks. The railways, postal service and central bank were, like the Nazis, opposed to the government's job-creation programme and took any opportunity to sabotage it. Not even the unions were on board. Meanwhile, Oskar von Hindenburg loathed Schleicher, and the old man never made a decision without consulting his son. The upshot was that the chancellor would never be granted authority to dissolve Parliament.

Had Gereke knocked back one too many glasses of wine? Was he frustrated? Or simply realistic? Whatever the reason, it was astonishing that such an important member of the cabinet would talk to journalists so candidly.

The reporters were baffled: Erich Marcks had just confirmed that the president had already given his permission.

What were they supposed to believe?

SATURDAY 14 JANUARY

On the Road to Resolution
Rural League's Attack and Ensuing Conflicts
Push Cabinet Reshuffle to the Fore
– *Tägliche Rundschau*

Schleicher Negotiating
Strasser–Hugenberg–Stegerwald Triad?
– *Vossische Zeitung*

Schleicher still knew how to work the machinery of public relations: the hints he'd dropped about an upcoming cabinet reshuffle had found their way into the newspapers as planned. The question now was how long Hitler could stay the course – how long he could dodge Schleicher and resist the conditional power being dangled before him. The man was under pressure from all sides.

January had been surprisingly mild the past couple of weeks, with temperatures remaining above zero even at night. The weather had been a blessing for Berlin's homeless and for people who couldn't afford heating, but now an icy wind was blowing in from the east, and the frost was hardening.

Hitler summoned Wilhelm Stegmann – the disgraced Franconian Brownshirts – to Lippe. Time to face the music.

Stegmann, an athletic former mercenary who stood nearly six foot seven, was a rabble-rouser who did not approve of Hitler's tactics. A member of the NSDAP since 1925, he'd put everything he had into the movement and was increasingly losing patience. He wanted to see the SA victorious on the streets and considered violence a legitimate means. Six months earlier he'd been in prison, he and two other NSDAP MPs having beaten up the journalist who had outed Ernst Röhm, the leader of the SA. How many Brownshirts still supported him in Franconia? At least a thousand. Stegmann was a provincial lord.

Although a head taller than Hitler, Stegmann had no choice but to endure the dressing-down. Dissent would not be tolerated, so on and so forth. The encounter ended in a staged reconciliation, and Stegmann issued a public statement: 'Today I went to see my Führer. I understand that he was right to rebuke me for my behaviour, so of my own accord I have placed my seat in the Reichstag at his disposal, and promised him to do my duty as a party member faithfully and obediently.'

Having said his piece, Stegmann promptly got up and left: humiliated, angry – and hell-bent on insurrection.

Christopher Isherwood was getting bored. As he wrote to a friend: 'The political situation here seems very dull. I expect there is a great deal going on behind the scenes, but one is not aware of it. Papen visits Hindenburg, Hitler visits Papen, Hitler and Papen visit Schleicher, Hugenberg visits Hindenburg and finds he's out. And so forth. There is no longer that slightly exhilarating awareness of crisis in the gestures of beggars and tram-conductors.'

Die Rote Fahne reported a shocking incident at the welfare office in Prenzlauer Berg, a district of Berlin. It had occurred the Thursday before, but the authorities had tried to keep it under wraps. A man by the name of Wilhelm Dämichen, a father of two who had lost his job with the tram company, had been found dead in the toilets. He'd hanged himself.

A reporter from *Die Rote Fahne* had investigated and found that Dämichen was married, with sons aged seventeen and nineteen. He was receiving 12.60 marks per fortnight to support his family.

Hounded by creditors, he could no longer afford to pay his electricity bill. His applications for emergency aid and clothing had been denied, although he was receiving vouchers for meat and coal. On one of the vouchers he'd written a message to his son:

> Dear Heini! Be good, the way you are now, and think of me in happier days. Always remember I wanted the best for you. Don't think badly of me.
> Your Papa.

On another, he wrote:

> Dear Heini! Try to persuade your mother not to think badly of me either.
> Farewell to you all.

Wilhelm Dämichen committed suicide on his forty-fourth birthday.

SUNDAY 15 JANUARY

HUGENBERG VISITS PRESIDENT

At lunchtime yesterday, President von Hindenburg met
with Alfred Hugenberg, the leader of the German National
People's Party. There can be no doubt their conversation
concerned the plans to expand Schleicher's cabinet.

– *Vossische Zeitung*

Today Lippe Will Be Liberated from Its November Rulers
Führer's Final Appeal / Schleicher Threatens New
Emergency Press and Terror Legislation

– *Völkischer Beobachter*

Chancellor Issues Sharp Warning
Against Rise in Sedition /
Wave of Terror Swelling

– *Tägliche Rundschau*

Christopher Isherwood was freezing. 'Here it is very cold and snow-
ing,' he grumbled. 'I am writing with a rug round my knees.'

Meanwhile, the Sportpalast was hosting an event organised by the
Kyffhäuser League, a national association of military veterans, who
were conducting their traditional celebration of the anniversary of
the German Reich, sixty-two years after Bismarck had proclaimed the
German Empire in the Hall of Mirrors at Versailles. It struck neutral
observers as a very monarchistic event.

This year Paul von Hindenburg attended in person instead of sending Otto Meissner to represent him: one of his rare public appearances.

The president was the Honorary Chairman of the League, and he took this honour seriously.

Several ministers were in the audience, as were the leaders of the Stahlhelm, Theodor Duesterberg and Franz Seldte, and Franz von Papen. So was Kurt von Schleicher, of course, giving a speech in his capacity as Defence Minister.

Among the former officers and soldiers, Schleicher knew his address would fall on receptive ears, but it was also being broadcast live on the radio. He referred to the armaments restrictions on Germany as 'degrading' but added that they had now been granted equality of military rights, which was the 'most decisive characteristic of the nation's sovereignty'. Compulsory military service was the ultimate goal, but first he was planning to establish a militia.

At the end of the celebrations, the audience sang 'Das Lied der Deutschen' by August Heinrich Hoffmann von Fallersleben, the third stanza of which is now Germany's national anthem. At the Sportpalast the league included a fourth stanza, as they and various other ultra-right-wing organisations had been in the habit of doing for a few years – it had been written after the Treaty of Versaille, and wasn't officially sanctioned.

Germany, Germany above all
Now less fortunate than ever.
Only in misfortune can love
Prove itself strong and true.
So let it sound for ever more
From generation to generation:
Germany, Germany above all
Now less fortunate than ever.

On this bitingly cold Sunday, Schleicher met with the Austrian Minister of Justice, Kurt von Schuschnigg, for a private chat. He told Schuschnigg cheerily that he was negotiating a cross-party alliance involving the trade-union movement, and in doing so he hoped to build a workable political platform.

'What about Herr Hitler?' asked Schuschnigg, who was familiar with the domestic political situation.

'Herr Hitler is no longer a problem,' answered Schleicher.

Not the response Schuschnigg was expecting.

What was Schleicher doing? He was considered a shrewd politician, a man never without some outrageous ploy or ulterior motive up his sleeve. His critics often accused him of putting himself first and – despite his protestations to the contrary – the Fatherland a distant second; but never in his long career had anybody ever accused the General of naivety or political blindness.

What was he really banking on, then? What was his trump card? He must have had one – we can be sure of that. A strategist of his calibre, however, never reveals his hand until the final denouement.

At last. The Lippe election was over.

The NSDAP had come out with 39.5 per cent of the vote, winning nine out of twenty-one seats in the regional assembly. That was eight more seats than at the previous local elections in 1929, but out of the hundred thousand votes cast in Lippe they had only garnered five thousand more than at the disastrous national elections in November. Even the Social Democrats won three thousand more than last time round. All that effort – for this?

Hitler was spending the day in Weimar, where he'd summoned party functionaries from across the country. Without waiting for the results to be announced, he greeted them by proclaiming: 'The party is in the ascendant!'

NSDAP MP Hans Frank was one of the attendees. When news of the results came in, he watched as Hitler beamed like an excited child, and later he went to see the Führer in his room at the Hotel Elephant.

Lippe had caught his imagination. 'This', said Hitler, 'has been the final battle of the greatest internal political struggle in German history.' It would not be long before the last triumphant march on Berlin.

In the capital, Theodor Wolff, editor-in-chief of the *Berliner Tage-blatt*, put the situation differently. 'Returning from his heroic struggle in Lippe, all Hitler has actually brought home is a fly impaled on the tip of his sword.'

MONDAY 16 JANUARY

The Oracle of Lippe
Hitler–Goebbels Redouble Claim to Absolute Power
– *Vossische Zeitung*

There was a cabinet meeting taking place at eleven fifteen. The ministers discussed the 'political situation'. The results from Lippe were in, and the NSDAP's collapse had been prevented. Yet Schleicher ignored the election, instead unveiling his plans to 'underpin' the cabinet by gaining the support of Nazis, Centre Party members, trade unionists and other groups.

In essence, continued Schleicher, it boiled down to one question: would they ever get the National Socialists on side, or was conflict inevitable? Before making a decision he'd have to speak to Hitler one more time. 'I'm convinced that Hitler doesn't want power,' said Schleicher. 'Recently he's been hankering to become Defence Minister. Obviously this means he doesn't want power, because the president will never trust him with Defence.'

Had Schleicher really swallowed Papen's canard?

And Strasser, someone asked – did he want a role in government? 'Yes,' said Schleicher, Strasser was keen to join the cabinet, but it was doubtful whether he had many supporters left. Hugenberg, too, would have to be won over, bringing the DNVP with him.

Then Commissioner Gereke piped up. He was worried. Even with the expanded cabinet, they still wouldn't have a majority in the Reichstag.

Schleicher responded in typical fashion. Self-assured, confident. Flippant, some would have said. He recognised, said the chancellor, that a parliamentary majority would only be possible with Hitler on board. They would have to hope for a gradual U-turn in public opinion, and that would never happen unless the cabinet did its job.

He meant Gereke, of course, and the job-creation scheme. But Gereke again protested: 'We won't start seeing real results until autumn 1933.'

Schleicher, as ever, had a back-up plan. When the Reichstag reconvened, he would dissolve Parliament. Given the state of the economy, nobody was going to suggest another national election. There was no support for that idea, even among the working class. So, he concluded, we'll simply postpone the election until the autumn!

Schleicher's ministry had drafted a paper on precisely this issue, a 'presentation re: action against the Reichstag', and the chancellor was now putting word into deed. The paper sketched out an 'active government policy' that largely bypassed the constitution. One of the major contributors had been Eugen Ott, Schleicher's legal expert, who knew the constitution and its loopholes inside out.

Ott's paper was intended to buy Schleicher time – time to convince the president about his policies. It proposed dissolving Parliament but set no deadline for a new election. Schleicher would simply continue to govern, and he wouldn't have to consult any annoying MPs. This was a clear violation of the constitution, which stipulated that new elections would have to be called within two months.

What would you call this method of governance under a general if not a military dictatorship? It was exactly what Schleicher had ruled out in his radio broadcast back in December. 'One cannot sit comfortably on the point of a bayonet,' he'd said.

There were now only two options: either the cabinet expansion would succeed, or the president would grant Schleicher free rein. Such was the chancellor's plan. Was it based in reality?

Suddenly Otto Meissner, Hindenburg's eyes and ears, interjected a warning: the proposed cabinet expansion swung the balance of power towards the Reichstag and away from the president.

What was Meissner playing at? Was he trying to prevent the left from gaining ground through the SPD-allied unions, perhaps? Hindenburg had previously forced Brüning to reject the Social Democrats' tacit support – and thus a majority in Parliament.

If Schleicher could scrape together a majority, on the other hand, then he would no longer need Hindenburg. The chancellor kept his cool. He'd already discussed it with the president, he said. Surely Meissner knew that? He was usually so hawk-eyed when it came to his boss.

The various branch leaders of the NSDAP had gathered for a conference in Weimar, and Strasser was at the top of their agenda. The branch leaders – known as Gauleiter in Nazi terminology – acted largely autonomously, forming the backbone of the party's organisational structure. Until his dismissal, Strasser had been their supervisor; but Adolf Hitler was and always had been their Führer.

In December he had shocked Strasser's supporters by reorganising the structure of the party. Now he was giving a three-hour speech, in a style Goebbels dubbed 'brusque intransigence'. First, Hitler celebrated the NSDAP's triumph in Lippe, before turning his attention to the feud with Strasser and those who backed him. Faith and loyalty, those were his demands, and if there was one thing the Nazis knew how to do, it was pledge allegiance: all Strasser's allies dissociated themselves from him.

'The Strasser matter is finished,' crowed Goebbels afterwards.

In Der Deutsche, the newspaper of the Christian Trade Union movement, Adam Stegerwald announced that he would refuse to join any cabinet of which Alfred Hugenberg was a member. Had Schleicher lost the conservative unions and thus the centre ground?

Stegerwald – previously Labour Minister under Brüning – was a co-founder of the Christian Trade Unions, and Schleicher had hoped he would represent this demographic in the cabinet. He was a cornerstone of the cross-party front.

In Der Deutsche, however, he launched a virulent attack on Hugenberg – and, indirectly, Schleicher's ambition to unite disparate political movements: 'An adversarial cabinet with Hugenberg and shaped by Hugenberg would turn Schleicher's government into a second Papen cabinet, an authoritarian, oppositional cabinet that without Hugenberg's party would be at daggers drawn with the entire Reichstag.'

Was Schleicher's strategy coming down around his ears? It seemed so. He couldn't win over the Nazis, the leftist trade unions were playing hard to get and now there was this broadside from the Christian lot.

That morning the beleaguered chancellor had a visit from Ludwig Kaas. He'd come to convey Stegerwald's message in person, and the two men ended up talking for hours.

Even a seasoned political veteran like Reinhold Quaatz was struggling to keep up with the pace of events. 'Situation developing,' he noted. 'Schleicher claims he intends to govern despite Parliament.'

How had that titbit from the cabinet meeting leaked out already?

Hitler travelled to Kassel, Hermann Göring at his side, where once again the Führer was confronted with trouble in the SA. The organisation was haemorrhaging members. Meanwhile, as Hitler and Göring addressed their fellow Nazis, a riot broke out in the street. National Socialists skirmished with Communists, the Brownshirts using spades to attack their opponents.

Pressure was building on the streets, and not just in Berlin.

TUESDAY 17 JANUARY

Schleicher! Step down!
– *Die Rote Fahne*

In this battle of competing interests, Schleicher is reaching the
heart of the fray. Industrialists and agrarians are at loggerheads,
and the country's economic policy is showing its fragility.
The general, having tried to placate all sides with a jovial
handshake, is getting nothing but declarations of war in return.
– *Die Weltbühne*, Carl von Ossietzky

National Socialist Victory in Lippe
Unstoppable Progress Despite Terror and Lies
– *Völkischer Beobachter*

Back in Berlin, Hitler met with Hugenberg at Göring's official residence. The two had never exactly hit it off. Hitler thought Hugenberg was an obstinate reactionary; Hugenberg thought Hitler was a
rabble-rousing vulgarian. His ideas were too radical, the Nazis' threats
against political opponents too alarming. Nor had he forgiven Hitler
for abandoning the Harzburg Front at the end of 1931, the right-wing,
anti-democratic alliance Hugenberg had painstakingly forged between
the DNVP, NSDAP, Stahlhelm and other extremist groups. The two
men had more differences than common ground.

At last the newspapers were allowed to print what Schleicher had told
them in confidence on 13 January: neither the parties nor the electorate, industry or trade unions would have any objection if new elections were held *after* the sixty-day period stipulated in the constitution.

Everybody had a theory. An interpretation. Schleicher, they

gasped, was trying to disenfranchise the electorate. Some commentators were even muttering about a dictatorship.

The chancellor's press office swiftly issued a denial: Schleicher had no intention whatsoever of violating the constitution.

Lutz Graf Schwerin von Krosigk became a father for the seventh time. He already had three sons and three daughters. The new arrival, a boy, was named Dedo Paul – Paul in honour of his famous godfather, Paul von Hindenburg. It wasn't quite the honour it sounds. Hindenburg was officially godfather to any seventh child from any family, whether labourer or aristocrat.

Hindenburg sent the leaders of the National Rural League a letter. His tone was cordial with no hint of rancour, the letter phrased as if from a landowner to his peers. Was he stabbing Schleicher in the back or trying to smooth his path?

There were still a few sensitive souls left in Berlin. Poet Oskar Loerke was taking a walk with another writer, Hermann Kasack, in a park near Alemannenstrasse. The landscape was covered in snow, while in Loerke's room at home, the forsythia he grew in jars had been blossoming since Christmas. 'At the tips of the sprigs green leaves are unfurling. Glories from our garden,' wrote Loerke. 'A little music nearly every day. A few little concertos by Mozart.'

So much now depended on how Schleicher's negotiations went with the DNVP. There were more pleasant conversationalists than the imperious, self-regarding Hugenberg. Quaatz didn't think there was any chance of his fellow party member reaching an 'understanding with Schleicher', adding that, 'in my opinion he has even less nerve than Papen'.

Hugenberg also told Quaatz about his recent exchange of words with Hitler. Apparently the Führer had declared: 'I must be chancellor, but I have no wish to form a party government. Schleicher I will tolerate if he gets out of my way. Marxism must be beaten down, but not by state institutions.' Moreover, Hitler had spoken very disrespectfully about the president: Hindenburg, he'd said, wasn't an independent force. His political vocabulary comprised about eighty sentences; the old man was nothing but a gramophone record.

All this seemed to have impressed Hugenberg, which alarmed Quaatz, and he warned his boss of the danger he saw in the Nazis.

It was good the DNVP had other options besides Schleicher, but Quaatz was sure of one thing: once Hitler was in the saddle, he wouldn't hesitate to crack the whip.

The Ufa-Palast am Zoo, a cinema in Charlottenburg, was playing the film *The Rebel* with Luis Trenker. The first showing began at six thirty, with the Ufa Symphony Orchestra providing a score.

The film had been released by UFA, a production company belonging to Alfred Hugenberg.

Konstantin von Neurath was hosting more than five hundred guests at the Palais Friedrich Leopold – the Foreign Office on Wilhelmstrasse simply didn't have the space for a gathering on that scale. Bella Fromm was among those invited to the soirée.

The chancellor, however, was conspicuously absent. He no longer had the time for parties. Fromm took it as a bad sign. She was relieved, at least, to see Colonel von Bredow, who explained how busy Schleicher was with countless meetings. The strain, he said, was 'almost inhuman'.

WEDNESDAY 18 JANUARY

Hitler and Hugenberg Talk
Exchange Ideas on New Alliance
— Vossische Zeitung

Outrageous Hitler Provocation!
SA Parade Outside Karl Liebknecht House Planned for Sunday
Red Berlin! To the Streets!
— Die Rote Fahne

Communist Students Attack National Socialists at University
— Völkischer Beobachter

The Reichstag Budget Committee had convened to discuss a controversial topic, one that not so long ago had cost Chancellor Brüning
the president's support: Eastern Aid, a programme that provided
state subsidies to bankrupt agricultural enterprises in East Prussia.
Hindenburg's good friends, close acquaintances and cherished neighbours all profited from it, and a group of them had even clubbed
together to buy him back his family estate and help him pay off a
portion of the debts incurred by a recent renovation. It was common
knowledge in political Berlin that Hindenburg had already interfered
in government business several times to defend the landowners'
interests.

And now Centre Party MPs were levelling a serious accusation
against the Prussian Junkers: that they had taken state funds and put
them straight into their own pockets. Millions of marks had been
siphoned off. The Centre Party backed up its accusations with detailed
financial reports about a number of prominent landowners who had
misappropriated the subsidies, including friends and relatives of the
president. Instead of paying off their creditors and investing in their

farms, they had used the funds to buy land, racehorses, expensive cars or holidays on the French Riviera. The country was in the middle of a depression!

Where had the Centre Party got its information? Who benefited from the 'Eastern Aid Scandal', as the papers were soon calling it? Who was trying to pressure Hindenburg? Was it Schleicher, perhaps, who'd instigated the political mudslinging?

His name came up, as it always did when people started playing dirty. But surely the scandal damaged the chancellor as well … Was it actually the Nazis who'd supplied those detailed reports? They could be trying to blackmail Hindenburg into appointing Hitler chancellor at last. Once again, Berlin was alive with rumours.

At noon, Hitler and Papen met again at the Ribbentrops' home in Dahlem. This time, Hitler brought Heinrich Himmler, Commander of the SS, and Ernst Röhm, his counterpart in the SA. Over lunch, the gentlemen debated how best to gain and share power.

Hitler had to be chancellor, he insisted. Especially after the victory in Lippe.

Papen answered that he didn't have enough influence with the president to break Hindenburg's opposition to the National Socialists and suggested again that the Nazis throw their support behind him as chancellor.

The suggestion was not well received.

Joachim von Ribbentrop encouraged Hitler to arrange a meeting with Oskar von Hindenburg. If they could win him round, then maybe the old man could be persuaded, too. There were rumours circulating in Berlin that Oskar's relationship with his former regimental brother-in-arms had grown noticeably chilly.

After the exhausting meeting with Papen, Hitler went to unwind at the cinema. *The Rebel* was his kind of film: students battling Napoleon's troops in Tyrol, Luis Trenker as a freedom fighter, stirring crowd scenes. The Führer was all 'fire and flame', remembered Goebbels. *The Rebel* was a 'supreme achievement' of the cinematic arts.

Late that night, news spread in journalistic circles that Hitler and Papen had been in talks at the Ribbentrops'.

The press office at the Chancellery was peppered with questions. Was there any truth to the rumours? Schleicher's staff made it sound as though the chancellor had approved the meeting in advance, or even that Papen had been acting on his instructions, that he'd been dispatched to smooth out the disagreements between Hitler and the current cabinet.

In fact, Schleicher had heard nothing about it. How had it slipped through the secret service's net? Hadn't he recently been boasting that nothing happened in Germany without his knowledge? Now there was a conspiracy unfolding right under his nose – and he hadn't even noticed.

THURSDAY 19 JANUARY

Disgusting Performances of Red 'Internationale'
Germany Is Not Their Fatherland
– *Völkischer Beobachter*

Hitler Dodges Schleicher
Papen's Mediation Fails
– *Vossische Zeitung*

Goebbels and Hitler visited Magda together at the Women's Hospital, and she was thrilled to see them. The Führer, meanwhile, took the opportunity to deliver a 'political lecture' to some of the doctors.

Magda's fever had gone down over the past few hours. 'Herr Hitler,' cried one of the medical staff, 'if your presence at Germany's sickbed is as effective as it was with Frau Goebbels, you'll have us back to health in no time!'

Der Alarm was a weekly newspaper published by the Central Association of German Citizens of Jewish Faith, an organisation with tens of thousands of members. The Nazis painted it as inflammatory propaganda, while the editors never tired of taunting and ridiculing the Nazis. It was often handed out at meetings of the Iron Front.

Somebody pressed a copy into Abraham Plotkin's hands, in which it was announced that Hitler had admitted being 5 million marks in debt. It didn't cross his mind that *Der Alarm* was using satire as a weapon.

Still, the paper wasn't entirely wrong. Hitler was in debt – to the German government. In 1932 he had declared an income of 65,000 marks. His book *Mein Kampf* had already sold several hundred thousand copies and was still flying off the shelves, but he wasn't paying enough tax on his royalties, and the arrears were adding up. Even if he did gain power, he might find himself with a six-figure bill.

Then again, power does come with certain privileges.

The *Deutschland*, Germany's first armoured battleship, was launched in Kiel. It had been built at the Deutsche Werke shipyard and would be handed over to the navy at the end of February. German rearmament continued.

Yet again, the NSDAP was in a lather. Wilhelm Stegmann was exiting the party with immediate effect, having founded the 'Freikorps Franken' – essentially a splinter group of disgruntled Franconian SA commanders – one day earlier, and in doing so he pre-empted his inevitable expulsion on the grounds of 'mutiny'. Stegmann's group instantly attracted over a thousand members, including many former Brownshirts.

With a circulation of 560,000 copies, the *Berliner Morgenpost*, published by liberal-leaning Ullstein, was Germany's largest newspaper. Unlike Hitler, its film critic had not enjoyed *The Rebel*. Despite its 'magnificent picture-book visuals of a magnificent landscape', the film was 'a simple, straightforward story told in a wooden manner; the tale of a young student who finds himself at the heart of a political battle, fights heroically against Napoleon and is finally shot by a firing squad alongside his comrades'.

The Rebel was the portrait of a fanatic, set against a gorgeous mountain backdrop. It had heroic posturing, and it had dead Frenchmen.

What would happen if the NSDAP imploded – might it have a negative impact on the Republic? Bernhard Wilhelm von Bülow, State Secretary at the Foreign Office, wrote to the German ambassador in

Washington: 'I cannot say the National Socialists are doing well. Structurally the party has been badly shaken, and their financial outlook is bleak. Some have even wondered whether the party might not be collapsing too rapidly – that it may not be possible to reabsorb all the voters, and that we may lose many of them to the Communists.'

In Berlin, under pressure from its creditors, the Rotter brothers' theatre company had gone bust. Fritz and Alfred Rotter – who had recently invited Bella Fromm to one of their extravagant parties – owned a complex tangle of major cultural enterprises in the capital, including opera houses and theatres. They had built their empire on borrowed money, and now it was crumbling.

The National Socialists pounced on the story. The labyrinthine structure of the Rotters' company was ideal fodder for their propaganda, and their newspapers milked Alfred's sudden departure from Berlin on 8 or 9 January – he'd bought citizenship of Lichtenstein long before – for all it was worth.

The Rotters were, of course, Jewish.

Elisabeth von Schleicher was throwing a tea party to benefit hospitals in Berlin. Bella Fromm saw a number of familiar faces from the 'old elite' of Berlin among the guests: civil servants, military officers, politicians. She discussed Papen's recent speech in Halle with a friend. 'It's characteristic of Papen to work both sides of the street,' remarked her friend. 'He praised Schleicher's speech at the *Kyffhäuser Bund*, in which he had proposed conscription. At the same time, he is waiting to kick the props out from under him.'

Hugenberg and Schacht, too, were known to have met with Hitler. Other members of the Gentlemen's Club were openly discussing whether the Führer hadn't earned a shot. 'It's maddening to watch this blindness,' sighed Fromm.

At least the National Socialists were still at each other's throats. Cold comfort.

Paris didn't understand the Germans. Why was the chancellor so unpopular? Ambassador François-Poncet explained the political situation in a dispatch to the French government: the right wing had been hoping Schleicher would install a military dictatorship, but the chancellor had taken off his uniform. He seemed weak. Unsoldierly. Instead of cracking down on the left, he'd let the unions force him into making concessions.

And now Schleicher had 'declared open war' on Hitler by associating with Strasser. 'Amid all the opposing currents in Germany, the General cannot bring himself to make a decision; one gets the impression he's waiting to see which current wins out before committing to one or the other.'

Lucky for the ambassador that diplomatic mail was sealed – Schleicher would not have taken kindly to François-Poncet's frank assessment. At the end of the letter, however, the ambassador revealed the underlying goodwill he felt for Schleicher. 'At present one can only say how quickly the General's star is fading and how thoughtless are those who are willing – without knowing who will succeed him – to sacrifice one of the most talented and intelligent men in Germany.'

Annelies von Ribbentrop made an entry in her private diary: 'Lengthy negotiations Joachim and Papen alone.' Was her husband, Hitler's latest acolyte, trying to convince Papen to let the NSDAP have the chancellorship?

Schleicher, meanwhile, was paid a visit by the Communists. No everyday event: after all, the KPD fought the General at every turn, and Schleicher wanted nothing more than to ban the party entirely. If only the consequences hadn't seemed so volatile!

Ernst Torgler, an MP since 1924 and chairman of the KPD parliamentary faction for the last three years, arrived with his colleague Wilhelm Kasper, his equivalent in the Prussian State Assembly. They asked Schleicher to forbid the SA from marching directly outside the KPD's headquarters, arguing that it was a deliberate provocation. A similar demonstration in Hamburg the previous summer had resulted in eighteen deaths, in a riot known as 'Altona Bloody Sunday'.

Torgler and Kasper were prominent men. A few months earlier they had been at the centre of a political cause célèbre when it emerged that they had met with senior SPD civil servants to explore how the KPD could help them tackle the NSDAP.

When the secret talks became public knowledge, Papen – then chancellor – had used it to justify why he'd deposed SDP Prime Minister Otto Braun. And now his successor, Schleicher, was consorting with the enemy!

Hitler was staying put. There was too much going on in Berlin at that moment. Even Strasser had approached him, wanting to talk. He was certainly not about to restore his reputation that way, sniffed Goebbels. In any case, there would be no meeting between the most powerful man in the NSDAP and his former second-in-command. Not initially. First Göring would meet with Strasser and discuss where to go next. Goebbels might not have wanted to admit it, but clearly Hitler was leaving the door ajar. As usual, he was postponing a final decision for as long as he could.

In Fallersleben, a district in the Lower Saxon city of Wolfsburg, 120 members of the SA were off to the cinema. But they hadn't come to see the show – they had come to prevent it. The theatre was playing *All Quiet on the Western Front*, an anti-war film based on the novel by Erich Maria Remarque.

Shortly before the film was due to begin, the SA stormed the cinema. Armed with spades, the same weapon soldiers on the Western Front had used to attack each other in the trenches, they threatened the audience. Men from the Reichsbanner stopped the situation escalating and called the police, but only twelve officers showed up – hardly enough to subdue so many angry Brownshirts.

The police immediately cancelled the showing.

FRIDAY 20 JANUARY

Landowners' Assault on German Volk – Reichstag
Brands 'Eastern Aid Profiteers' – Minister Silent
– Berliner Morgenpost

New National Socialist Electoral Victory in Hanover
Rural Front against Schleicher Administration Still Growing
– Völkischer Beobachter

BÜLOWPLATZ OKAYED

Schleicher–Bracht Dictatorship Wants Fascists Marching
Outside Karl Liebknecht House / KPD Demonstration to be
Suppressed / Workers of Germany, Mobilise Against Fascism!
– Die Rote Fahne

Schleicher Faces Barrage
Papen's Mediation Fails
– Tägliche Rundschau

The Council of Elders convened once more. Wilhelm Frick, leader of
the NSDAP faction in the Reichstag, demanded the government present its budget for 1933 as early as possible; only then should Parliament
be recalled. Since that could easily drag on for weeks, the Communists
and Social Democrats rejected his proposal.

Erwin Planck, speaking on the chancellor's behalf, said that the
government believed the most urgent order of business was to clarify
the political situation. Evidently he'd lost track of what was going on.
It seemed Schleicher still didn't understand how the Nazis viewed him
or what the DNVP were going to do next.

He was out of his depth.

Eventually the Council of Elders decided not to recall Parliament on 24 January, as originally planned; 31 January would be the first session, and on 27 January they would meet again to confirm the date.

A week's grace. A decisive week, perhaps.

Berlin was on tenterhooks: what was going to happen on Sunday if the Nazis demonstrated outside the Communists' head office? Thousands of Brownshirts massing outside Karl Liebknecht House – sparks were bound to fly.

All this talk of 'bloodshed' was unnerving Abraham Plotkin. 'Overnight,' he wrote, 'there has come into the air a tenseness that is new and startling.' The Communists had already said they wouldn't take such an insult lying down.

He went to visit Kurt Zielenziger, head of the Berlin Press Bureau. Zielenziger, who came from one of the oldest Jewish families in Berlin, had a thin moustache and hair slicked back sharply from his forehead. His uncle was President of the Berlin Stock Exchange. Plotkin and Zielenziger discussed the rising anti-Semitism in German society. Only the influential Jews were relatively safe, he said. 'The vast majority of Jews don't have that. Thousands of Jewish shopkeepers have been driven out of business, many thousands more in white-collar occupations also have been driven out. Where can they turn?' Hitler's rise, he added, had fuelled the worrying uptick in anti-Semitism.

'The future of the Jew in Germany', he observed thoughtfully, 'is uncertain.'

Swathes of the country were in the grip of a flu epidemic. Schools in Brunswick and Göttingen had to be closed. In Hamburg hundreds of new cases were admitted to hospital every day. Only Berlin, as if by a miracle, had largely been spared.

Hitler was to give a speech at the Sportpalast. Clad in a brown jacket, brown riding trousers and black boots, he strutted into the arena to the sound of his baying supporters. 'You may strike us, but you will never defeat us!' he roared. 'Again and again we will start the battle afresh, and we will never abandon the flag. My mission as standard-bearer of the movement is to press ceaselessly onwards. For as long as fate allows me to live, I will carry the standard. Never will I cover it, never roll it up.'

There was more in that vein.

Franz von Papen wasn't going to get any further by himself – he had to break cover. Turning to Oskar von Hindenburg and Otto Meissner, Hindenburg's closest advisers, he let them in on the plan. Neither was remotely averse to ousting the chancellor, even if it meant sharing power with Hitler.

That evening he gave Ribbentrop an update: both Meissner and Hindenburg had said they were willing to meet with Hitler. It would happen on Sunday. The wheels were already in motion.

Goebbels sat up with the Führer and Ernst Hanfstaengl at his apartment until three in the morning. Hanfstaengl was accompanied by two ladies. 'Dreadful,' shuddered Goebbels. Was he thinking of Magda, still in hospital? It had been a good day for the patient, and she was recovering rapidly. Goebbels could focus all his attention on Sunday's SA march, the biggest in a long time – right outside the Communists' HQ.

SATURDAY 21 JANUARY

Bülowplatz Tomorrow!
Showdown Gets Go-Ahead
– *Vossische Zeitung*

Outrage in Factories and Welfare Offices
Oppose Hitler's Provocation! Oppose Schleicher–Bracht Dictatorship!
– *Die Rote Fahne*

New Agrarian Declaration of War on Schleicher:
'So Far We've Been Given Nothing But Sops!'
– *Völkischer Beobachter*

By now everybody knew it: the National Socialists had permission to demonstrate outside Karl Liebknecht House, the head office of the KPD. Rumour had it the Communists were already arranging a counter-demonstration. As Plotkin noted in his diary: 'The place where the meeting is to be held is in the heart of a working-class district: that blood will be spilt is a dead certainty.' Police spokesmen insisted that they had given the Nazis permission to demonstrate there ages ago, but Plotkin wondered what they hoped to achieve. 'It was inconceivable that Schleicher was unaware of what this meeting may result in.' Was he trying to stir the pot?

The general consensus was that Schleicher was deliberately pitting the Nazis against the Communists, waiting until they'd worn each other out before stepping in. Nobody could talk of anything but the march, and the whole city was on edge. Tomorrow there would be columns of people marching on Bülowplatz from every corner of Berlin.

'I wanted excitement,' wrote Plotkin, 'and I must confess that I am getting it.'

Accompanied by Martin Plettl, Plotkin went for a drink at the Imperator, one of the largest restaurants in Berlin, which was divided into several salons on the first floor. Four orchestras were playing waltzes by Johann Strauss, while patrons lounged in plush armchairs and sipped beer or coffee. That Saturday it was packed.

'What do you suppose', he asked Plettl, 'Schleicher's motives are?' Both assumed the chancellor knew exactly what he was doing. Plettl, a member of the SPD, described a similar situation from a few years earlier, when the Communists had marched outside the Social Democrats' headquarters. 'We remained passive. We placed the responsibility wholly on the police department.' Plettl's theory was that Schleicher knew Hitler would lose the ongoing power struggle within the NSDAP. 'It may be that Schleicher is using Hitler as a cat's paw. Hitler on the downgrade, supplying Schleicher with provocative means for eliminating the Communists, will clear the roads in the coming elections for Schleicher.'

It was a neat theory.

Plettl continued:

To split Hitlerism, eliminate Communism as much as is possible and to entrench himself so thoroughly that nothing can budge him, I think is Schleicher's game. The only effective opposition to him will come through our party, but when we will run afoul against each other is hard to say. But of all the political parties in Germany, we are the only ones who for the present are keeping our heads. Let Schleicherism, Hitlerism and Communism fight it out. The road will be a little less foggy then.

There was driving snow in the wintry garden. Oskar Loerke was working on his poetry. He'd stayed up reading late into the night and decided a brisk walk to the village of Stolpe on the outskirts of Berlin would clear his head. At first the sun shone, but then – as Loerke sketched it in his fluid style – 'clouds gathered; every so often little flurries of snow'.

All day long Goebbels and other National Socialists had been planning the march. Officially it was in honour of Horst Wessel, an SA commander murdered by the Communists in 1930. The party's anthem had been named after him, partly because he'd written the lyrics himself. Unofficially the demonstration was intended as a show of strength, and as a way of humiliating the chancellor. Only one thing worried Goebbels: the police might still forbid the march. After all, the press – full of Jews, he lamented – were calling for it to be cancelled.

Actually, there was something else bothering him. He'd heard from a visitor that there was a rumour going around about him in the party. People said he was lining his pockets by playing dodgy tricks with foreign currencies. It was an accusation the Nazis liked to lob at Jewish businessmen. For a senior figure in the NSDAP, an allegation like that could prove dangerous. Who was spreading lies about him? It certainly did pay to have a thick skin, thought Goebbels bitterly.

A report by the Munich Police observed that the local SA was shrinking fast. Thirty-five men had been expelled from the organisation in December 1932 for dereliction of duty and another fifteen in January.

In hospital, Magda Goebbels was able to get out of bed for the first time in weeks. 'Overjoyed!' wrote Joseph Goebbels. On the downside, he was now worried about his boss: Hitler was sleeping and eating too little.

Everything was set for tomorrow evening, Ribbentrop assured the Führer. Meissner and Hindenburg Jr would come to Dahlem in secret. Hitler said he would bring Göring and probably another confidant. Schleicher, he insisted, must not under any circumstances be invited. In case anybody was wondering. It seemed Hitler didn't wholly trust his new friend Papen.

Meanwhile, the chancellor had turned to Interior Minister Franz Bracht for advice. Schleicher was torn between right and left – the classic political dilemma. If he cancelled the Nazis' demonstration, he would antagonise a potentially important partner. If he forbade the planned counterdemonstration, he would be accused of being anti-democratic. As usual, the chancellor found himself stuck between a rock and a hard place – and all eyes were on him.

Strasser went to see Göring at his apartment. He was conceding defeat. At least, that's what Göring told Goebbels.

The *Neue Zürcher Zeitung* had nothing but praise for the Pepper Mill, Erika Mann and Therese Giehse's cabaret company. 'Charm – that is the quality one sees in this young Munich cabaret!'

The entire run was sold out. The Bonbonnière was turning out to be too small, and the company had to pick a new space. Sometimes they even had Nazis in the audience. Were they secretly laughing at the Führer? Or quietly taking note of every jibe?

SUNDAY 22 JANUARY

Anti-Fascists – Defend Red Berlin!
– *Die Rote Fahne*

Across Bülowplatz
Quick March Through Total Police Blockade
– *Vossische Zeitung*

It was bitterly cold in Berlin, and the clouds hung low. Late on Sunday morning, uniformed police officers seized control of Karl Liebknecht House, driving staff out into the street – at gunpoint, in the case of one *Rote Fahne* editor. While they searched the building, other officers appeared and took up their positions in the snow-covered square. They cordoned off the area ready for the march, putting armoured police vehicles at the crossings, and patrolled the streets with their guns at the ready. Officers with binoculars were dotted across the rooftops, and residents were instructed to keep their doors and windows shut. Nobody was allowed onto their balconies. Then they waited. The column of Nazis was on its way.

The *Betriebsräte* – the umbrella organisation of works councils in Germany – was holding a conference, and Theodor Leipart was giving the opening speech. Plotkin was in the audience, although more out of duty than interest. Leipart addressed the accusation that the unions were tacitly supporting Schleicher. The unions were not a political party, he argued. 'We have our Social Democratic Party. As trade unions we have neither the authority nor even the option to overthrow a government, so there can be no question of tacit support.'

Plotkin was exhausted and uneasy. He went out into the cold, setting off towards Bülowplatz.

Around one o'clock the first Brownshirts came marching onto Bülow-platz, flanked by the police. 'We don't give a shit about freedom!' they screamed. 'We don't give a shit about the Jewish republic!' Almost sixteen thousand members of the SA had turned out, and roughly the same number of police officers were escorting the procession.

What happened? Nothing.

Afterwards the Nazi press were exultant. 'Commies hopping mad in the side streets,' gloated Joseph Goebbels. 'Armoured cars, machine guns. Police made sure nobody shot at us from the windows.' All in all, he decided: 'We have won a battle!'

Oskar Loerke was off to a friend's birthday party in Neu-Westend, an area to the west of Berlin. 'Delightful reception with superb drinks and every hospitality. Music: Mozart, the Birthday Sonata (the little E-flat Major), "Gelobet sei der Herr", and Handel, D Major Sonata.' The birthday boy, noticed Loerke, had a lovely new violin, still unvarnished.

The Nazis were pushing ahead with their propaganda campaign. In the early afternoon, Hitler unveiled a memorial to Horst Wessel at the Nicolai Cemetery in Prenzlauer Berg. Many thousands of sympathisers attended the ceremony, including the sixteen thousand Brown-shirts who had marched over from Bülowplatz.

Joseph Goebbels went to see his wife at the clinic, Hitler at his elbow. The doctors had virtually written her off, and now he thanked God for giving Magda back to him. He found Hitler's attentiveness 'moving'.

Especially as Hitler's day was far from over. He was speaking again at the Sportpalast, giving another speech about Horst Wessel. In it the Führer praised 'those fanatics who are consumed by the great task of their age, who live for that task and who die for it'.

That evening, two famous men and their wives entered the Berliner Staatsoper and took their seats in a box. Performed that night was *Das Liebesverbot* (The Ban on Love), Richard Wagner's version of Shakespeare's *Measure for Measure*. During the interval, they mingled with the other guests before returning punctually to their box as the gong sounded for the second act.

When the lights dimmed and the music started, they rose softly and crept outside, leaving via the back exit. Finding themselves in the thick of a snowstorm, they hailed a taxi. The destination? Dahlem. No specific address. They didn't want the driver knowing where they were headed, so Oskar von Hindenburg and Otto Meissner walked the final stretch to the Ribbentrops' villa, where Papen, Göring and Hitler were waiting.

Papen had been there since nine, Hitler a little later. Hindenburg's two confidants arrived at ten o'clock.

Henkell champagne was poured – although Hitler drank only water – and the gentlemen exchanged pleasantries. After a while Hitler managed to get Oskar von Hindenburg alone. This would not be plain sailing. Oskar was no friend to National Socialism, and he'd warned his father against appointing Hitler. Only a few weeks earlier he'd told the president that 'once Hitler gets his hands on power, he won't stick to the initial list of ministers or any agreements in the long term – we'll end up with a party dictatorship'. It was Oskar who had insisted Meissner join them that evening.

He and Hitler withdrew to the parlour.

They spoke for two hours before returning to the group. Not a word was said about the content of their discussion, but it was clear they shared a common goal: Schleicher had to go. The gentlemen ate a light meal and drank a little more champagne, served by a liveried, white-gloved footman, then Meissner and Hindenburg Jr left in a taxi.

Afterwards, Hitler and Papen talked long into the night. Alone. Papen said he'd decided to back Hitler for chancellor – although, if Hitler didn't trust him, he'd drop the issue immediately.

Naturally the president had been apprised of this meeting in advance. His permission signalled that Papen's course of action was under serious consideration.

Excitement at the Staatstheater: *Faust II* was being performed at a major Berlin venue for the first time in more than twenty years, and Gustaf Gründgens was playing Mephistopheles. Alfred Kerr was fascinated by Gründgens' portrayal of this diabolical, seductive character, in which he sensed 'immense mental strength, intellectual ability'; Mephistopheles was a 'richly animalistic creature of the thinking mind – yet shadowed by melancholia'.

Kerr was a giant of literary journalism, writing for the *Berliner Tageblatt* and the *Frankfurter Zeitung*. Since the autumn of 1931, whenever he went to the studio to record his radio broadcasts, he'd been under police protection. Then, in August 1932, the new Political Commissioner for Broadcasting – a member of the NSDAP – cancelled them entirely. The Nazis had their eye on him.

Kerr, a supporter of the Iron Front, wasn't squeamish when it came to conflict. He'd made no secret of his contempt for Hitler, calling him 'riff-raff who's read Nietzsche'. In 1931, he published a poem in the *Berliner Tageblatt*:

See the Nazi unimpeded
Claims mass murder is what's needed.
He invokes mass murder
And legality.

Not long before, a Communist newspaper had conducted a survey among leading intellectuals, asking: 'How do we combat the Third Reich?' Kerr responded in no uncertain terms. In the Third Reich he expected 'the hard-won intellectual bar to be lowered by sergeants and unemployed mystics; ethics will be undermined'. He advocated a 'campaign plan' in which they began 'training officers on the left as soon as possible – not to start a civil war but to be there when it does'.

In August 1932, when the NSDAP's official newspaper, the *Völkische Beobachter*, printed a list of writers who would be banned after the Nazis came to power, Kerr's name was on it. He was in good company: the list also included Stefan Zweig, Carl Zuckmayer, Bertolt

Brecht, Franz Werfel and Klaus Mann. In *Der Angriff*, meanwhile, Goebbels had called for 'putting the writing scum up against the wall'.

What *would* happen if the Nazis wielded all the power of the state? Would Kerr and his family be able to stay in Berlin? In recent months the sixty-five-year-old journalist had been deeply uneasy and restlessly productive, penning one long article after another.

As if his time were running out.

Another gala performance in Berlin, and another unmissable event in the social calendar – this time to benefit the winter welfare programme. Hindenburg was the patron, although he wasn't there in person.

'An exceptionally glamorous affair,' thought Bella Fromm, 'with the general mood at freezing point.' Hjalmar Schacht was conniving with Hitler, she heard, having 'hitched his horse to the National Socialist star'. And Papen? He and his scheming were also a topic of conversation. As Fromm put it: 'the old to and fro between Wilhelmstrasse and Kaiserhof is in full swing'.

MONDAY 23 JANUARY

Deadline for Parties
Government Statement on 31 January
— *Vossische Zeitung*

Unity Needed! Unity, Not United Front Tactics!
Proletarian Germany, Unite!
— *Vorwärts*, special edition

At half past eight Schleicher called Meissner. He wanted to know what had been discussed at the Ribbentrops' the previous evening, and asked sarcastically how the stew had tasted.

Schleicher's network of informants was working after all!

We don't know what Meissner said in reply. Schleicher had arranged an appointment with Hindenburg at eleven thirty. He was evidently seething.

That morning Papen went to see the president and explained his proposals for reorganising the government. He suggested dismissing Schleicher. Hindenburg was listening.

Then Papen recommended Hitler as the next chancellor.

Hitler?

Hindenburg bridled. He summoned Meissner and Oskar. Meissner was on Papen's side: Hitler should be made chancellor and Papen Vice-Chancellor. That way responsibility would be shared, and the Nazis would be controlled. No, said both Hindenburgs. Only Papen could be chancellor.

SA and SS commanders had assembled at the Hotel Kaiserhof, where

Hitler favoured them with a two-hour speech. Things were looking up for the movement, he declared – the NSDAP was stronger and better than ever before. As 'political soldiers of the German popular uprising', they had a historic task ahead of them.

Joachim von Ribbentrop dropped in on Hitler to update him on the trouble Papen was having with Hindenburg. He then put forward another permutation: a cabinet led by Hjalmar Schacht. Schacht, the former President of the National Bank and a well-known Nazi sympathiser, might be more palatable. Hitler refused all options that didn't involve him becoming chancellor.

Fromm went to see the chancellor, and the two had a brief chat. Schleicher seemed to know what was going on behind his back, that his colleagues were plotting to unseat him. He told Fromm he no longer had any access to Hindenburg. 'The slanderous whispers against him have persuaded the childish old man that a revolt in the Reichswehr will break out soon, if the appointment of a strong man is postponed much longer.'

Why hadn't Schleicher been vigilant enough to see it coming? Fromm was wondering the same thing. She concluded that Meissner had lulled him into a false sense of security by constantly remarking that Hindenburg despised Hitler.

Before Schleicher walked the few metres across to the president's office, he probably skimmed once again the list of potential approaches his staff had prepared. How should he deal with the Reichstag?

Option one: dissolve the Reichstag, postpone new elections beyond the sixty-day deadline then simply continue to govern. But that would be unconstitutional. Papen had suggested exactly the same thing two months earlier and been rebuffed. It would also put Schleicher on the defensive – although, frankly, he already was.

Option two was an equally unconstitutional approach. He would adjourn the Reichstag indefinitely and only recall it once he had a workable parliamentary majority. But how could he convince the parties represented in the Council of Elders to defer scheduling the first session?

Option three exploited a loophole in the constitution that experienced legal theorists like Carl Schmitt had pointed out many times before: the authors of the constitution had never considered the possibility of a negative majority that would bring motions of no confidence and topple governments but refused to form a cabinet. What if Schleicher simply ignored any vote of no confidence and continued to govern? It wasn't technically a breach of the constitution – but it might result in a general strike, mass protests or even civil war. And the Reichstag could always reverse his emergency decrees. Still, it would buy Schleicher time. Valuable time.

What had Schleicher been doing in the last few hours? Had he been wrestling with the decision? Had he debated his options with his brightest staff, perhaps especially Eugen Ott, his legal expert? Or had he simply sat alone and brooded?

Unemployment had risen by 250,000 since Schleicher took office, Abraham Plotkin was told. The chancellor was in a bind, he decided. 'Schleicher is being criticized by the industrialists for counteracting von Papen's industrial program, by the Communists for failure to solve the unemployment problem, and by the Nazis for encouraging the trade unions and the Jews.'

Schleicher had made his choice. The only feasible path was to dissolve Parliament and then to put off reconvening it. He wasn't going to stall, he wasn't going to feint. He was going all in.

The chancellor was now dependent on the president.

Alfred Klieforth, First Secretary at the American embassy, wrote to the State Department that one of Göring's trusted aides had approached him about 'obtaining a loan for the Nazi party in the United States'.

The NSDAP was evidently trying frantically to raise some cash. How long could the movement sustain its momentum?

It was half past eleven, and Schleicher was asking Hindenburg to grant him the authority to dissolve the Reichstag and postpone elections so that he could push through the 'national emergency'. That would be the argument: that desperate times called for desperate measures.

This step, as Meissner noted afterwards, would be 'perceived by all sides as a breach of the constitution'. It would mean outrage in the newspapers and fierce criticism directed at Hindenburg. Before even contemplating it, he wrote, they would have to ask all the party leaders in advance whether they would acknowledge the state of emergency.

He would consider, said Hindenburg, whether or not to let Schleicher dissolve the Reichstag, but under no circumstances would he postpone the subsequent election. Consider it? Was Hindenburg breaking the promise he'd made in December? At the time he'd assured Schleicher he would be granted permission at any time.

Now it seemed he was setting the chancellor up to fail. As soon as Parliament reconvened, the Communists would table a motion of no confidence and try to get him booted out of office – and he didn't have the majority to vote them down.

Unless Hindenburg changed his mind.

Hitler left Berlin for Munich, but not before issuing a peculiar warning: in twenty-four hours a bomb would drop, and it would be curtains for General von Schleicher.

What was he insinuating?

TUESDAY 24 JANUARY

Brown March Dominates Berlin
20,000 Warriors Honour Horst Wessel
Adolf Hitler: 'His Spirit Remains among Us!'
– *Völkischer Beobachter*

Parliament and Parties Must Be Disabled
– *Tägliche Rundschau*

Show Fascism Our Strength Tomorrow!
Red Berlin, Onto the Streets for Stormy Week of Anti-Fascist Action
Everybody, Everybody to Bülowplatz!
– *Die Rote Fahne*

The newspapers were still analysing the events around Bülowplatz. To Abraham Plotkin, it was clear the Nazis considered themselves the victors. They were the lords of Berlin.

Now the SPD was announcing a march for the coming Sunday – at the Lustgarten. Its supporters had been waiting a long time. 'It should offer an interesting comparison both of temper and methods between the different groups in Germany,' observed Plotkin.

At a rally in Nuremberg, renegade SA commander Wilhelm Stegmann savaged Hitler's strategy. 'The historic moment of the movement has been missed,' he said, and the party would 'lose every future election'. The SA could no longer play 'fire brigade' or 'palace guard' – there could be no more of this 'obsession with legality'. The battle for power must be fought 'more brutally and with more revolutionary spirit'.

How influential was Oskar von Hindenburg, really? And that isn't the only question – it's also unclear how much he really understood. Hitler, at least, was unimpressed by Oskar's intellect, commenting to Goebbels that he was a 'remarkable model of stupidity'.

Ribbentrop's villa was rapidly becoming conspiracy central. On 24 January Franz von Papen had tea there with Wilhelm Frick and Hermann Göring, as well as with Ribbentrop himself.

What would make Hindenburg appoint Hitler chancellor? The group agreed: only if the leading figures on the right were prepared to form a cabinet. The 'national front' must be made a reality. For that, however, they needed the cooperation of Alfred Hugenberg and Franz Seldte, Commander of the Stahlhelm. The problem? Both men were at loggerheads with Hitler.

And yet. That could change.

Hugenberg was finally becoming a key figure in the battle for power, although hardly anybody in German politics had a good word to say about the conceited sixty-eight-year-old leader of the German National People's Party. His speeches in Parliament were ferociously boring, and he liked to be addressed as 'Privy Councillor', the title he'd been given under the Kaiser in recognition of his faithful service to the crown.

François-Poncet found Hugenberg something of an enigma. 'Stout, with gold-rimmed glasses and a shaggy white moustache, he looks as upright and conventional as a country doctor. In reality he has a slow and narrow mind, is obstinate in the extreme, a fierce sectarian, wildly partisan and one of the most malevolent spirits in Germany.'

Hugenberg's party, the DNVP, was refusing to cooperate with Schleicher, insisting he 'rebuild the cabinet from the ground up in order to ensure effective and unified governance, especially in terms of economic policy. The increasingly desperate situation and growing bitterness among the people demand clarity.'

Another unmistakeable declaration of war. The chancellor was running out of lifelines.

In Munich, Hitler was telling Goebbels over coffee what steps he planned to take next. Goebbels wasn't allowed to participate directly in the Wilhelmstrasse negotiations – his image was too tarnished, the president's dislike for him too pronounced – so his information usually came piecemeal. 'Schleicher's position very precarious,' he noted later. 'Seems he still doesn't have a clue. Poor simpleton!'

WEDNESDAY 25 JANUARY

Hugenberg Attacks Cabinet
First Unseat Schleicher, Then 'State of
Emergency' – Pressure on Hindenburg
– *Tägliche Rundschau*

Schleicher Isolated!
Whole Volk Against Policy of Immiseration
Catastrophic Rise in Unemployment
Chancellor's Position Untenable
– *Der Angriff*

Battle Against Unemployment
Job-Creation Scheme Comes Into Force
Unemployment for the first half of January seems to be looking up.
– *Vossische Zeitung*

Now it was the Communists' turn to march through Bülowplatz. Ernst Thälmann and the other leaders of the KPD stood on a stage outside Karl Liebknecht House, and from the balustrades hung the hammer and sickle, the symbol of Marxist–Leninism.

A hundred and thirty thousand people marched past, their fists raised.

There were far fewer police around, because this time they weren't worried about snipers picking off the protesters. On Bülowplatz, the authorities knew, the KPD were kings.

A meeting of the Fighting League Against Fascism – the successor organisation to the banned Red Front Fighters' League – in Dresden ended in a shootout with the police. All of the nine dead and eleven wounded were Communists. Officers insisted they had only fired in response to shots. The authorities announced an investigation.

The SPD's key strategists held a council of war, the results of which were published as a 'resolution':

> The party executive of the Social Democratic Party of Germany and the board of the Social Democratic faction in the Reichstag protest in the strongest terms against the forthcoming proclamation of a so-called state of national emergency. Implementing such a measure would be tantamount to a coup, robbing the people of their constitutional rights and benefitting those cliques that represent special interests while disregarding the nation as a whole and the working class in particular – cliques which thus have every reason to avoid the criticism of Parliament.

Should the DNVP participate in the next government, even if that meant making concessions to the NSDAP? It was a dangerous calculation. Reinhold Quaatz knew how eager Hugenberg was to gain power, so he never tired of reminding his boss that command of the military and the police could not be given to the Nazis. They could not allow 'terror on the streets'.

'The matter may founder over that,' hoped Quaatz.

Ribbentrop was serving tea to another political guest at his Dahlem villa, this time Oskar von Hindenburg. The idea of a 'national front' under Hitler as chancellor wasn't a hopeless one, said Oskar. He promised his host he'd be in touch again before his father made a final decision.

How was Kurt von Schleicher bearing up? His hopes of forming a cross-party front somewhere in the middle ground had been dashed. The trade unions had deserted him. Gregor Strasser had been neutralised. At least he had the cabinet behind him. And the military.

Was he prepared to fight? Was he still banking on the job-creation scheme gaining sudden traction? Or was he on the verge of throwing up his hands? Politicians about to have power snatched away from them are sometimes overwhelmed by a feeling of helplessness, of being undeservedly misunderstood. Fine, they think. Try it without me and see what happens! He could simply go skiing – he could retreat into the mountains with his wife. Lick his wounds and recuperate in peace. Wait for Wilhelmstrasse to get in touch. They were bound to, surely, probably within a few weeks at most.

Schleicher never explained how he felt during those days, but from what he did say it's clear he was terrified Hindenburg would appoint the one man who would inevitably plunge the military into a bloody civil war. No, not Adolf Hitler. Hitler, he believed, would be the lesser of two evils.

Schleicher feared the return of Franz von Papen.

It was an awful journey. Goebbels had travelled to Gleiwitz in Upper Silesia to give a speech – in an open car in sub-zero temperatures. But the SA received him with huge fanfare, and he arrived to find the hall packed to bursting. 'A smash hit', Goebbels noted in his diary. Then it was onwards to Beuthen, where he gave another speech, although not before a breakdown on the road and half an hour in the searing cold. Campaigning was a nightmare.

Social Democrat Rudolf Hilferding had invited guests for dinner, and Harry Graf Kessler kept a close eye on Heinrich Brüning throughout. Brüning, still with the Centre Party, was a man who knew what it felt like to achieve power only to have it slip through his fingers.

He seemed fresher and more youthful than Kessler had expected, almost jolly. They discussed the revolutionary days of 1918–19, when the Weimar Republic was born. It was only fifteen years ago, yet it felt like another era.

After wallowing in the past, Brüning turned to the present. He wondered aloud whether they might see a Papen cabinet next.

It was enough to make you sick, replied Kessler, the thought of having to endure that semi-deranged imbecile back as chancellor. They risked an explosion of violence if Papen was appointed yet again. There would be an uprising of extremists on both left and right.

Brüning shook his head. Schleicher staying in office was just as dangerous. Schleicher, he argued, was no different politically from Papen – he was just going about things more cautiously. It would come to revolution either way.

THURSDAY 26 JANUARY

Schleicher's Last-Ditch Rescue Attempt:
New Emergency Decrees!
— *Der Angriff*

Streets Lined with Jubilant Masses During March!
This Is Red Berlin!
— *Rote Fahne*

Hugenberg: Swing and a Miss
Baseless Attack
— *Tägliche Rundschau*

A powerful anticyclone had settled over Europe, driving cold air from the Baltic and northern Russia towards Germany. The nights were clear and icy. In East Prussia and Pomerania, temperatures plummeted to minus 28 degrees. To the west of the country, drifting ice on the Rhine made shipping difficult. Soon it would probably have to be abandoned.

Berlin reached minus 20 in certain areas, with water pipes freezing solid in many apartment blocks. Homeless shelters – there were seventy in the city – were hopelessly overcrowded. The authorities insisted they had enough supplies of coal. But how were people coping in Meyer's Hof?

More fuss in Wilhelmstrasse. Arguments, ruses, water-testing. Political Berlin was reaching fever pitch, and Schleicher was stuck in the middle.

He met with leading trade unionists close to the SPD again, trying to convince them to support his plan to postpone fresh elections. It was a fool's errand. The unions were distancing themselves, and the Social Democrats responded starkly. Otto Braun wrote a letter to Schleicher, copying in the president, in which he described the plan as 'an invitation to high treason'.

Braun was one of the few Social Democrats Hindenburg liked. Both men were fond of hunting, and had occasionally bumped into each other while out deerstalking.

Erwin Planck told Schwerin von Krosigk that Schleicher would be asking for permission to dissolve Parliament the day after tomorrow. As Hindenburg was extremely unlikely to agree, added Planck, the cabinet was going to resign.

Oskar von Hindenburg's abrupt change of heart hit Schleicher hard, and he found Papen's activities unfathomable.

But why was he bringing matters to a head? Why force a decision instead of simply watching the situation develop? If he'd been more passive, he might perhaps have weathered the storm.

The Reichstag committees met again, as though there weren't a political earthquake in the offing. The Committee on Foreign Affairs held a four-hour session on the government's 'minorities policy'. All concerned were jittery, of course. 'The game continues back and forth,' wrote Quaatz.

His boss, Hugenberg, received a letter from Joachim von Ribbentrop, who was now negotiating with the DNVP on Hitler's behalf. Only a few months earlier he'd played no role in political life at all.

Schleicher was never one to hesitate. Now he was going all in. Appearing before the president, he asked him to 'dissolve the Reichstag, postpone the next election and invest me with absolute and unrestricted executive authority'.

The chancellor's move was either brave or brazen, depending on your perspective. Permission, if granted, would have dislodged Hindenburg as supreme commander of the armed forces. Meissner reported later that Schleicher intended to ban the KPD as well as the SA. Doing so could have provoked exactly what he'd always striven to avoid: a civil war.

Hindenburg refused, uncharacteristically softening the blow: 'My dear young friend, soon I will be up above. From there I will be able to see whether I acted rightly or not.'

And how was the mood among the Nazis?

Hitler would be back in Berlin the following day. He still didn't know whether he'd get what he wanted this time. He had to be patient, but patience didn't come easily. Once again, the final word would be the president's, and the old man had disappointed him often enough. What if he appointed Papen again? What if Hitler was made chancellor, but none of his allies was given an important cabinet post?

The Führer was facing a weighty decision, Joseph Goebbels knew. It still wasn't clear what the new government would look like. Only one thing was obvious: Schleicher's role was played out. 'He is absolutely isolated,' wrote Goebbels. 'All his big plans have fallen through.' Yet he didn't let himself get too euphoric – there had been too many let-downs over the past few months.

That evening Harry Graf Kessler attended a packed reception given by the French ambassador. Everybody was gossiping about Schleicher's imminent fall from power, and it seemed increasingly likely that Papen would replace him. Kessler could scarcely believe it. 'There is an orgy of backstairs politics', he wrote, 'not seen since Wilhelm II.'

Tempo, an evening paper published by Ullstein, printed a 'sensational story', as Plotkin put it in his diary. 'A new government was being formed, composed of Hitler, von Papen and Hugenberg!'

Immediately he telephoned some friends whom he assumed would know the latest news and read them the headline. Herbert Kline of the *Chicago Tribune* replied that 'anything is possible'. Another friend warned him against giving the tabloids any credence. A third simply laughed. 'They would never dare resurrect von Papen again. Von Papen is the most hated man in all Germany.'

FRIDAY 27 JANUARY

BLOODSHED IN DRESDEN

In the Name of 'Social Equity': Authorities Estimate
9 Dead and 11 Badly Injured – Fruits of Murderous
Bolshevist Agitation Increasing Under Schleicher
– Emergency Terror Decree Announced

– Völkischer Beobachter

To Battle Stations!
Papen, Göring, Hugenberg, Frick, Stülpnagel Cabinet Ahead?
Redouble the Anti-Fascist Struggle! Defend Your Party!

– Die Rote Fahne

Amid the barrage of assumptions and guesswork, General Kurt von Hammerstein-Equord decided to act. That morning he sought out his friend Schleicher. Was there any truth in the rumour that Hindenburg was reappointing Papen?

Schleicher replied that the president no longer trusted him, and that he expected to be replaced within a day or two. He would, however, remain Minister of Defence.

Had he given up? Or did he just know Hammerstein?

The Commander-in-Chief marched straight to Meissner's office, where he delivered a stern warning: the military would not support a second Papen cabinet! Schleicher must remain chancellor.

Shortly afterwards, Hammerstein and General Erich von dem Bussche-Ippenburg, head of the Army Personnel Office, had a private word with Hindenburg. The generals warned him that installing Papen as chancellor would risk a civil war – and Hammerstein cautioned him specifically about appointing Hitler.

The president was furious. The military, meddling in politics yet again? It wasn't their job!

Nevertheless, he assured them he had no intention of making Adolf Hitler chancellor.

André François-Poncet was one of the best-informed diplomats in Berlin, yet even he couldn't predict how the situation would develop. He'd heard the gossip about Schleicher the night before and passed it back to Paris.

As Hitler was still in Berlin, Ribbentrop visited him at Göring's apartment to report on the situation: Hindenburg was still reluctant.

He would leave the city at once, said Hitler.

The matter wasn't hopeless, replied Ribbentrop. There was another solution – the 'national front'. Hitler had to join forces with Hugenberg. Ribbentrop offered to host another conversation with Papen that evening at ten o'clock. He and Hitler could iron out the details.

Goebbels had met with some influential figures in the National Rural League, the powerful group of agriculturalists out for the chancellor's blood. They all agreed that Schleicher had to go – and that Hitler ought to be chancellor.

Afterwards, Hitler, Göring, Frick and Goebbels held a council of war. But what could they do? Not much. Schleicher was still chancellor, and Papen was still the president's preferred candidate. Hitler was close to power, but it wasn't yet his. He had to bide his time. And if Hindenburg did summon him, the Kaiserhof was only two minutes from the Chancellery.

There was something in the air. Everybody felt it, including Plotkin, who had been surprised by Hugenberg's hostility towards the chancellor. What was that about?

He was perplexed. 'I ask questions, but the answers are as clear as mud. Everyone is doing exactly what I am doing – guessing; and no one knows exactly what will happen, although everyone agrees that the whole thing is impossible.'

Berlin was an enigma. German politics were an enigma.

A 'tower of Babel', Plotkin sighed.

The Council of Elders confirmed that Parliament would reconvene on 31 January. There was no move on the part of the government to postpone that deadline.

All was set for that afternoon. Joachim von Ribbentrop had convinced Hitler to meet with Hugenberg, arguing it was his best shot at the chancellorship. The time had come to act – to forge a nationalist alliance. This time they'd gathered at Göring's apartment, although Ribbentrop was also invited.

It turned into a duel. Neither side – Hitler, Frick and Göring for the NSDAP, Hugenberg and parliamentary faction leader Otto Schmidt-Hannover for the DNVP – trusted the other. The Nazis were acting as though the DNVP had no choice but to fall in line: Franz Seldte and the Stahlhelm, said Göring, had already agreed, while Hitler began by demanding the Interior Ministries of Prussia and of the entire Reich. They weren't exactly subtle negotiators. Their opening move was a slam.

Absolutely not, responded Hugenberg. The Prussian Interior Ministry was off the table – and the roles of chancellor and cabinet press officer belonged to the DNVP.

Politics is a racquet sport, and Hugenberg's return volley matched Hitler's for vehement inflexibility. The Führer broke off the negotiation and flounced out of the room.

The moment Papen heard about the disastrous encounter, he insisted on seeing Hitler at once.

No! Hitler decided. No more talking to Papen! Göring and Ribbentrop got to work, and eventually the Führer acquiesced. He would stay in Berlin. For now.

Reinhold Quaatz made an entry in his diary. 'Hindenburg doesn't want Hitler. Papen foolishly shares that with Hitler, yet nonetheless invites Hugenberg to discuss the options regarding Hindenburg with Hitler.'

Quite the merry-go-round. Did anybody really know what was going on?

Papen was flexible, Papen was determined, Papen was in his element. He told Ribbentrop that the Hugenberg issue didn't matter very much. From now on he would be supporting Hitler's claim to both the Interior Ministry and the office of chancellor.

Papen wanted to be Commissioner of Prussia, succeeding the Prime Minister – which would make him senior to the Prussian Interior Minister.

Gereke's telephone rang. Oskar von Hindenburg was on the line. He was calling on behalf of his father, said Oskar, and he wanted to arrange a discreet chat in the Tiergarten. Oskar suggested they meet at dusk near Siegesallee, 'as if by chance'. Gereke, disconcerted, turned up as agreed.

'Are you with the house of Hindenburg or with the traitor Schleicher?' demanded the president's son.

'How is he a traitor?' asked Gereke.

He knew from reliable sources, said Oskar, that Schleicher was planning to mobilise the Potsdam garrison and depose Paul von Hindenburg on the pretext of his age before proclaiming himself president. To mollify the people, Schleicher would then make Hitler chancellor. The word 'traitor' was surely too mild.

Gereke was scandalised. This was a fantasy, he said. A despicable insinuation. He spoke to Schleicher nearly every day, and the chancellor would never come up with such a plan. He went to see the president without a moment's delay but found Hindenburg in a dismal mood. The old man sat in silence. He'd made up his mind. Conversation was impossible.

Gereke was Schleicher's ally. What could he do? Tell him, at least – he had to.

'Oskar Hindenburg is a snake in the grass,' replied the chancellor. 'He forced me out of his father's confidence. If Oskar says the Potsdam garrison want a coup, it's pure deception. As bitter as I am about the old gentleman's behaviour towards Papen and the Nazis, my oath forbids me from even entertaining such a thought.'

SATURDAY 28 JANUARY

Schleicher Government on Last Legs: Desperate Rescue Attempts
– *Völkischer Beobachter*

Courting a Presidential Crisis?
Schleicher Visits Hindenburg – Tension Builds
– *Tägliche Rundschau*

The country was still in the grip of a cold snap. In Silesia and in the south of Germany the temperature dropped to 10 degrees below zero, while in East Prussia it reached minus 25. But warmer air was on its way from Scandinavia, and in the next few weeks the punishing cold would lift. A thaw was coming, although it would probably bring showers.

Paul von Hindenburg had been scheduled to meet with people from the Christian and Free Trade Unions that morning, but his office cancelled at the last minute. Even the Foreign Minister and Finance Minister, as well as representatives from Germany's largest business associations, were sent friendly requests to postpone their appointments.

Hindenburg was reshaping the fate of the country, and that took concentration.

Around eleven o'clock, Ribbentrop popped in to see his old comrade Papen. 'Where's Hitler?' asked the former chancellor. Ribbentrop thought he'd already left and could probably be reached in Weimar. Papen insisted that he be recalled at once. They were reaching a turning point, he exclaimed, and the chancellorship was now a real possibility. Ribbentrop rushed off to find Göring, who knew that Hitler was still at the Kaiserhof. Göring telephoned the Führer, and the Führer stayed in Berlin.

Even so, he wouldn't see Papen today. Tomorrow. Tomorrow was soon enough.

At half past eleven the cabinet met at the Chancellery. Would it be the last time? They'd not been in office two months – certainly not long enough to affect the job market.

The ministers' eyes wandered outside, where the magnificent trees were rigid with frost.

Schleicher was the first to speak. In a few minutes he had an audience with Hindenburg, and he would ask again for permission to dissolve Parliament. He expected the president to refuse. And then – he would resign. He couldn't make himself and his cabinet a laughing stock. In all likelihood the next administration would be a Papen cabinet supported by Hugenberg and the DNVP.

Several ministers protested. Shouldn't they warn the president against such a coalition?

Schleicher pushed back his chair and rose to his feet.

12.15 p.m. Everything hung on this one conversation. Hindenburg sat at his desk. He knew he didn't have long to live but believed that God was on his side.

The chancellor outlined the president's options.

A Hitler cabinet supported by a parliamentary majority. Very unlikely, noted Schleicher.

A presidential cabinet under Hitler, but that ran counter to the president's principles. Also ruled out.

The third option was to keep Schleicher as chancellor but grant him sweeping emergency powers.

There was no other way. Papen and Hugenberg? They'd have a revolution on their hands.

Deep down Hindenburg was a military strategist. He understood the nuances of conflict. He knew how to read the signs. And he was well aware of the chancellor's close affiliation with the *Tägliche Rundschau*.

The newspaper had printed an outrageously impudent article only that morning. 'Presidential Crisis'? Did Schleicher honestly believe he could intimidate the field marshal with such blunt tools?

No. Hitler and Papen were offering a solution that meant he could act constitutionally and stop relying so excessively on his authority as president. It would be a huge relief.

I am requesting permission to dissolve Parliament, said Schleicher.

'No,' said Hindenburg. 'You're not getting it.' Those were his exact, contemptuous words. Such was his opinion of Kurt von Schleicher.

He was grateful, continued Hindenburg, 'that you tried to win over the National Socialists and create a majority. You were not successful, and now other options must be sought.'

The chancellor responded: 'You have the right to remove me from office, but you do not have the right to make deals with somebody else behind the back of a chancellor you appointed against his will. That is a betrayal.'

He announced he would step down. His entire cabinet would be joining him.

Hindenburg had expected that, of course. The letter of resignation had already been prepared. Meissner fetched it. Meissner, who always thought of everything. Meissner, who had laid so many snares with Schleicher in the past. Meissner, always loyal to whomever had the upper hand.

Schleicher could remain in office until the new cabinet was in place.

The chancellor returned to his cabinet in less than fifteen minutes. Crushed. It was over. Only fifty-six days in office.

It was like talking to a brick wall, he told his ministers.

The news spread rapidly through the city. Schleicher had resigned!

The Communists were instantly on the alert. They had to be ready for anything, and quickly. Ernst Thälmann told his colleague Otto Franke that the Central Committee had to convene as soon as possible, but somewhere safe. 'Do you know a suitable place?' he asked. 'Two, off the top of my head, Comrade Thälmann,' answered Franke. They had known each other for many years, Franke having taken part in the very first KPD party conference. He was a rock. Utterly reliable.

Thälmann opted for the Sporthaus Ziegenhals near Königs Wusterhausen, south-east of Berlin, a restaurant owned by a Communist called Willy Mörschel. They arranged for all the KPD leaders to meet there on 7 February.

Franz von Papen's day had only just begun. Hindenburg had now officially tasked him with assembling a government, and he didn't need to be asked twice. He spoke with Hugenberg in the afternoon, who was half grouchy and half greedy. Papen, promising him Economics and Agriculture, realised the DNVP chairman was coming around to the idea of the Nazis being given both the national and the Prussian Interior Ministries.

He held talks with members of the current cabinet until the evening. Some were happy to stay on. At midday he telephoned Schwerin von Krosigk at home and told him there were only two options: a Hitler cabinet with Papen as Vice-Chancellor, or a Papen–Hugenberg cabinet, which would immediately find itself on an adversarial footing. Tomorrow he would continue negotiations with Hitler, as well as with the leaders of the Centre Party and the Bavarian People's Party. Papen was nearly at the finish line.

The leaders of the Centre Party and the BVP, both Catholic parties, had already heard Papen was exploring options for a new government. Fritz Schäffer, chairman of the BVP, immediately told the Führer he was willing to cooperate with a Hitler cabinet as part of a coalition. He, too, wanted to stymie Papen.

But Hitler turned him down: he wasn't the one tasked with

building a government, he said, and hence he couldn't start negotiating a coalition.

The situation was tricky. Papen knew that if Hindenburg got wind of the Catholic parties' suggestion and took it seriously, any chance of him appointing Hitler chancellor without a parliamentary majority would be off the table. Yet Hitler was refusing to enter a coalition, or to accept any situation in which he had to justify his actions to others.

There had to be another solution!

Schleicher was gone. That awful man Papen had been asked yet again to form a government. Harry Graf Kessler was appalled: confronted with the goings-on at Wilhelmstrasse, he thought, all a person of good taste could do was turn away in disgust.

Kessler wondered how it had got to this point, especially when replacing the chancellor seemed so unnecessary. Some sort of intrigue, that much was clear, probably with the Eastern Aid Scandal behind it.

> The corrupt grandees thought Schleicher was too slapdash in covering up their mess; that's why the old man had to be quickly presented with his favourite again, who is willing to proceed more robustly in such cases. The whole thing is a mixture of corruption, backroom dealing and cronyism. It reminds me of the worst periods of the absolute monarchy.

Journalists were beginning to compete for news. Who would be the first to break the next big story? Editorial offices were obsessed with the idea that they were witnessing a sea change, and Bella Fromm was swept along with the general tide. She, however, was concerned with more than getting a scoop – she was worried about her friend. The office at Ullstein was so thick with tension and excitement it was unbearable, so she jumped into her car and raced across to see

Schleicher. What was going on? 'Don't worry so hard, Bella, dear,' said Schleicher, trying to reassure her. 'I'll see you tonight at the Press Ball. I'll come to the Ullstein box to have the second dance with you.' It was two o'clock in the afternoon.

If any Nazi was likely to inspire confidence in Hindenburg, it was First World War veteran Hermann Göring. The former flying ace had been chosen to deliver a message to the president: once they were in power, the National Socialists would continue to respect Hindenburg's authority; they had no intention of breaching the constitution or gaining influence over the armed forces.

It made an impression on Hindenburg – the word of honour, he thought, from a man who knew what honour meant.

The theatre on Schiffbauerdamm was premiering a comedy entitled *Caution! Wet Paint!*. Written by the Frenchman René Fauchois, the play left the usually earnest critic Alfred Kerr in stitches. Charmingly constructed, he decided, with a sparkling cast. After the performance he went home to Douglasstrasse 10 in Grunewald, around the corner from the Rot-Weiss Tennis Club. He would write his review the following morning, assuming he was spared by the flu epidemic still sweeping across Germany. Perhaps he'd also settle down to work on the libretto for his opera *Der Chronoplan*, which he was writing with his wife. Julia loved composing, and they'd been working on the opera for two years. Only the finale was left.

Kerr wasn't overly concerned by the political rumblings. His suitcases weren't packed. He'd stashed no money abroad. His valuable collections – first editions of Heinrich Heine, original engravings, paintings, musical scores – were scattered across the apartment in all their glory. If the Nazis did seize power, there'd be time to see whether they really would govern as advertised, surely. There'd be time to sort everything out.

Eight o'clock. Hundreds of Communists had poured into Bülowplatz, chanting banned leftist songs. Police quickly descended. An illegal demonstration, the officer in charge decided. Break it up! The police cleared the square, attacking the demonstrators with rubber truncheons. One hour later, officers broke up another Communist protest in Karlstrasse.

Meanwhile, at the Rostock Sportpalast, Joseph Goebbels was giving a lecture to an audience of students. Only after leaving the stage did he learn that Schleicher had stepped down, and instantly he dashed back to Berlin, full of scepticism: he didn't trust the 'gang of swindlers', as he called the president's advisers, and he considered Hindenburg himself faithless and unpredictable, despite the old man's constant harping about loyalty.

At the Kaiserhof, Hitler brought him up to speed on the latest developments. Papen was sounding things out. Everything was looking good. Yet the Führer was moody. He didn't believe Papen. He suspected he'd abuse his mandate, maybe even proclaim himself chancellor at the last minute. Eventually his grievances devolved into a monologue. He railed against the faithless aristocrats and their caprices, against the whole lot of 'vons'. His entourage, who'd heard it all before, listened in silence, supplying the audience Hitler needed.

Late that evening, Papen trekked through the snowy garden once again to speak to Hindenburg. The NSDAP's demands were reasonable, he argued. They only wanted a few ministerial posts, and many of the current cabinet would continue as before. He was careful not to mention the spat between Hitler and Hugenberg.

Hindenburg insisted the two most important roles, Foreign Minister and Defence Minister, go to his own allies.

Konstantin von Neurath would stay in office as Foreign Minister, said Papen.

Very good.

But Schleicher can't be Minister of Defence.

No, agreed Hindenburg.

He named Lieutenant-General Werner von Blomberg, who had taken part in the disarmament conference in Geneva.

Before Papen left, Hindenburg made him promise to join Hitler's cabinet as Vice-Chancellor.

Papen said yes.

The Press Ball, which took place in the function rooms at the Berlin Zoo behind the Memorial Church, was a highlight of the social calendar. Kurt von Schleicher, however, did not attend. Nor did most of his ministers. The box reserved for the government was almost empty. Instead, there was a cast of literary figures, actors and musicians, who did not let the political tug-of-war dampen their mood: Erich Kästner, Roda Roda, Carl Zuckmayer, Wilhelm Furtwängler and Edgar Ansel Mowrer rubbed shoulders in the cheery throng. New guests were still showing up even after midnight; the rooms were packed. Berlin was back to its old self.

Bella Fromm was there, of course. Did she wait in the Ullstein box for Schleicher and the promised dance? More likely work distracted her. It was her job to attend, after all. To observe 'who flirted with whom, who wore what, who escorted whom, and who shared which table with whom'. She plastered an appropriately festive smile on her face, which suited her outfit, a pale rose velvet dress with a long train and chinchilla trim. Ordered especially from Paris. But the chancellor wasn't there to see it. Fromm was no fool – she was filled with foreboding. 'My heart was heavy,' she sighed in her diary.

'An anguish of suspense and waiting hung over the Press Ball,' she remarked afterwards in her column. 'Chancellor-less! Schleicher no longer felt the responsibility, while Hitler, Papen and Hugenberg did not feel it yet.'

Abraham Plotkin was at a competing event that evening: a masked ball thrown by a socialist magazine. There were plenty of journalists at this party, too. The ball was spread across three rooms, with a jazz orchestra playing in each. All were filled to bursting. The dancing, it struck Plotkin, 'was exactly what it would have been in an ordinary jazz palace on Broadway'. Huge bottles of wine could be bought for approximately 3 marks each, and Plotkin's party of six shared three bottles over the course of the evening. Nobody got drunk; their jollity struck Plotkin as forced. He went home around three in the morning, while the dancing continued until five.

Tomorrow was Sunday, a day of rest.

SUNDAY 29 JANUARY

Our Demand after Schleicher's Departure: Hitler for Chancellor
— *Völkischer Beobachter*

Alert! Alert!
United Front: Take Action against All-Out Fascist Attack
Emergency Measures Threaten Red Party of Freedom
— *Die Rote Fahne*

Negotiations with Hitler
Tuesday Reichstag Session Cancelled
All Communist Demonstrations Banned
— *Vossische Zeitung*

Trade Unions Mobilising
Storm against Papen – What Will Hindenburg Decide?
— *Tägliche Rundschau*

How had they slept last night? How did the denizens of Wilhelmstrasse feel as they awoke on Sunday morning?

The future of the German nation would be decided on a day that never really grew light. The weather wasn't quite as frosty, but temperatures were still hovering below zero. At least the worst of the cold had receded. Scattered showers of rain and snow – or both at once. That was the forecast.

Around ten o'clock in the morning, Hindenburg arrived at his study. This Sunday he had little time for his beloved family, or for prayer. Summoning Meissner to his side, he announced his decision: Schleicher was to be relieved of his duties as Defence Minister. Immediately.

A telegram was dispatched to Geneva, ordering Blomberg back to Berlin. Blomberg, the commander in charge of the military in East Prussia, was a frequent visitor at Wilhelmstrasse, and Hindenburg was fond of the tall general, who had often expressed his disagreement with Schleicher's policies.

Not even Papen was told.

A copy of the telegram landed promptly on Schleicher's desk. His spies were still spying, his informants still informing. Blomberg, recalled to Berlin? Picking up the telephone, Schleicher learned from Blomberg's staff that the General was coming back by train because of the weather.

He would be in Berlin tomorrow. Blomberg, a military-history enthusiast, was mild mannered and well educated. Not a man to think for himself. Schleicher had never taken him seriously as a rival; not so far.

Hitler postponed all his travel plans. He had to be on the spot. He had to think ahead. He called Hans Heinrich Lammers, an undersecretary who had worked for many years as a constitutional lawyer at the Ministry of the Interior. Formerly a strict monarchist, he had joined the NSDAP one year earlier. Did Lammers want to be State Secretary? 'I am a politician,' said Hitler, 'and I'm not familiar with all this bureaucratic red tape. I don't want to bother with it, but nor do I want to make a fool of myself. I need a civil servant who knows the ropes. Are you willing to accept this office?

Yes, answered Lammers. He was willing.

Another mass march at the Lustgarten, this one organised by the SPD. The Iron Front was gathering. These were the defenders of the Republic: the Reichsbanner, the Federation of German Trade Unions, the Workers' Gymnastics and Sports Federation, and the General Federation of Salaried Employees. According to their own estimates, the Reichsbanner alone comprised three million members.

A banner hung outside the former palace of the Hohenzollerns: 'Berlin Is Staying Red'. Roughly twenty thousand uniformed men had assembled, many of whom had marched fifteen or twenty kilometres that morning. Another eighty thousand people had squeezed into the Lustgarten, and a hundred thousand more lined the streets.

Plotkin was among them, of course. It was the first time he'd seen the Iron Front. 'They marched with a zip as effective as that of the Nazis,' he observed. Holding their red banners high in the air, they were 'a stirring sight'. The protectors of the Republic seemed determined.

Franz Künstler, a member of Parliament and head of the Berlin branch of the SPD, addressed the crowd. 'Berlin belongs to the Reds,' he shouted. 'The Iron Front has saved the Republic on two occasions. It may be necessary for the Iron Front to save it again. We will not permit the Nazis or the monarchists to destroy the edifice that we have so painfully built.'

It was a powerful speech. Shoulders straightened. Heads were lifted. Plotkin thought it was 'the most effective fifteen minutes of oratory I have ever listened to'.

As they left, the crowd sang the 'Internationale'.

So comrades, come rally,
And the last fight let us face.
The Internationale
Unites the human race.

Then the Iron Front dispersed.

Even Harry Graf Kessler had been at the demonstration. He'd kept a lookout for Communists but couldn't find any, although they'd announced they would be marching, too, since whole units of the Reichsbanner had taken part in a KPD march on Wednesday. Still, Kessler was pleased to see so many people turn out, despite the miserable weather. It gave him hope.

Papen's apartment was a hive of activity that morning. Hitler and Göring had arrived, and the negotiations resumed. It was an endless, psychologically draining rally. Which members of the NSDAP would be ministers?

Frick had to be Interior Minister, declared Hitler, and Göring Interior Minister for Prussia, so that the Prussian police would 'finally be in safe hands'. Papen didn't demur. In return, Hitler accepted Papen as Vice-Chancellor and Commissioner for Prussia.

Then, however, he came out with a new condition: the Reichstag must be dissolved as soon as possible and new elections arranged. As chancellor he would want to pass an Enabling Act, which the Reichstag would have to approve with a two-thirds majority – only then would his cabinet have total control.

Papen agreed to that, too. He went straight to see Hindenburg.

Meanwhile, Schleicher was discussing the situation with several generals at the Ministry of Defence. They had to stop Hitler or Papen becoming chancellor – but how?

With violence, said one of the generals. The military had to remove the president from office. Seize Hindenburg – treating him respectfully – and take him to Neudeck. Then notify the troops and declare martial law. Ferdinand von Bredow agreed.

It would be a coup.

No, said Schleicher. Never!

Then he went home. Schleicher wanted to stay Minister of Defence at any cost, and he hadn't yet heard anything to the contrary.

So, the chancellor was history. Carl von Ossietzky decided to address it in the next edition of the *Weltbühne*. 'We're going through saviours at quite a rate,' he observed.

Another one bites the dust. If the authoritarian regime keeps managing its affairs like this, everyone in Germany will be getting a turn!

How long is it since the last chancellor, hailed by all and sundry as a statesman of genius, appeared on the scene? And today General von Schleicher, wound-riddled as Caesar's corpse, lies in the abandoned Capitol. The 'social general', trying to lift every heavy weight at the same time, has been exposed as a dilettante, bested in his own specialist area: scheming.

That afternoon, Hitler and Goebbels were having a quiet cup of tea when Göring came hurtling into the room. Everything was going perfectly, he cried. The Führer would be appointed chancellor the very next day! For a long time no one said a word. Then Hitler and Goebbels stood and shook hands.

Even when they were alone, the Nazis had a weakness for theatre.

Papen's official residence – which had been supposed to transfer to Kurt von Schleicher's when he entered office – became the new hub of the negotiations. That afternoon, he sent for Hugenberg and the two leaders of the Stahlhelm, Seldte and Duesterberg. He gave them an update on the situation, if one strategically incomplete: he neglected to mention that Hitler had stipulated that they call a fresh election.

Instead, he offered Seldte the post of Labour Minister, and to Hugenberg he said that the president wanted him in charge of both Economy and Agriculture, for the Reich as a whole as well as for Prussia. Hugenberg was going to be a super-minister.

Papen was cunning. He knew how to play on Hugenberg's inferiority complex.

Hugenberg accepted. 'We'll box Hitler in,' he said. Better still, not a word had been said about the Centre Party, which he loathed. It all sounded good. Very good.

Some of his colleagues, however, urged their leader to refuse the offer. Hitler was a fanatic! 'What do you want?' asked Papen. 'I have

Hindenburg's confidence. In two months we'll have pushed Hitler so far into a corner that he squeals.'

Theodor Duesterberg also objected. Although he was a well-known anti-Semite, he had been repeatedly denigrated in the Nazi press because of his Jewish ancestry.

By the time they finished, nothing had been set in stone. Yet Papen told the National Socialists that the road to government was finally clear.

Even though he still needed another chat with Hindenburg.

The Reichstag faction of the DVP published a statement deploring the political agitation that had led to this new crisis. And the German State Party demanded of the president and the Reichstag a government with 'democratic authority'. If the state ended up 'at the mercy of a revolution because every opposing position became increasingly entrenched', then all hope of freedom would be lost.

General Kurt von Hammerstein-Equord wanted an urgent word with Hitler. He had come to advocate for his friend Schleicher. Did he also threaten retaliation? Certainly a rumour quickly started circulating that the military was planning a coup to prevent a change of government.

Germany was reaching the point of no return.

It wasn't the only rumour in Berlin. François-Poncet heard Papen had dropped his plan to build a Hitler government, and similar news reached the ears of the non-partisan Finance Minister, Schwerin von Krosigk – even though Papen had told him only that morning that a Hitler cabinet was in the pipeline.

The puffed-up busybody's time had come. Schwerin von Krosigk had also heard that Hugenberg was calling for Papen's return as chancellor, while another informant told him the president was no longer in his right mind, and Schleicher was poised to get the military involved. What ought one to believe?

General Hammerstein-Equord paid Schleicher another visit that evening, and he brought somebody else with him: Werner von Alvensleben, the shadowy conservative power broker who combined excellent connections with nearly everybody on the right with a willingness to act as Schleicher's go-between and informant.

Hitler and Göring visited Goebbels at his apartment on Reichskanzlerplatz, where the three shared a meal. The doorbell rang – Werner von Alvensleben. He had come to make enquiries. Alvensleben said the military was preparing for the possibility that the new government wouldn't be to their liking.

What did that mean? asked the Nazis. Was it a threat? They sent Alvensleben packing without a reply.

He had left the NSDAP in a fluster. What was all that mysterious stuff about the army? Were they launching a coup after all?

Or it was nothing but a cock-and-bull story, thought Goebbels. Either way, it was getting Hitler all riled up. Goebbels didn't believe Schleicher had the courage to take action against Hindenburg. Still, better safe than sorry. He summoned Graf von Helldorff, Chief Commander of the SA in Berlin, and instructed him to take 'measures' – what measures, exactly, Goebbels did not confide in his diary.

Finally, Göring contacted Papen and Meissner. Was there any truth to these rumours about a coup?

The disconcerting news had also reached Hindenburg's ears. Of course. There was a constant stream of gossip coming down the grapevine. The latest was that Schleicher had mobilised the Potsdam garrison, who were on the verge of seizing Hindenburg and taking him to Neudeck in a sealed train.

Nobody on Hindenburg's staff checked whether this was true.

Instead, they listened anxiously for the sound of marching boots.

The moment had come. Franz von Papen knew how to make a compelling case, and late that night he presented his list of ministers to Hindenburg. Göring's name was on there, as a minister without portfolio on the national level, as Interior Minister for Prussia, and as Commissioner for Air Traffic. Frick would be Interior Minister for the Reich as a whole. Goebbels' name was missing. The conservatives hated him – he'd be too difficult a sell.

Some posts were still vacant. The Justice Minister, for instance. Maybe the Centre Party would want one?

If not, the new government wouldn't have a majority. The NSDAP and DNVP weren't enough by themselves. Of course, Hitler had no intention of entering a coalition: he wanted power. But Papen didn't mention that. Instead, he gave Hindenburg the impression that they were in intensive talks with the Centre Party.

It was a trick. Hitler saw it for what it was, Hugenberg saw it for what it was, and Meissner saw it for what it was. Anyone with an ounce of political savvy could see it for what it was. Maybe even Hindenburg.

But it was the chance he'd been looking for, a chance to finally offload responsibility. He *wanted* to believe that the new government already had a majority behind it.

The DNVP was also in a state of high tension. On the one hand, Reinhold Quaatz was pleased with himself. His party's declaration of war had, he noted, 'dealt Schleicher the death blow', even though Schleicher was telling everybody he'd be back inside three weeks, after 'this Papen experiment blows up in Hindenburg's face'.

On the other hand, the party knew the risk they were running.

'The ultimatum has had a galvanising effect on the party. At a single stroke we are now in the centre of events,' continued Quaatz. 'If we go with Hitler, we'll have to harness him. Otherwise we're finished either way, whether he manages to seize power for himself or whether he fails.'

If the Hitler government fell flat, then Papen, Meissner and possibly even Hindenburg would try to pin the blame on the DNVP. As Quaatz observed: 'we'll also have to prevent a Hitler–Centre coalition, although we can't fall out with the Centre completely. It's a juggling act. Luckily everybody else is reliant on us.'

And what were the SPD doing? The Social Democrats were discussing the united front they would soon have to build with the Communists. They were discussing which was more effective, to act or to wait, in order to seem most impressively aware of their responsibility.

The SPD talked. And readied themselves.

TAKING POWER

30 JANUARY 1933

MONDAY 30 JANUARY

President Hindenburg bears ultimate responsibility, as
history will judge. His re-election expressed the will of
the people to put a guardian of the entire nation in the
highest office – a man of reconciliation, of domestic peace,
a representative of equal rights and equal duties.
The signs point to an oncoming storm.

– Vossische Zeitung

The Social Democrats and the entirety of the Iron Front,
with both feet planted in the constitution and the law, stand
opposed to this government and its threatened coup.

– Vorwärts

Hitler and Göring conferred with Goebbels until five o'clock in the
morning. What *was* Schleicher up to? 'A coup?' wondered Goebbels.
'A threat? Is he serious? Is he being childish?' They surmised. Debated.
Brooded. Hitler paced up and down the room. What should they do?
There was nothing they could do. Finally they went to bed. It was time
for a few hours' rest.

Shortly after seven, an agitated Franz von Papen opened the door of
his apartment to Theodor Duesterberg. 'If we don't have a government by eleven o'clock,' he cried, 'the military will act. We're facing a
Schleicher and Hammerstein military dictatorship.'

'Where did you hear that?' asked Duesterberg.

'From Hindenburg's son,' replied Papen.

Duesterberg hurried across to the Chancellery, where Oskar von
Hindenburg lived with his family. There was a soldier outside the
door. Was Oskar under arrest? No, he was just standing guard. Then

the door burst open, and Oskar came charging out. He was off to the railway station.

Blomberg was expected to arrive at Anhalter Bahnhof at half past eight.

Paul von Hindenburg had sent his son to fetch him; he had orders to bring him to the presidential office.

Hammerstein, meanwhile, had sent his adjutant, a major; he had orders to bring Blomberg to see Schleicher.

The station was busy that morning, a confusion of steam, whistles and puffing trains. The commuters' breath froze in the chilly air. The night train pulled in, and out stepped Blomberg.

He was greeted by the Major. Hurry, General, there's a car waiting. It's urgent!

Then Oskar von Hindenburg stepped forward.

Blomberg chose the higher-ranking officer, Oskar, and the ultimate authority he represented: Hindenburg.

Arriving at the Chancellery, Oskar von Hindenburg described what had occurred at the station.

The coup had to be imminent!

The president didn't hesitate. Shortly after nine o'clock, he swore in Werner von Blomberg as the new Minister of Defence. Hindenburg, who only two days earlier had barred Schleicher from breaking the constitution, was now acting unconstitutionally himself: in the Weimar Republic, a president could not swear in any minister not put forward by the chancellor.

Meissner fetched the official letter of appointment.

Just like that, Schleicher was dethroned. He was no longer in charge of the armed forces, as he discovered when Meissner telephoned him.

'It's a violation of the constitution!' blurted Schleicher.

Well, the president had to act, was Meissner's response.

After the ceremony, Blomberg was about to set off for the Ministry of Defence when Oskar von Hindenburg issued a few words of caution: show your face around there, and they'll arrest you!

Abraham Plotkin spent that morning with trade-unionist friends. Furtwängler, from the Federation of German Trade Unions, kept assuring him that Hitler would never be appointed. Hindenburg would sooner resign than make him chancellor.

'White Week', marking the annual winter sales, was beginning. The shops were offering special discounts on sheets, pillowcases, towels, fur rugs and similar items. Long white flags hung from department-store roofs, and window displays were full of cut-price wares.

Pandemonium all around. Schleicher's State Secretary, Erwin Planck, had been on the telephone with Finance Minister Schwerin von Krosigk and was now reporting that Hitler had broken off negotiations – that he'd probably already left Berlin. Hindenburg had called for Papen and was going to summarily swear him in as chancellor.

Moments later, Schwerin von Krosigk received a call from the office of the president. He was invited to present himself at eleven o'clock, when he would be officially reappointed as Finance Minister. Who was going to be chancellor? No information on that score.

Next, Schwerin von Krosigk contacted Neurath, the Foreign Minister; both agreed they wanted no part in another Papen cabinet. Neurath, too, had been curtly summoned to the presidential study.

Then, at last, Schwerin von Krosigk got hold of Franz von Papen. He sounded unruffled. 'Pay no attention to the rumours,' he said. The Hitler cabinet was as good as sworn in.

That morning, the British ambassador, Sir Horace Rumbold – another

Wilhelmstrasse resident – informed London that Papen was almost certainly going to be the next chancellor. He'd heard about the rumoured coup, but his political instincts told him there was nothing in it.

Between nine and ten o'clock, Duesterberg and Seldte, leaders of the Stahlhelm, arrived at Papen's apartment to meet with Hugenberg and Otto Schmidt-Hannover, chairman of the DNVP's faction in the Reichstag. Papen, now anything but unruffled, insisted they couldn't sit on their hands any longer – they *had* to swear in the cabinet if they wanted to prevent a military coup.

Yet the DNVP were still implacable. Neither Schmidt-Hannover nor Duesterberg would accept Hitler's conditions. At the very least, he would have to relinquish the Prussian Ministry of the Interior.

Both men hurried across the see the president – but Hindenburg's door was shut. They had to settle for Oskar, who was still up in arms and fulminating against Schleicher's alleged treachery.

Back at Papen's apartment, Hitler and Göring had appeared.

The situation was complicated. Seldte wanted to join the cabinet, but his colleague had to agree. Yet Duesterberg, having been so viciously maligned in the Nazi press, refused even to shake Hitler's hand.

The two Nazis briefly conferred, then Hitler approached Duesterberg. Putting on his most solemn voice, the Führer seemed genuinely affected. 'I regret the malicious abuse levelled against you in my press. I give you my word that it was not done on my instructions.'

The little performance served its purpose.

Out into the cold they went. Through the back door of the Interior Ministry, down the garden path and via the rear entrance into the Chancellery. Papen could probably have found his way even on a moonless, snowless, pitch-black night, he'd made the trip so many times. Their leather-soled shoes fumbled across the packed snow.

The procession reached Meissner's office on the ground floor shortly before eleven o'clock, where they bumped into the two former ministers who had come to be sworn in one more time.

When Graf Schwerin von Krosigk had entered the Chancellery minutes earlier, he'd been greeted humorously by a long-time servant: 'All the holes are already full.' A presidential adviser offered him and Neurath a seat in his office, and then they were left to wait.

Now Schwerin von Krosigk was meeting Adolf Hitler for the first time. He tried briefly to outline a responsible fiscal policy for the new chancellor: introduce no measures that would result in inflation and keep a balanced budget. The Führer made an awkward impression on Schwerin von Krosigk. 'Discuss the details with Göring,' said Hitler. 'He's more concerned with these matters than I am.'

As it happened, Schwerin von Krosigk knew perfectly well that Göring had read up on the issues.

A discussion arose in Meissner's office.

Hitler repeated his demand for fresh elections.

Excuse me? Hugenberg was hearing this for the first time, and he refused outright.

Things were getting heated. Was Papen's house of cards – painstakingly constructed through diplomacy, half-truths, omissions, charm and lies – about to collapse?

Again Hitler played his ace. He gave his word of honour that he wouldn't alter his cabinet, no matter the results of the election. It had always worked for him before: an honourable man's word of honour. This was Prussia, after all.

No! Hugenberg was unyielding.

Meissner had slipped out of the room during the squabble.

Papen now appealed to Hugenberg. You're endangering nationalist unity! How can you doubt this man's word?

Hugenberg dug in his heels.

The door was thrown open, and Meissner appeared, pulse racing.

In his hand he held a watch. The old man wasn't happy. 'Gentlemen, you were due to be sworn in at eleven o'clock. It's now eleven fifteen. You cannot keep the president waiting any longer.'

Now.

Did they feel it in the room? That in this heightened hour, everything hung in the balance?

Finally Hugenberg's resistance collapsed. He could no longer withstand the lure of power when it was so close. It was up to the president, he said, whether to dissolve Parliament or not.

Göring was the first to speak. 'Well, that's everything sorted!' he cried. 'We can go up now.'

And so they rushed, stumbling and bounding, up the staircase.

It was Hindenburg's turn to keep his chosen cabinet waiting. After a few minutes he appeared, wearing a frock coat. There was no trace of ceremony in his manner or words.

Papen read the list of ministers aloud, excluding only the name of the Justice Minister. Negotiations with the Centre and the BVP would have to begin immediately. No jumping to conclusions there, of course.

Around half past eleven, Adolf Hitler, forty-three years old, was sworn in on the Weimar Constitution. 'I swear I will devote all my energies to the welfare of the German people, protect the laws of the German nation, diligently fulfil the duties incumbent upon me and conduct my affairs without party bias and equitably towards all people.'

The new cabinet had 248 out of 560 votes in the Reichstag. Less than half. Yet Hindenburg was still telling himself this wasn't a presidential cabinet, that they would scrape together a majority somehow. The hero of the Battle of Tannenberg had fallen into Papen's trap. Because he wanted to.

Paul von Hindenburg only had one thing to say, something he'd probably said long ago to his officers before sending the troops into combat: 'And now, gentlemen, go forth with God!'

A crowd of people had been massing in Wilhelmstrasse since the morning, necks craning. Had it happened yet?

SA commander Ernst Röhm peered through binoculars from a window at the Kaiserhof, watching the door of the Chancellery. Hitler would have to emerge at some point, and he'd be able to read on his face what had occurred.

First out was Göring, shouting something. Then Hitler. The Führer climbed into an open-topped car and was driven to the Kaiserhof. He stood upright in the vehicle, tears streaming down his cheeks. 'We did it,' he cried, over and over, his voice cracking.

In the lobby of the Kaiserhof there was clapping and cheering. A chorus of *heils*. Hitler stepped into the lift. 'We are ready,' he said before he disappeared.

Seconds later he was standing opposite Goebbels. Hitler said nothing. Neither did anybody else. Goebbels saw tears in the Führers' eyes.

An impromptu victory celebration broke out in the hotel restaurant, with nearly all the NSDAP bigwigs taking part. Having fought so long, having suffered so long, they were now overcome with the unfamiliar sensation of power.

Earlier that morning, in their conference room at the Reichstag, senior Social Democrats had met with leading trade unionists to review the situation. Rudolf Breitscheid, SPD faction leader in the Reichstag, believed that if Hitler was appointed chancellor then Parliament would probably be adjourned or dissolved. 'We would then enter a new phase of National Socialism in which it would be necessary for us to drive the Fascists out of power.' But they would have to do it without the KPD. For now, the SPD's only option was to 'demonstrate their resolve'. One of the Social Democrats left the room after Breitscheid's speech to telephone an official statement to the party newspaper, *Vorwärts* – but he never made the call. Just as he was picking up the receiver, he heard a wild shout go up in the corridor: Hitler was chancellor.

The KPD immediately started printing flyers.

Now was the time for a general strike!

The Central Committee issued a resolution: 'This new cabinet of an openly Fascist dictatorship is the most brutal and blatant declaration of war on working people, on the German working class.'

Would the SPD and the trade unions support them?

The official announcement read as follows:

The President of the Reich has appointed Herr Adolf Hitler as chancellor, and at Herr Hitler's suggestion the government will be reshuffled:

Former Chancellor von Papen as Vice-Chancellor and Commissioner of the State of Prussia;

Freiherr von Neurath as Foreign Minister;

MP and former Prime Minister Dr Frick as Minister of the Interior;

Lieutenant General Freiherr von Blomberg as Minister of Defence;

Graf von Schwerin-Krosigk as Finance Minister;

MP and Privy Councillor for Finance Hugenberg as Economics Minister and Minister for Agriculture;

Freiherr von Eltz-Rübenach as Minister for Postal Services and Transport;

Reichstag President Göring as minister without portfolio and Commissioner for Air Traffic.

Minister Göring has been entrusted with safeguarding the affairs of the Prussian Interior Ministry.

Commissioner for Work Gereke remains in office.

The role of Justice Minister remains unassigned. The chancellor will begin negotiations today with the Centre Party and the Bavarian People's Party. The first cabinet meeting will take place this afternoon at five o'clock.

Goebbels hurried back to his office at the local branch of the NSDAP and updated his staff. The atmosphere was solemn. 'Like in a church,' wrote Goebbels in his diary. 'The first stage!' Papen as Vice-Chancellor, Seldte as Labour Minister? Minor blemishes, he told his colleagues. 'They'll have to be erased.'

Then, accompanied by Ernst Hanfstaengl and Auwi, the Kaiser's son, he went to see his wife, who was still recovering in hospital.

At half past one, Kurt von Schleicher assembled his cabinet for the final time. He expressed his 'sincerest thanks' to all members of the cabinet for the work they had done together, which was marked by a high degree of 'trust'. Then, that was that.

As Schwerin von Krosigk noted later: 'he gave no outward sign of his profound shock and distress. But this experience has been a matter of life or death to him.'

Harry Graf Kessler heard the news from a friend at about two o'clock. He was astonished: he hadn't expected it to come so quickly. From the street outside came a cheer – the 'Nazi doorman', as he called the building's concierge, was celebrating.

History was unfolding before his eyes, and Abraham Plotkin watched half fascinated, half alarmed. Still, he consoled himself with the thought that the military remained in the hands of Hugenberg and his allies. 'Dictators are not in the habit of trusting each other with armies,' he wrote.

The victorious National Socialists posed for a group shot at the Kaiserhof: a team photograph of exactly eleven men. Hitler clasped his hands in front of him, while Göring stood with one hand in the pocket of his voluminous trench coat and the other clutching his hat. Goebbels was there, too, of course, as were Röhm, Himmler, Hess and Frick.

Later, Hitler left the hotel through rows of enthusiastic supporters, Rudolf Hess close at his heels. Tears welled in every eye. Arms
were raised, *heils* roared. The chancellor wore a dark tie with a tight
knot and a pale trench coat. His parting looked like it had been cut
with a knife.

Millions of Germans had been waiting for the SPD to respond. Many
were determined to fight; it was what they'd prepared for. Then the
party executive and Reichstag faction issued a statement.

'Cool heads, determination, discipline, unity and, again, unity,'
the SPD demanded of its supporters, urging them to keep their pow-
der dry. 'Undisciplined activity by individual organisations or groups
working on their own initiative would be to the serious detriment of
the whole working class.' The 'rules of democracy' had to be obeyed.

Trade union bosses similarly exhorted their members to 'be pru-
dent and keep cool heads'. Was this a plea? An order? 'Don't be misled
into premature and harmful individual actions.' Theodor Leipart, the
valiant head of the Federation of German Trade Unions, emphasised
that 'organisation, not demonstration, is the watchword of the hour.
This is the spirit in which the trade unions have acted for decades.'

The defenders of the Republic held fire. What were their leaders
waiting for?

What else had to happen? And, if something did happen, were
they leaving it too late to respond?

The revolving door at the Kaiserhof hadn't stopped spinning. Press
Officer Ernst Hanfstaengl had his hands full, besieged by hordes
of foreign journalists falling over themselves to interview the new
chancellor.

Kurt Schumacher, chair of the SPD and the Reichsbanner in Stuttgart,
telephoned orders to a colleague in the region: the members of the

Iron Front must obey only their own organisation. Nothing they heard from the other side – i.e. the Communists – was in the interests of the working class. 'In Berlin,' he added, 'in the thick of it, there is no trace of defeat or despondence in our ranks. There is not the slightest reason for such a thing.'

There was no proof that Kurt von Schleicher had been plotting anything treasonous, so he simply handed over the affairs of state to his successor as normal before retreating to his apartment. Rumour had it he was going to write a book.

Acting on instructions from Ernst Thälmann and the Central Committee of the KPD, Walter Ulbricht, head of the party's Berlin branch, approached the SPD executive and suggested they form an alliance. 'Join your Communist class comrades in all industries and working neighbourhoods to carry out mass demonstrations, a mass strike, a general strike.'

The SPD declined.

Early that afternoon, Hitler sat down at his desk in the Chancellery for the first time. A photograph was taken. Gazing into the middle distance, the Führer put his hands into his jacket pockets. Behind him were flowers, before him sharpened pencils.

The most recent national census, conducted in 1925, had put the total population at nearly 62.5 million. Of those, 563,733 people described themselves as members of the Jewish community. As a proportion of the population, their numbers had been sinking for decades. At the beginning of 1933, there were probably around five hundred thousand Jewish people living in Germany.

The first cabinet meeting commenced at five o'clock. Hugenberg and Hitler immediately began to argue about whether to call a new election. Most of the ministers sided with Hitler. The cabinet was only a few minutes old, and already Hugenberg was on the back foot.

Christopher Isherwood couldn't help smiling at the thought of the new government. He spoke excellent German, and had quickly sized up the cabinet. 'As you will have seen, we are having a new government, with Charlie Chaplin and Father Christmas in the ministry. All words fail.' Still, he reassured himself, Hitler would now be exposed as a windbag – he'd never be able to cope with the country's shambolic economy.

Goebbels' propaganda machine had not stopped whirring. The first interviews with the new administration appeared, painting the ministers as immensely hard-working straight from the word go.

How was the news received by intelligent neutral observers?
    Camill Hoffmann, a diplomat with the Czech embassy, wrote in his diary, 'The cabinet has been hurriedly cobbled together. Hitler is in there, with Dr Frick and Göring, but Hugenberg, Papen and Defence Minister Blomberg have been added as gendarmes, as well as several old ministers, including Neurath. So this isn't a nationalist, revolutionary government, although it bears Hitler's name. It's not the Third Reich, barely 2½.' A *Sunday Times* reporter wondered: 'Have President von Hindenburg and his "comrade", Herr von Papen, got Hitler into a cage before they wring his neck, or are *they* in the cage?' while a journalist with the *Basler Nachrichten*, a Swiss newspaper, was more ominous still: 'A bear is still a bear, even if you stick a ring through his nose and put him on a lead.'
    And Bella Fromm's response? 'It seems an ironic foreshadowing that the new Hitler cabinet should start off without a Minister of Justice.'

There was frantic activity at the *Völkische Beobachter*, the official news-paper of the NSDAP. The transfer of power was going to be splashed all over the next day's edition. There was a sense of pride and excite-ment in the newsroom, but also pressure to find words adequate to such a historic day. One editor's attempt was as follows:

THE FOUNDATION STONE OF THE THIRD REICH

30 January 1933 will someday be written into the history books as a moment of radical change in the development of Germany. After fourteen years of extraordinary sacrifice and work, today Adolf Hitler has risen to the position he has long deserved. A feeling of unbounded pride is shared by all the millions of people whose longing, struggle and devotion during these years repre-sented their desire to redress the ignominy of 9 November 1918.

Some responses took less time than others. A colleague had taken the opportunity to slip an advertisement into the right-hand corner:

BOOK OF THE DAY: *MEIN KAMPF* BY ADOLF HITLER.

What will Adolf Hitler do? – today millions of hopeful Germans are wondering! – This question can be answered by anybody who knows his work and thus his desires and goals. Nobody, whether friend or foe, can now afford to overlook Hitler's opus.

2 editions: 2 paperback volumes 2.85 marks each. Both volumes in full cloth binding 7.20 marks.

Available in every German bookshop! Verlag Frz. Eher Nachf., Munich 2 NO.

That evening Plotkin tried to buy tickets for *Faust II* at the Staatstheater – Gründgens was supposed to be fantastic – but it was sold out. As he walked down Markgrafenstrasse towards Leipzigerstrasse, he glimpsed the first torchlight parade of Nazis. The further he went, the more of them he saw. Thousands, streaming towards Wilhelmstrasse. Here and there among the marchers, he noticed members of the Stahlhelm.

At the central square in the Tiergarten, Hitler's supporters gathered in the darkness, creating a sea of torches. In Berlin alone, an estimated twenty-five thousand members of the SA and SS were on the march that night, as well as thousands of Stahlhelm troops. Shortly after seven, the column began to move, heading through the Brandenburg Gate, around the Hotel Adlon and along Wilhelmstrasse.

Similar scenes played out across the Reich. Swastika flags were hoisted. Brownshirts marched through the streets, bursting their way into town halls, newsrooms, and SPD and KPD offices in an eruption of excitement that would have been impossible to orchestrate.

In Bamberg, a young man in uniform walked at the front of the procession: Lieutenant Claus Schenk Graf von Stauffenberg.

When Ernst Thälmann realised that the SA were marching triumphantly through the Brandenburg Gate, he sent all his leading functionaries back to their branch offices. All comrades had to be mobilised; the party was switching gear. They'd known all along they'd have to defy the law at some point. They were prepared. And now the time had come. In parting, Thälmann told his people: 'We'll see each other in a few days, when the Central Committee reconvenes. You'll be given more information.'

Many members of the KPD had packed their things. Whatever weapons they could muster were kept close at hand. They awaited only the signal to attack.

Only a signal.

Only a spark.

It was Goebbels who'd come up with the torchlight procession. Who else? Afterwards, he would claim on the radio that half a million people had joined them; the British embassy put it closer to fifty thousand, while Bella Fromm estimated twenty thousand.

The Fridericus Rex March was played around eight thirty, as the head of the procession reached the Chancellery.

Emmy Sonnemann, Göring's new girlfriend, was watching the parade from a window in Hitler's suite at the Kaiserhof. Hermann was only a few hundred metres away, at a window on the first floor of the Chancellery.

The Reich's new lords watched the train of torches, listened to the bands, the songs, the shouts of 'heil!' – Hitler, Goebbels, Göring, Papen. At another window Paul von Hindenburg listened.

At the Kaiserhof, prominent National Socialists surged onto the balconies. Joachim von Ribbentrop was among them. He doffed his hat as the SA and SS carried their flags past in the street below. He'd brought his eleven-year-old son to witness the historic event.

More cries of heil, over and over. *Heil Hitler!*

Something was ending. Something was beginning.

Hitler turned to Papen. 'What a tremendous task lies ahead of us, Herr von Papen. We must never part company until our work is done.'

At the function rooms near Hallesches Tor, the Association for the Protection of German Writers was conducting a meeting. Among those present was Erich Mühsam, the anarchist, who urged everyone to stand firm. Most of the other authors favoured doing absolutely nothing – simply waiting it out. The nightmare would pass. Then Carl von Ossietzky stood up, and the room fell silent. In his soft voice, he said: 'All this will last much longer than you think. Maybe years. We are powerless against it. But each of us can decide not to give them so much as an inch.'

At Wannsee, the Hungarian-born director Paul Fejos was visiting German film star Heinrich George. Fejos, who had been working in Hollywood for five years, considered George the 'king of actors'. While the SA were marching a few kilometres to the east, the two men discussed whether George should continue his career in America. It was safer there, and the jobs paid well. Ernst Lubitsch, another director, wasn't the only one who'd fled to California to escape the Nazis. Many artists had already left Berlin – and not just the Jewish ones. And Heinrich George? In 1930 he'd signed a contract with Metro-Goldwyn-Mayer for a fee of 20,000 dollars, an enormous sum.

That evening Harry Graf Kessler went to the Kaiserhof, as he often did on a Monday. There, among the celebrating National Socialists, he was due to attend a dinner followed by a lecture given by Richard Nikolaus von Coudenhove-Kalergi. The topic was 'Germany's European Mission'. Kessler was troubled to learn that the half-Japanese, half-Austrian intellectual considered his concept of 'pan-Europeanism' a bulwark against Bolshevism.

A banker at the table, Emil Georg von Stauss, on the board at Deutsche Bank and connected to the NSDAP's financial department, was boasting about his wonderful relationship with Hitler: anything he wished, the Führer would grant. Somebody else, meanwhile, was gossiping that Hugenberg and Hitler had already locked horns at the first cabinet meeting.

Kessler got home late, writing in his diary that

> there's practically a carnival going on in and around the Kaiser-hof. Uniformed SS are arrayed outside the main entrance and in the hall; SA and SS people patrol the corridors. As we came out after the lecture, an endless file of SA were goose-stepping past various bigwigs (second-tier, Hitler himself was at the Chancellery), who had planted themselves outside the main gate and were greeting them with the Fascist salute; a proper parade. The whole square was crammed with people gawping.

Kurt von Schleicher had a visitor, someone he'd not spoken to for a while: Wilhelm Groener, the one-time father figure who'd felt so betrayed by his protégé. Today, when Schleicher was at his lowest ebb, Groener had come to show his support.

Schleicher was deeply moved by the gesture. He had lost power but regained a friend.

After the procession of torches the crowd dispersed, the revellers traipsing back to their various neighbourhoods. Sturm 33 of the SA went home shortly before midnight, taking a route down Wallstrasse in Klein-Wedding. Their leader's name was Hans Eberhard Maikowski. In December 1931 he'd shot a Communist and fled to Italy before returning to Germany, where he'd been arrested in October; he'd been released shortly before Christmas under Schleicher's amnesty.

Wallstrasse was Communist territory. Messengers had passed on news of the approaching SA unit, and the Max Hölz Häuserschutz-staffel (a Communist Party organisation designed to protect locals from Nazi violence) was waiting for them. It was accompanied by a police officer by the name of Josef Zauritz, ordered to the scene by his superiors. Were the Brownshirts planning an attack?

The Häuserschutzstaffel came to meet them. Insults were fired back and forth, then fists were swung. Dozens of Communists streamed out of the Zum Hirsch pub. Attempts were made to calm the situation. Then shots rang out.

Zauritz crumpled to the ground, fatally wounded. So did Maikowski.

Only Communists were arrested.

The shooter was never identified.

Goebbels heard the news that night. As soon as their position was unassailable, Göring would deal with the Communists.

It was late, but Adolf Hitler was still strolling through the snowy ministry gardens with some colleagues. Soon they would cross the road to the Kaiserhof and collapse, exhausted, into bed.

Germany's new chancellor allowed himself to rest.

CLOSING CREDITS

André François-Poncet remained in Berlin until 1938, when he was appointed ambassador to Italy. He later worked as an adviser to the Vichy Regime, then from 1949 to 1953 was the French High Commissioner in Germany and subsequently the ambassador in Bonn. He died in Paris in 1978 at the age of ninety.

Bella Fromm was prohibited from working in 1934. Four years later she left Germany and emigrated to the USA. She died in New York in 1972 at the age of eighty-one.

Günther Gereke was arrested a few days after the transfer of power, accused of embezzlement. By 1945 he had served three custodial sentences. After the war he continued his career in West Germany but decided in 1952 to emigrate to the GDR, where he worked with the East German Christian Democratic Union. He died in 1970 at the age of seventy-six.

Joseph Goebbels was made Minister for Public Enlightenment and Propaganda on 13 March 1933 and later President of the Chamber of Culture. On his orders, countless intellectuals were banned from working, forcing them into exile. His speeches whipped up the German population into hysteria, building support for the Nazis and for the Second World War. He committed suicide on 1 May 1945, probably with cyanide.

Magda Goebbels also took her own life on 1 May 1945 after the couple had killed their six children.

Hermann Göring was appointed Minister for Aviation, Prime Minister of Prussia and a general of the infantry in 1933. He remained a leading figure in the Nazi regime until the end. He killed himself in 1946, aged fifty-three, after he was sentenced to death at the Nuremberg Trials.

Wilhelm Groener kept out of politics, dying of liver disease in May 1939 at the age of seventy-one. Officers were forbidden to appear in uniform at his funeral.

General Kurt von Hammerstein-Equord tendered his resignation in October 1933, but was recalled in 1939. Shortly afterwards, however, Hitler relieved him of command. He was active in the resistance movement, but died of cancer in 1943.

Ernst Hanfstaengl became a critic of Hitler's regime, and in 1937 he fled the country. When war broke out he was arrested in England. The Gestapo put him on a list of people to liquidate, but Hanfstaengl survived until the age of eighty-eight, when he died in 1975 in Munich, his home city, where he'd first met Hitler fifty years before.

Oskar von Hindenburg spoke out publicly in favour of making Hitler president in 1934 after his father's death. During the Second World War he served as a general in the Wehrmacht. He died in 1960 at the age of seventy-seven.

Paul von Hindenburg, President of the German Reich, died on 2 August 1934 at the age of eighty-six. To the end, he remained convinced that he had invested power in the right people.

Adolf Hitler became President of the German Reich shortly after Hindenburg's death in August 1934. The Führer and Chancellor of the Reich instigated the persecution of German Jews, artists and anyone who opposed him, banned other political parties and muzzled the press. On 30 April 1945, at the end of an unprecedented war and after the systematic murder of much of Europe's Jewish population, Hitler shot himself.

Alfred Hugenberg resigned from his ministerial post on 29 June 1933 but remained a member of the Reichstag (by then under Hitler's control) until 1945. After 1941 he was the oldest member of Parliament. He died in 1951 at the age of eighty-five.

Christopher Isherwood left Germany in May 1933, and from 1939 lived in America. He died in 1986 aged eighty-one.

Mascha Kaléko gave birth to a son in 1936. Her books were banned by the regime. She emigrated to the United States with her son and husband in 1938. She died in Zurich in 1975 aged sixty-seven.

Alfred Kerr fled to Prague on 15 February 1933 and was joined by his family shortly afterwards. He was among the first Germans to be deprived of citizenship by the Nazis. Labelled an enemy of the state by the Reich, he lived in London. Kerr died in 1948 at the age of eighty.

Harry Graf Kessler left Germany in 1933, subsequently living in Mallorca and France. He died in 1937 at the age of sixty-seven, his fortune depleted.

Theodor Leipart tried to reach an understanding between the Federation of German Trade Unions and the Nazis, but in May 1933 he was arrested, although he was quickly released. The unions were crushed. In 1946 he joined the Socialist Unity Party of Germany in the Soviet occupation zone and died in 1947 at the age of seventy-nine.

Oskar Loerke continued to work as an editor. He led a quiet life, dying in 1941 at the age of fifty-six.

Otto Meissner worked for Adolf Hitler as Chief of the Presidential Chancellery of the Führer and the Chancellor until 1945. He was tried after the war but acquitted. He died in 1953 at the age of seventy-three.

Edgar Mowrer received death threats after the Nazis came to power, and in 1933 he left the country. After postings to Tokyo and Paris he returned to America, his home country. He died aged eighty-seven in 1977.

Carl von Ossietzky was arrested again on 28 February 1933 and taken to a concentration camp. Seriously ill, he was released in November 1936. He was later awarded the Nobel Peace Prize. He died of tuberculosis in 1938, aged forty-eight.

Eugen Ott was sent to Japan on 1 June 1933 as a military observer, then from 1938 – the year he joined the NSDAP – to 1942 he was the German ambassador there. Throughout his life he defended Kurt von Schleicher's policies. He died in 1977 at the age of eighty-seven.

Franz von Papen was removed as Vice-Chancellor in 1934 and sent as Hitler's ambassador to Austria and later to Turkey. In 1947 the Allied prosecutors deemed him a 'Hauptschuldiger', a main perpetrator, and he spent two years in prison. He died in 1969 at the age of seventy-nine.

Abraham Plotkin stayed in Berlin until 8 May, arriving in New York on 1 July 1933. He continued to work on behalf of leftist politicians, trade unions and Jews in Germany, founding an organisation that enabled hundreds of people to escape to the USA, including several people he had met in Berlin. He died in Los Angeles in 1988, ninety-five years old. His diaries were published posthumously.

Reinhold Quaatz, classed by the Nazis as half Jewish despite his own anti-Semitism, remained a member of the Reichstag until November 1933. After the war, he was a member of the Christian Democratic Union in Berlin. He died in 1953 aged seventy-seven.

Joachim von Ribbentrop was given various diplomatic posts after the Nazis came to power. Between 1936 and 1938 he was the German ambassador to London, then from 1945 Foreign Minister for the German Reich. Found guilty of war crimes at the Nuremberg Trials, in October 1946, at the age of fifty-three, he was executed. His wife, Annelies, lived to be seventy-seven, dying in 1973.

Frederic M. Sackett left Berlin in 1933, returning to the USA and leaving the diplomatic service. He died of a heart attack in 1941, at the age of seventy-one.

Kurt von Schleicher and his wife, Elisabeth, were murdered by the SS on 30 June 1934 at their home in Berlin. Many of their private documents were taken by the killers.

Kurt Freiherr von Schröder joined the NSDAP on 1 February 1933 and the SS in 1936. He was one of the most influential businessmen in the Third Reich. After the war he was sentenced to a year in prison and given a fine. He died in 1966 at the age of seventy-six.

Kurt Schumacher was taken into custody in July 1933 and spent nearly all the subsequent period until 1945 in concentration camps. His health was badly affected, but after the war he was a crucial figure in rebuilding the SPD in Germany. In 1949 he became head of the party's faction in the first Bundestag. He died in 1952 at the age of fifty-six.

Gregor Strasser initially stayed out of politics after the NSDAP rose to power, but on 13 June 1934 Hitler offered him the Economics Ministry. Strasser was willing to accept but insisted Göring and Goebbels be dismissed from the cabinet. A few days later, on 30 June, Strasser was shot by the SS.

Ernst Thälmann made efforts during the first weeks of the Hitler government to organise a leftist resistance. On 3 March 1933 he was arrested. Eleven years later, in 1944 – when the KPD leader was fifty-eight years old – he was murdered at Buchenwald concentration camp.

Dorothy Thompson was given twenty-four hours to leave Germany in August 1934 and returned to the USA. She divorced Sinclair Lewis in 1942. Thompson died in 1961 at the age of sixty-seven.

Hans Zehrer's newspaper *Tägliche Rundschau* was forced to cease publication in July 1933. After the war, Zehrer became editor-in-chief at *Die Welt* and a columnist with *Bild-Zeitung,* as well as one of the publisher Axel Springer's most important advisers. He died in 1966 aged sixty-seven.

SOURCES AND LITERATURE

We spent many hours researching this book in libraries and archives, scouring databases and reading hundreds of books and papers on our search for the most vivid descriptions of each day. Our goal was to reconstruct events as precisely as possible. To this end, we primarily focused on transcripts and minutes, diaries, letters, newspaper articles and government documents. The Chancellery's official transcripts were an invaluable resource, as was the *Vossische Zeitung*, which appeared twice daily and was astonishingly rich in information.

The most glaring gap in our research was definitely Kurt von Schleicher's missing papers. Schleicher and his wife were murdered in June 1934, and the killers, working on orders from the government, also took numerous documents. Otherwise, however, the period is relatively rich in source material, and, of course, we are also gratefully indebted to the standard works of historical research. We also consulted more in-depth studies, including on the underground activities of the KPD during the period, on the 1932 transport strike in Berlin and on street violence.

We incorporated all the sources that seemed important into an archive system and subsequently evaluated them. Whenever possible, we checked the facts against a second source, and, when in doubt, avoided using descriptions that seemed implausible.

THE MAKING OF

The last ten weeks of the Weimar Republic were a phase of social hysteria, of energy and fear, of political threats, presumptuous arrogance and string-pulling. In this short space of time careers and fates were decided; what we commonly call a historical process was compressed in an extraordinary fashion.

There were two impulses that prompted us in the conception and research of this book. As journalists at home with narrative historical material, we stumbled across a topic two years ago that fascinated us: the battle between Franz von Papen and Kurt von Schleicher over the chancellorship at the end of the Weimar Republic. At school we were simply taught to think of Papen as the Republic's 'gravedigger', but it soon became clear to us how complex their struggle had been, and that various forces were at work in the months between late 1932 and early 1933, all of which were co-responsible for ending the first German democracy. We also realised that events could have gone very differently: at the end of 1932 the NSDAP was on the verge of collapse – the number of its seats in the Reichstag dwindling, its finances precarious – and the German economy was slowly beginning to recover.

Around the same time we happened to be watching the American series *House of Cards*, featuring Kevin Spacey as a diabolical, power-hungry politician who wants to become – and eventually does become – president. As we chatted about it over coffee, it seemed to us that the end of the Weimar Republic and the driving forces behind Papen, Schleicher, Hitler and the others, were fundamentally more exciting than *House of Cards*. It was just as subtle and complex, but it actually happened. It had terrible consequences for millions of people. It was an extraordinary subject.

We looked around. Then we got to work. There are many books about the Weimar Republic, including some outstanding ones, but we'd never seen one that described those climactic weeks in detail, as though laying the groundwork for a script. Our goal was to construct the book like a documentary montage, allowing the characters to speak for themselves, to get inside their heads if at all possible, without knowing commentary or the wisdom of hindsight. To let the drama unfold of its own accord, to watch as it emerged from the moment.

What was the most important thing we realised? It would be too banal to say that Hitler's seizure of power was by no means inevitable. Yet it wasn't until we came to write this book that we understood how cunningly, selfishly and unscrupulously the major German politicians of the age had behaved. How many opportunities there had been to bring down the Nazis.

The gravediggers didn't have to triumph.

ACKNOWLEDGEMENTS

Needless to say, this book would never have been published without the support of many generous people. We owe them a huge, heartfelt thanks. First, to our agent, Thomas Hölzl, whose persistence, patience and precision was crucial in finding the right tone and dramatic arc for this book. To Tanja Hommen and Nina Sillem, our editors at S. Fischer Verlag, whose sensitivity and capacity for enthusiasm throughout the process was inspiring, and also to the entire publishing team in Frankfurt.

We are grateful to the wonderful editorial staff at *P.M. History* – it was while working for the magazine that we came up with the idea for *The Last Winter of the Weimar Republic*. Thank you, Bettina Daniel, Julia Franz, Florian Gless, Ruth Hoffmann, Katharina Jakob, Imke Keyssler, Jan Krummrey, Gunhild Lübeck, Andreas Pufal, Thomas Röbke and Martin Scheufens!

To all the archivists and documentalists at the state and university libraries and research institutes in Hamburg, Schleswig and Berlin whom we pestered with our pleas and requests, thank you for being so helpful. Another thank you goes to Irene Strenge, who gave us a deep insight into the environment around Kurt von Schleicher, and also to Wolfgang Kopitzsch, who was indispensable in helping us research Altona Bloody Sunday.

Rüdiger Barth

This book is dedicated to my family, to my wife, Petra, and to Tom and Kim – the three of you simply make life a perpetually new source of joy. To my father, Günter, whose scepticism ('why are you messing about with old news?') was transformed into enthusiasm once he read the first chapter. And to my mother, Silke, for her confidence, strength and love.

To my friends and colleagues at Looping Studios in Hamburg, Munich and Berlin, thank you for your team spirit and your taste for adventure, especially Robin Houcken and Dominik Wichmann. Thanks also to Johannes Erler for his expert advice.

Hauke Friederichs

My son Jonathan was born while I was working on this book. *The Last Winter of the Weimar Republic* is dedicated to him and his mother, Martina. I deeply hope my son never experiences such dark days as in the winter of 1932–3, and I'm proud that my wife is fighting for a vibrant democracy in the Hamburg Parliament.

Thanks are due to my doctoral supervisor, Franklin Kopitzsch, who is a constant source of good advice in my journalistic work, and to Monika and Wolfgang, who bring tremendous interest and support to all my projects. My father also played his part in the making of this book: when I was still in primary school, he took me to the state and university library, kindling my enthusiasm for history.

TIMELINE

The Brink

17 November 1932
The parliamentary elections on 6 November were a disaster for the parties faithful to the Republic. Chancellor von Papen announces his cabinet's resignation.

18 November 1932
President Hindenburg begins the search for a new chancellor.

19 November 1932
A letter reaches Hindenburg: prominent figures in the business community urge him to give the chancellorship to Adolf Hitler, the leader of the strongest party in the Reichstag.

21 November 1932
Hindenburg offers Hitler a mandate: draw together a parliamentary majority that would support him as chancellor.

23 November 1932
Defence Minister von Schleicher asks Hitler whether he would be willing to join a cabinet under his own stewardship. Hitler refuses and suggests to Hindenburg that he be appointed chancellor and given presidential powers without a parliamentary majority.

24 November 1932
Hitler declares in a letter to Hindenburg that he has no intention of seeking a parliamentary majority.

25 November 1932

A pledge of loyalty to the Führer signed by several National Socialists – Frick, Goebbels, Göring, Röhm and Strasser – appears in the *Völkische Beobachter*. The Defence Ministry begins to run its simulation testing the capability of the army to respond to civil unrest.

30 November 1932

Hitler and his intraparty opponent Gregor Strasser fight. Strasser demands the NSDAP agree to join a coalition.

1 December 1932

Hindenburg again tasks Papen with building a government.

The Plan

2 December 1932

The results of the simulation are presented. Several members of the cabinet refuse to cooperate with Papen. General Schleicher is appointed the Weimar Republic's twelfth head of government.

4 December 1932

Schleicher meets with Strasser and explores whether he would be willing to join the government.

5 December 1932

The NSDAP holds a summit of senior party leaders at the Hotel Kaiserhof in Berlin.

6 December 1932

The first session of the new Parliament takes place.

7 December 1932

The power struggle inside the NSDAP escalates.

8 December 1932
Strasser announces his resignation from his roles in the party and leaves Berlin.

15 December 1932
Chancellor Schleicher gives a radio address in which he presents his government's agenda: 'create jobs'.

Silent Night

16 December 1932
The conservative Gentlemen's Club throws its annual dinner. The former chancellor, Papen, gives a speech in which he criticises his successor's fiscal policy.

21 December 1932
Schleicher's amnesty comes into force, freeing hundreds of prisoners before Christmas. Carl von Ossietzky is among them.

28 December 1932
The Cologne-based banker Kurt von Schröder arranges a conversation between Hitler and Papen for 4 January.

In the Maelstrom

4 January 1933
Hitler and Papen meet secretly in Cologne, but news of their conversation is leaked. In Berlin, Hitler's rival, Gregor Strasser, visits President Hindenburg.

9 January 1933
Papen and Schleicher have a long talk.

11 January 1933
At the president's office, the National Rural League complains to Hindenburg and Schleicher about the pressing struggles of large-scale agriculturalists.

12 January 1933
A clandestine meeting takes place between Papen and Hitler at the home of prominent businessman Joachim von Ribbentrop.

13 January 1933
Hugenberg offers the DNVP to Chancellor Schleicher as a coalition partner. In return he demands two ministries – Economics as well as Food and Agriculture – for himself. Schleicher hesitates.

15 January 1933
An election takes place in Lippe. The NSDAP receives just under 40 per cent of the ballot, becoming the largest faction in the Regional Assembly.

16 January 1933
Addressing the cabinet, Schleicher clings to his notion of a 'cross-party front' incorporating Strasser.

18 January 1933
East Prussian landowners are accused of misappropriating state funds through the Eastern Aid scheme at the meeting of the Reichstag Budget Committee. The newspapers begin calling it a 'scandal'. Papen and Hitler meet again at Ribbentrop's villa.

22 January 1933
The SA demonstrates outside the KPD's head office in Bülowplatz, guarded by the Prussian police. That evening another meeting between Hitler and Papen takes place at the Ribbentrops' home; also present are State Secretary Meissner and Hindenburg's son, Oskar.

26 January 1933
Schleicher asks President Hindenburg to grant him quasi-dictatorial plenary powers.

28 January 1933
Schleicher steps down as chancellor when Hindenburg refuses to give him the authority to dissolve Parliament.

Taking Power

30 January 1933
Adolf Hitler is appointed chancellor by President Hindenburg. Franz von Papen becomes Vice-Chancellor, and Commissioner of Prussia; Hugenberg becomes Minister for Economics and Agriculture. Hermann Göring and Wilhelm Frick are also given cabinet posts. The KPD calls for a general strike. The SA, SS and Stahlhelm conduct a torchlight procession through the Brandenburg Gate.

SELECTED FURTHER READING

Baedekers Berlin und Umgebung (Berlin and Surrounding Area), Leipzig 1927.

Bahne, Siegfried: *Die KPD und das Ende von Weimar: Das Scheitern einer Politik 1932–1935* (*The KPD and the End of Weimar: A Failure of Policy, 1932–1935*), Frankfurt am Main 1976.

Benz, Wolfgang: *Geschichte des Dritten Reiches* (*A History of the Third Reich*), Munich 2000.

Beuys, Barbara: *Verteidigung der Republik: der sozialdemokratische Reformer Theodor Haubach (1896–1945)* (*Defending the Republic: Social Democratic Reformer Theodor Haubach (1896–1945)*), Hamburg 2000.

Blasius, Dirk: *Weimars Ende: Bürgerkrieg und Politik 1930–1933* (*The End of Weimar: Civil War and Policy, 1930–1933*), Göttingen 2005.

Bracher, Karl Dietrich: *Die Auflösung der Weimarer Republik: Eine Studie zum Problem des Machtverfalls in der Demokratie* (*The Break-Up of the Weimar Republic: A Study of the Problem of Declining Power in Democracy*), Stuttgart/Düsseldorf 1955.

Bracher, Karl Dietrich/Funke, Manfred/Jacobsen, Hans-Adolf (eds): *Die Weimarer Republik 1918–1933* (*The Weimar Republic 1918–1933*), Bonn 1987.

Burke, Bernard V.: *Ambassador Frederic Sackett and the Collapse of the Weimar Republic, 1930–33: The United States and Hitler's Rise to Power*, Cambridge 1994.

Büttner, Ursula: *Weimar – die überforderte Republik, 1918–1922* (Gebhardt Handbuch der Geschichte, Vol. 18, 10th edition) (*Weimar: The Overwhelmed Republic, 1918–1922*), Stuttgart 2010.

Collomp, Catherine/Groppo, Bruno (eds): *An American in Hitler's Berlin: Abraham Plotkin's Diary, 1932–33*, Champaign 2008.

Conradi, Peter: *Hitler's Piano Player: The Rise and Fall of Ernst Hanfstaengl, Confidant of Hitler, Ally of FDR*, New York 2004.

Demant, Ebbo: *Von Schleicher zu Springer: Hans Zehrer als politischer Publizist* (From Schleicher to Springer: Hans Zehrer as Political Journalist), Mainz 1971.

Easton, Laird M.: *The Red Count: The Life and Times of Harry Kessler*, Berkeley 2006.

Engel, Hartmut/Ribbe, Wolfgang (eds): *Geschichtsmeile Wilhelmstrasse* (Wilhelmstrasse: The Historic Mile), Berlin 1997.

Fest, Joachim: *Hitler: Eine Biographie* (Hitler: A Biography), Berlin 2002.

Fischer, Conan: *Stormtroopers: A Social, Economic and Ideological Analysis*, 1929–1935, London 1983.

François-Poncet, André: *Als Botschafter im Dritten Reich: Die Erinnerungen des französischen Botschafters in Berlin, September 1931 bis Oktober 1938* (An Ambassador in the Third Reich: Memoirs of the French Ambassador in Berlin, September 1931 to October 1938), Mainz 1983.

Frank, Hans: *Im Angesicht des Galgens: Deutung Hitlers und seiner Zeit auf Grund eigener Erlebnisse und Erkenntnisse* (Facing the Gallows: A Reading of Hitler and his Period, Based on His Own Experiences and Insights), Munich 1953.

Friedrich, Thomas: *Die missbrauchte Hauptstadt. Hitler und Berlin* (The Abused Capital: Hitler and Berlin), Berlin 2007.

Fromm, Bella: *Blood and Banquets: A Berlin Social Diary*, New York 1942.

Glatzer, Ruth: *Berlin zur Weimarer Zeit. Panorama einer Metropole* (Berlin in the Weimar Era: Panorama of a Metropolis), Berlin 2000.

Goebbels, Joseph: *Die Tagebücher. Vol. 2/III: Oktober 1932–März 1934* (The Diaries: Vol. 2/III: October 1932–March 1934). Edited by Angela Hermann, Munich 2006.

Golecki, Anton (ed.): *Das Kabinett von Schleicher: 3. Dezember 1932 bis 30. Januar 1933 (Akten der Reichskanzlei. Weimarer Republik)* (The Schleicher Cabinet: 3 December 1932 to 30 January 1933 [Chancellery Files, Weimar Republic]), Boppard am Rhein.

Groener-Geyer, Dorothea: *General Groener: Soldat und Staatsmann* (General Groener: Soldier and Statesman), Frankfurt am Main 1955.

Hanfstaengl, Ernst: *Zwischen Weissem und Braunem Haus* (Between the White House and the Brown House), Munich 1970.

Harter, Johannes: *Wilhelm Groener: Reichswehrminister am Ende der Weimarer Republik (1928–1932)* (Schriftenreihe des Militärgeschichtlichen

Forschungsamtes; 39) (*Wilhelm Groener: Defence Minister at the End of the Weimar Republic 1928–1932*), Munich 1993.

Heuss, Theodor: *Hitlers Weg: Eine historisch-politische Studie über den Nationalsozialismus*, 7th edition (*Hitler's Way: A Historical-Political Study of National Socialism*), Stuttgart, Berlin, Leipzig 1932.

Hömig, Herbert: *Brüning: Kanzler in der Krise der Republik* (*Brüning: Chancellor During the Crisis in the Republic*), Paderborn et. al. 2000.

Kaléko, Mascha: *Grossstadtliebe: Lyrische Stenogramme* (*Big City Love: The Book of Lyrical Shorthand*), Reinbek 1996.

Kaufmann, Bernd et al.: *Der Nachrichtendienst der KPD 1919–1937* (*The KPD Intelligence Service 1919–1937*), Berlin 1993.

Kellerhoff, Sven Felix: *Hitlers Berlin: Geschichte einer Hassliebe* (*Hitler's Berlin: Story of a Love-Hate Relationship*), Berlin 2005.

Kellerhoff, Sven Felix: *Die NSDAP: Eine Partei und ihre Mitglieder* (*The NSDAP: A Party and Its Members*), Stuttgart 2017.

Kempner, Robert M. W.: *Das Dritte Reich im Kreuzverhör: Aus den unveröffentlichten Vernehmungsprotokollen des Anklägers in den Nürnberger Prozessen* (*The Third Reich under Cross-Examination: From the Unpublished Interrogation Transcripts of the Nuremberg Trials Prosecutor*), Munich 2005.

Kerbs, Diethart / Stahr, Henrick (ed.): *Berlin 1932: Das letzte Jahr der Weimarer Republik* (*Berlin 1932: The Last Year of the Weimar Republic*), Berlin 1992.

Kershaw, Ian: *Hitler 1889–1936*, London 1998.

Kessler, Harry Graf: *Das Tagebuch 1880–1937. Vol. 9: 1926–1937* (*The Diary 1880–1937*), ed.: Gruber, Sabine / Kamzelak, Roland S. / Ott, Ulrich, Stuttgart 2010.

Kissenkoetter, Udo: *Gregor Strasser und die NSDAP* (*Gregor Strasser and the NSDAP*), Stuttgart 1978.

Lange, Annemarie: *Berlin in der Weimarer Republik* (*Berlin in the Weimar Republic*), Berlin 1987.

Longerich, Peter: *Deutschland 1918–1933: Die Weimarer Republik* (*Germany 1918–1933: The Weimar Republic*), Hannover 1995.

Longerich, Peter: *Goebbels: Biographie* (*Goebbels: A Biography*), Munich 2010.

Longerich, Peter: *Hitler: Biographie* (*Hitler: A Biography*), Munich 2015.

Meissner, Hans-Otto: *Junge Jahre im Reichspräsidentenpalais: Erinnerungen an Ebert und Hindenburg 1919–1934* (*Early Years in the President's Palace: Reminiscences of Ebert and Hindenburg*), Munich 1988.

Möckelmann, Reiner: *Franz von Papen: Hitlers ewiger Vasall* (*Franz von Papen: Hitler's Eternal Vassal*), Darmstadt 2016.

Nagel, Anne C.: *Johannes Popitz (1884–1945): Görings Finanzminister und Verschwörer gegen Hitler* (*Johannes Popitz (1884–1945): Göring's Finance Minister and Conspirator against Hitler*), Cologne / Weimar / Vienna 2015.

Nagorski, Andrew: *Hitlerland: American Eyewitness to the Nazi Rise to Power*, New York 2012.

Papen, Franz von: *Der Wahrheit eine Gasse* (*Make Way for the Truth*), Munich 1952.

Paschen, Joachim: *Hamburg zwischen Hindenburg und Hitler: Die nationalsozialistische Machteroberung in einer roten Festung* (*Hamburg between Hindenburg and Hitler: The Nazi Takeover in a Red Stronghold*), Bremen 2013.

Plehwe, Friedrich-Karl von: *Reichskanzler Kurt von Schleicher: Weimars letzte Chance gegen Hitler* (*Chancellor Kurt von Schleicher: Weimar's Last Chance against Hitler*), Frankfurt am Main / Berlin 1990.

Plieber, Ulla: *Theodor Leipart (1867–1947): Persönlichkeit, Handlungsmotive, Wirken, Bilanz – ein Lebensbild mit Dokumenten* (*Theodor Leipart (1867–1947): Personality, Motives, Work, Outcome – A Life in Documents*). Vol. 2: documents. Berlin 2001.

Pufendorf, Astrid von: *Die Plancks: Eine Familie zwischen Patriotismus und Widerstand* (*The Plancks: A Family between Patriotism and Resistance*), Berlin 2006.

Pünder, Hermann: *Von Preussen nach Europa* (*From Prussia to Europe*), Stuttgart 1968.

Pyta, Wolfram: *Hindenburg: Herrschaft zwischen Hohenzollern und Hitler* (*Hindenburg: Ruling between the Hohenzollerns and Hitler*), Munich 2007.

Pyta, Wolfram: *Hitler: Der Künstler als Politiker und Feldherr: Eine Herrschaftsanalyse* (*Hitler: The Artist as a Politician and Strategist: An Analysis of Control*), Munich 2015.

Reuth, Ralf Georg: *Goebbels: Eine Biografie* (*Goebbels: A Biography*), Munich / Zurich 2012.

Ribbentrop, Rudolf von: *Mein Vater Joachim von Ribbentrop: Erlebnisse und Erinnerungen* (*My Father Joachim von Ribbentrop: Experiences and Memories*), Graz 2008.

Röhl, Klaus Rainer: *Die letzten Tage der Republik von Weimar: Kommunisten und Nationalsozialisten im Berliner BVG-Streik von 1932* (*The Last Days of the Weimar Republic: Communists and National Socialists during the Berlin Transport Strike of 1932*), Vienna 2008.

Rosenkranz, Jutta: *Mascha Kaléko: Biografie* (*Mascha Kaléko: A Biography*), Munich 2012.

Rott, Joachim: *»Ich gehe meinen Weg ungehindert geradeaus«: Dr Bernhard Weiss (1880–1951): Polizeipräsident in Berlin. Leben und Wirken, (Aus Religion und Recht)* (*'I Go My Way Straight On, Unhindered': Dr Bernhard Weiss [1880–1951]: Deputy Police Chief in Berlin: Life and Work*), Berlin 2010.

Salewski, Michael: *Preussischer Militarismus – Realität oder Mythos? Gedanken zu einem Phantom* (*Prussian Militarism – Myth or Reality? Thoughts on a Phantom*), in: Zeitschrift für Religions- und Geistesgeschichte 2001, Vol. 53, pp. 19–34.

Schäfer, Claus W.: *André François-Poncet als Botschafter in Berlin (1931–1938)* (*André François-Poncet as Ambassador in Berlin (1931–1938)*), (Pariser Historische Studien; 64), Munich 2004.

Schober, Volker: *Der junge Kurt Schuhmacher* (*The Young Kurt Schumacher*), Bonn 2000.

Schulze, Hagen: *Weimar: Deutschland 1917–1933* (*Weimar: Germany 1917–1933*), Munich 1998.

Schwerin von Krosigk, Lutz Graf: *Es geschah in Deutschland* (*It Happened in Germany*), Tübingen / Stuttgart 1952.

Schwerin von Krosigk, Lutz Graf: *Memoiren* (*Memoirs*), Stuttgart 1977.

Strenge, Irene: *Machtübernahme 1933 – Alles auf legalem Weg?* (*Takeover 1933 – Was It All Legal?*) (Zeitgeschichtliche Forschungen; 15), Berlin 2002.

Strenge, Irene: *Ferdinand von Bredow: Notizen vom 20.2.1933 bis 31. 12. 1933: Tägliche Aufzeichnungen vom 1. 1. 1934 bis 28. 6. 1934* (*Ferdinand von Bredow: Notes from 20.2.1933 to 31.12.1933: Daily Records from 1.1.1934 to 28.6.1934*) (Zeitgeschichtliche Forschungen; 39), Berlin 2009.

Thompson, Dorothy: *Kassandra spricht: Antifaschistische Publizistik 1932–1942 (Cassandra Speaks: Anti-Fascist Journalism 1932–1942)*, Wiesbaden 1988.

Turner, Henry Ashby, Jr: *Hitler's Thirty Days to Power: January 1933*, Boston 1996.

Turner, Henry Ashby: *German Big Business and the Rise of Hitler*. Oxford, 1985.

Ullrich, Volker: *Adolf Hitler: Biographie, Vol. 1: Die Jahre des Aufstiegs 1889–1939 (Hitler: Ascent 1889–1939)*, 2nd ed., Frankfurt am Main 2013.

Vogelsang, Thilo: *Die Reichswehr und die Politik 1918–1934 (The Military and Politics 1918–1934)*, Niedersächsische Landeszentrale für Heimatdienst, Vol. 1, 1959.

Vogelsang, Thilo: *Kurt von Schleicher: Ein General und Politiker (Kurt von Schleicher: A General and Politician)*, Göttingen/Frankfurt/Zurich 1965.

Wandel, Eckhard: *Hans Schäffer: Steuermann in wirtschaftlichen und politischen Krisen (Hans Schäffer: A Helmsman in Economic and Political Crises)*, Stuttgart 1974.

Weiss, Hermann/Hoser, Paul (eds): *Die Deutschnationalen und die Zerstörung der Weimarer Republik: Aus dem Tagebuch von Reinhold Quaatz 1928–1933 (The DNVP and the Destruction of the Weimar Republic: From the Diary of Reinhold Quaatz 1928–1933)*, Munich 1989.

Winkler, Heinrich August: *Weimar 1918–1933: Die Geschichte der ersten deutschen Demokratie (Weimar 1918–1933: The Story of the First German Democracy)*, 4th edition, Munich 2005.

Winkler, Heinrich August: *Der lange Weg nach Westen (The Long Way to the West)*, (Vol. 1: *Deutsche Geschichte vom Ende des Alten Reiches bis zum Untergang der Weimarer Republik (German History from the End of the Old Reich to the Downfall of the Weimar Republic)*), Munich 2012.

Wirsching, Andreas: *Die Weimarer Republik: Politik und Gesellschaft (The Weimar Republic: Politics and Society)*, Munich 2000.

Newspapers

Der Angriff: National Socialist Berlin daily newspaper
Berliner Tageblatt: national daily newspaper

B.Z.: Berliner Zeitung: tabloid
Die Rote Fahne: KPD newspaper
Tägliche Rundschau: conservative daily newspaper with close military
  connections
Völkischer Beobachter: NSDAP daily newspaper
Vossische Zeitung: independent and liberal newspaper
Die Weltbühne: left-leaning, intellectual weekly journal
Vorwärts: party newspaper of the SPD
Die Sonntags-Zeitung: independent newspaper based in Stuttgart

INDEX